ALEX SALMOND:
MY PART IN HIS DOWNFALL

ALEX SALMOND:
MY PART IN HIS DOWNFALL

THE COCHRANE DIARIES

ALAN COCHRANE

Biteback Publishing

First published in Great Britain in 2014 by
Biteback Publishing Ltd
Westminster Tower
3 Albert Embankment
London SE1 7SP
Copyright © Alan Cochrane 2014

ISBN 978-1-84954-826-7

10 9 8 7 6 5 4 3 2 1

A CIP catalogue record for this book is available from the British Library.

Set in Adobe Garamond Pro

Printed and bound in Great Britain by
CPI Group (UK) Ltd, Croydon CR0 4YY

MIX
Paper from
responsible sources
FSC® C020471
FSC
www.fsc.org

For Jenny: with love, and without whom

we wouldn't have got this far.

CONTENTS

FOREWORD

THE GENESIS FOR this diary was the fact that although I'd been involved in political reporting and, latterly, commentating on politics for more than thirty years, the campaign to take Scotland out of the United Kingdom was, as far as I was concerned, easily the most important event I'd ever covered or am ever likely to cover.

This is not, and was never intended to be, an attempt at writing a history of the referendum campaign. Instead, I decided to record not so much the everyday happenings as the campaign unfolded, but my own reaction to what was going on and the conversations I had with those involved in the decision-making process associated with what was, in every sense, the Battle for Britain.

If I have let anyone down through reporting what they may have thought were off-the-record conversations, I can only apologise for any embarrassment caused and confidences breached.

My only defence is that I never, and have never, made any secret of my occupation. And in documenting, in an unvarnished way, its hopes and fears, its incredible mood swings and enormous complexities, I hope I may have provided a clearer insight into this truly remarkable campaign than might have been possible with 'on the record' interviews.

Given my open and oft-declared support for the Union, it is inevitable that this diary deals primarily with what became known as the Better Together effort. However, I make absolutely no apology for that. I was and am biased in favour of Scotland remaining part of the Union.

The views expressed here are my own and were expressed spontaneously. They represent what I thought about people and events at the time, often in the heat of argument, and are in no way considered opinions. In consequence, these initial judgements often turned out to be spectacularly wrong.

I should like to express my gratitude to all those who helped me – whether knowingly or not – in compiling this diary. I owe a particular debt to my close friend and sometime colleague Iain Martin. Other than Jenny, my wife, he was the only person who knew, right from the start, that I was keeping a diary. He gave me continued encouragement and much sound advice.

My colleagues at the *Telegraph* office in Edinburgh, Auslan Cramb and Simon Johnson – as well as, for a time, Ben Riley-Smith – provided me with much support and even greater amusement, even if they weren't aware until the very last moment what I had been up to.

I want to say thanks and pay tribute to Murdoch MacLennan,

CEO of Telegraph Media Group, for his unstinting encouragement of me and unflinching enthusiasm for the Union.

I should also thank all of those politicians, civil servants, officials
and others who spoke to me readily and, in most cases, frankly,
without realising that I planned to record their comments and
opinions at a later date.

And a special thanks to Olivia Beattie, an editor extraordinaire,
for her forbearance and encouragement.

Finally, let me say that the campaign to keep Scotland in the
United Kingdom is often said to have lasted for something like
three years – since, probably, that sensational SNP victory in the
2011 election for the Scottish Parliament. That, however, is an out-
sider's conclusion. For me, and people like me inside the political
'bubble', it has been going on for much, much longer – for most
of my adult life, in fact.

However, the Scottish people have spoken. The referendum has
been won. Alex Salmond has resigned as First Minister. It's over.

Isn't it?

CHRONOLOGY

1997

MAY: Tony Blair leads Labour to a landslide victory in the general election, promising devolution for Scotland. Former Prime Minister John Major warns that Scotland risks sleepwalking towards separatism.

SEPTEMBER: A referendum on devolution is held, backed by 74.3 per cent of voters.

1998

The Scotland Act 1998 is approved, paving the way for a Scottish Parliament with control over most domestic policy.

1999

MAY: The Scottish Parliament meets for the first time in 292 years. The legislature is reconvened by the SNP's Winnie Ewing, the oldest MSP, with the words: 'The Scottish Parliament, which adjourned on 25 March 1707, is hereby reconvened.'

2007

MAY: The SNP is the biggest party after the Scottish Parliament elections, winning forty-seven seats, ahead of Labour's forty-six seats. The SNP forms a minority government; Alex Salmond becomes First Minister.

AUGUST: Salmond launches his government's 'national conversation', a White Paper setting out the 'full range' of options for Scotland's constitutional future.

2009

JUNE: A commission chaired by Sir Kenneth Calman finds that the Holyrood administration should take charge of half the income tax raised in Scotland, along with other powers.

The SNP announces that the Referendum (Scotland) Bill 2010 will be included in its third legislative programme for 2009/10, outlining details of a referendum on Scottish independence.

2010

FEBRUARY: The Scottish government publishes a draft bill on a referendum on independence, proposing giving Scots either new powers for the Scottish Parliament or full independence from the UK.

SEPTEMBER: The Scottish government announces that no referendum will occur before the 2011 elections.

2011

MAY: The SNP wins the Scottish Parliament elections, with sixty-nine seats, ahead of Labour (thirty-seven seats), the Conservatives (fifteen seats), the Liberal Democrats (five seats) and others (three).

David Cameron, the Prime Minister, concedes that the First Minister now has a mandate to secure a referendum on independence, one that the PM says he'll fight 'with every fibre I have'.

OCTOBER: The SNP formally launches its drive for independence, announcing details of an 'unprecedented' campaign to win the forthcoming referendum.

2012

8 JANUARY: David Cameron tells the BBC's Andrew Marr that clarity is needed over the independence referendum, which should be held 'sooner rather than later'.

10 JANUARY: Scottish Secretary Michael Moore tells MPs that the Scottish government does not have legal power for a referendum. Salmond replies that he intends to hold the referendum in the autumn of 2014.

25 JANUARY: Salmond sets out his ideal question in any referendum: 'Do you agree that Scotland should be an independent country?' The question is 'short, straightforward and clear', he says, arguing that Scots are about to make the most important decision facing the country in 300 years.

MAY: The Yes Scotland campaign for independence is launched, with Blair Jenkins, former head of news at the BBC, as chief executive.

JUNE: The Better Together campaign to defend the Union is launched, with former Chancellor Alistair Darling fronting an event in Edinburgh, which unites Labour, the Tories and the Lib Dems.

OCTOBER: Cameron and Salmond sign the Edinburgh Agreement, which commits to holding a one-question referendum by the end of 2014. It will also allow sixteen- and seventeen-year-olds to take part in the ballot.

2013

JANUARY: Following advice from the Electoral Commission, new wording is agreed for the Yes/No question: 'Should Scotland be an independent country?'

12 MARCH: The law is changed to give the vote to anyone who is sixteen or seventeen years old on the day of the referendum in autumn 2014.

21 MARCH: The Scottish independence referendum will take place on 18 September, Salmond announces.

NOVEMBER: A 667-page White Paper – titled 'Scotland's Future: your guide to an independent Scotland' – is published by Salmond. He describes it as the 'most comprehensive blueprint for an independent country ever published'.

2014

MARCH: The Conservatives, Labour and the Lib Dems rule out a formal currency union with England in the event of Scottish independence, saying, 'If Scotland walks away from the UK, it walks away from the UK pound.'

5 AUGUST: The first live TV debate between Salmond and Darling, which the latter wins.

25 AUGUST: Salmond wins the second TV debate against Darling.

7 SEPTEMBER: A YouGov poll puts the Yes campaign in the lead, by two points, for the first time.

16 SEPTEMBER: Cameron, Clegg and Miliband sign the Vow, a pledge to give Scotland more powers in the event of a No vote.

18 SEPTEMBER: Four million Scots (84.59 per cent of the electorate) vote on whether Scotland should leave the United Kingdom, with 55.3 per cent voting No and 44.7 per cent voting Yes. The Union is saved.

19 SEPTEMBER: Alex Salmond announces he is resigning as leader of the SNP and Scotland's First Minister.

2015

JANUARY: Deadline set by Gordon Brown for draft laws to set out a 'modern form of Scottish Home Rule'.

MAY: General election.

With thanks to Christopher Hope.

2012

9 JANUARY

I had a long talk to David Mundell[1] very early and he gave me the whole shooting match on what was about to happen on the referendum front. I thought I had a brilliant exclusive and phoned London to tell Chris Evans, who does all the Sunday editing now, what was going to happen.

However, unknown to me, while I was talking to Munners, David Cameron was on the *Marr* show blabbing the lot.[2] So everyone had it.

Although it was a good story, there seems little doubt that it went off at half cock and there are suspicions that No. 10 nicked

---

1　Conservative MP for Dumfriesshire, Clydesdale and Tweeddale; the only Scottish Conservative Member at Westminster.

2　David Cameron used the *Marr* interview to call for the independence referendum to be held 'sooner rather than later', thus forcing the issue, and said he was prepared to let the Scottish Parliament hold a legally binding ballot.

it from Michael Moore[3] because DC wanted to do it himself.

Still, it completely buggered the Nats. Unfortunately for DC, the Nat press operation up here is pretty well oiled and the local hacks are so used to being spoon-fed by Kevin Pringle[4] that they all bought Eck's[5] line about 'how dare' the British PM tell Scotland what to do. This total dependence on Kevin for lollipops, plus their innate dislike of anything emanating from London, means they'll always bash whatever comes up from the south, whether it's Thatcher/Major/Blair/Brown or now Cameron. Pathetic, really. Devolution was supposed to end that. Instead, it's got worse. Independence will make it a bigger nightmare.

10–13 JANUARY

Frantic efforts by the Nats and their tame civil servants to catch up. All of them burned the midnight oil to get their response to Cameron out. Brilliant operation by DC, but sadly for him the locals think he's lecturing them. What a bloody chippy race we are.

21 JANUARY

Had dinner in Edinburgh with David Hunt – now Lord Hunt and putative chairman of the new PCC.[6] He's a good lad and

---

3   Lib Dem MP and then Scottish Secretary.

4   Senior political spokesman for Alex Salmond.

5   Alex Salmond's nickname, 'Wee Eck'.

6   Lord Hunt of Wirral, who served in Margaret Thatcher's and John Major's governments, took over at the Press Complaints Commission in October 2011.

used to give me lots of stories when he was in the Cabinet; he always hated Maggie[7] but pretended he liked her. I suspect he's a bit of a shit. But a nice one. He told me a good story about how after she'd pulled out of the leadership race she phoned him and told him to ask Hezza[8] if he (Hezza) would release Hunt from his promise to vote for him. He phoned Maggie back to tell her that Michael was keeping him to his promise. He said Maggie put the phone down and never spoke to him again.

David said he was seeing all sorts of nonentities like the editors of *Scotsman*, *Herald* and *Record*. I asked him when he was seeing DC Thomson but he didn't seem to know who they were! Astonishing. I think the PCC is a waste of time. We do need privacy laws or tabloids will just get worse again, after a few years of good behaviour. But I can't write that or say it – it's deemed to be treachery in hacks' world. But I told Hunt not to get too close to the press bosses – it looks bad. I also told him that I thought Wakeham and Chris Meyer[9] were useless PCC bosses as they let the hacks away with murder and got us into the present state.

---

7   Margaret Thatcher, Prime Minister from 1979 to 1990.

8   Former Cabinet minister Michael Heseltine, who challenged Thatcher for the party leadership in 1990.

9   Lord Wakeham was PCC chairman from 1995 to 2001 and Sir Christopher Meyer, a former British ambassador to the US, ran it from 2003 to 2009.

4 FEBRUARY

I eventually got through to John Reid[10] – it took umpteen phone conversations with his secretary and with the noble lord himself before he agreed to meet me.

JR – they really are appropriate initials for the great man – came down to the special entrance to the House of Lords to meet me. It's an amazing place; there is nothing like the security there that there is at the Commons.

Anyway, John took me to the Pugin Room, where we had tea – he doesn't drink now. He's very funny about his drinking days. When asked if he had a drink problem, he always says: 'Aye, my problem was I couldn't get enough of the fucking stuff!'

I remember him well from those days – long nights, and afternoons, in the Strangers' Bar before John Smith[11] and George Robertson[12] got him off the sauce. But what a credit he's been to Labour and to himself ever since. Brilliant.

I tried to get him interested in taking over the anti-Nationalist campaign but right from the start he said he wasn't interested, wasn't the right man and wouldn't do it, no matter who asked him. He suggested all sorts of people who would be better than him, Alistair Darling[13] and Jim Murphy[14] being the two most often mentioned.

His initial reluctance, he says, is because he's still chairman of

---

10 Lord Reid, former Labour Cabinet minister.

11 Leader of the Labour Party from 1992 until his death in 1994.

12 Now Lord Robertson, former Labour Defence Secretary and Secretary General of NATO.

13 Former Chancellor, Labour MP for Edinburgh South West.

14 Labour MP for East Renfrewshire.

Celtic, which he's due to be for another six months or so. And he doesn't have to explain why that would stop him being a unifying figure in a campaign to save Britain – half of West Central Scotland, the Rangers half, would say, 'We're no' listening to a bloody Tim like John Reid.'

He was very warm in his praise for Jim Murphy and although he didn't say as much, it's clear that he thinks that Jim will keep the Blairite flag flying in the Labour shadow Cabinet. But doesn't Jim have that 'Celtic thing' hanging over him, too?

After we parted I met up with Mundell and told him what had happened and said that Cameron should ask Reid directly to do the job. Surely JR couldn't reject a direct appeal from the Prime Minister, I suggested.

But David said that Cameron was reluctant to involve Reid because he knows, or suspects, that Miliband[15] doesn't like him because he has made it pretty plain that he doesn't think much of the new Labour leader. And Cameron knows he has got to keep Miliband on side in the fight for the Union because it will be Scottish Labour's foot soldiers who will have to do most of the work.

So if Cameron recruits Reid, he risks losing, or at least annoying, Miliband. Jesus – talk about wheels within wheels.

I think it's worth the risk as Reid would be great at tackling Eck's bombast. But I think I'm going to lose this one.

Great night later in the Commons. Much plotting. I met Margaret Curran[16] in the Central Lobby and we went to the Pugin

---

15   Ed Miliband, Labour leader since 2010 and Leader of the Opposition.
16   Labour MP for Glasgow East.

Room for a drink. We were joined there by – at various stages – Thomas Docherty,[17] Lords Robertson and Foulkes[18] and various other passing Labour MPs and peers and then Mundell – a real Unionist cabal. At one stage, Pete Wishart[19] looked in and appeared horrified by these forces of darkness ranged against him. Great fun, but serious business being done. Everyone is very keen on a united front against the Nats. The trouble is, as Margaret points out, Labour is very wary of being seen to be getting too close to the Tories. It's really pathetic: they're more worried about saving their own skins than saving the Union. It won't change, either, I don't think, until after the May council elections, when Labour appears resigned to losing Glasgow.

7 FEBRUARY

Sent an email to Jeremy Paxman to tell him that BBC Scotland isn't showing his *Empire* programme at normal time, but very late on Sunday nights. They say it isn't because it glorifies imperial days – which it doesn't, but they probably thought it would – but for some other stupid reason. Old Paxo is clearly very miffed and sends me back an email about all sorts of badness by BBC Scotland. He obviously thinks they're all bigoted. And he might not be too wrong, either.

---

17 Labour MP for Dunfermline and West Fife.
18 George Foulkes, former Labour MP and MSP.
19 SNP MP for Perth and North Perthshire.

14 FEBRUARY

After months of buggering about over whether I should be working for DC as a special advisor and then nothing happening, I told them at Christmas that I'd rather forget it, if they don't mind, as I want to get on with the rest of my life. I don't like people describing me as a Tory, as I've hardly ever voted for them, but I like Cameron and I'd have worked for him on fighting independence. Still, I'm probably better where I am.

So, it was a bit of a surprise when out of the blue I got an email from Julian Glover – ex-*Guardian* political correspondent who is the new speech-writer at No. 10 – telling me that the PM had said I should be shown a copy of his speech due to be delivered in Edinburgh on Wednesday. It eventually arrived and it looked very good. I made a couple of minor suggestions – one was not to compare Scotland to Latvia, as this would annoy the natives – and I also pointed out, as I'm sure they were aware, that his offer to think about more powers if the Scots voted against independence would be the story. And so it proved.

Bigger surprise later when I was asked if I could have dinner with the PM on Wednesday at the Peat Inn in Fife. Oh, very well, I said. As if! Phoned Peat and got a room – it turned out to be the last one, as Andrew Dunlop,[20] the new special advisor, and Michael Moore, the Secretary of State, had to stay in St Andrews. No. 10 probably had a hand in booking my room. Still, the *Telegraph* had to pay for it.

---

20 Former advisor to Thatcher, political lobbyist and appointed in February 2012 to be Cameron's advisor on Scotland.

Dunlop is a good guy; I remember him from when he worked for George Younger[21] eons ago. He's been some sort of lobbyist but although a Scot he's out of touch and it will take him ages to get back up to speed. Mundell is a bit miffed about the appointment but I told him not to be and that Dunlop might get those buggers in Downing Street moving at last.

Dinner was very good. DC came in an open-necked shirt with a sweater around his shoulders. The rest of us were in suits – private secretary; Craig Oliver,[22] the new press secretary; Dunlop; Cameron and me. Very relaxed. DC called me Cochers, which is better than Cock, which is what Charles Moore[23] used to use. Venison and moderately priced Burgundy – 'we can't spend too much of the taxpayers' money', he said.

It is pretty clear that Oliver is a TV man, much more interested in that side of things than in what the papers are saying and doing. I suppose it was he who was responsible for making DC go to a porridge factory the next day. For Chrissake, a porridge factory! As the jovial man from the *FT* said when he heard about it, 'What happened? Were all the haggis factories closed?'

Still, DC is up for the fray. No mistake about that. Kept asking things like: 'If I say x, what will Salmond say to that?' And made clear that while he might be able to do a deal on timing or on teenagers voting, there was no way – absolutely no way – that he would agree to a second question. If it came to it, he said he

---

21 Former Conservative Secretary of State for Defence (*d.* 2003).

22 Appointed Cameron's director of communications in February 2011.

23 Former editor of the *Daily Telegraph*.

had his final option – what I call his nuclear option – of West-minster holding the referendum. 'Let him boycott it,' he said. He also asked what would be Salmond's final position and was told by Dunlop that it would be to hold an illegal referendum and tell the PM: 'I'll see you in court.'

Dunlop sat and listened, which is a good sign. Private secretary said nothing, which is proper. I told DC that he's got to do more to get to know the Scottish editors and told him about how Blair, who I said was as 'disliked as you are', used to have little infor-mal gatherings of editors and senior hacks, just sat and chewed the fat and had a beer or a coffee, nothing too much. He seemed to like the idea and told Oliver to do something about it. But I doubt if anything will happen.

I don't know if I'm right, but there seems to be a lack of grip and direction about No. 10 on the Union. I'll probably be proved wrong but the contrast with the Blair operation – fast, hard, instant – seems stark. But what do I know?

DC loved my line about my son and daughters and how I don't want them to be foreigners to each other just because some live in Scotland and some in England. Everyone likes it – German newspapers, French TV. The Nats hate it, so it must be good.

DC says he might use it in his speech when we meet at break-fast the next morning. Moore is surprised to see me there, as was Donald Martin, *Sunday Post* editor in chief, who was supposed to be having an interview. But he was left in an ante-room while we had bacon and eggs. DC had been for a run with the cops. Looks fit, not tired at all.

I gave him a spare Caledonian Club[24] tie, which looks very like the SNP one, and he says he'll wear it next time he's up.

Cameron got it in the neck from the Scottish hacks after his speech, thanks to Eck's sound bite 'Where's the beef?' If I was Cameron or Moore I would have said: 'From the look of you, Alex, and all the weight you are putting on, it looks like you've eaten it.'

Aus and Simon[25] urge me to write that line and I have – twice – but I delete it just before filing. Bad taste? Or am I being squeamish?

Cameron couldn't counter Eck on this jibe at the time because he had to rush back to London to see the Queen. Pity.

On a personal note, and as we were eating venison, DC moaned about the fact that he couldn't go deer stalking any more. I've known him since he was a Central Office press officer and I remember stalking with him at Glenfernate,[26] which the Brute (Bruce Anderson)[27] and Alan Duncan[28] used to take; George Osborne was there as well.[29] (In fact, also at Glenfernate at various times were Norman Lamont,[30] Jonathan Aitken[31] and William

---

24 Belgravia home from home for Scots.

25 *Telegraph* colleagues Auslan Cramb and Simon Johnson.

26 The Scottish estate of Conservative MP David Heathcoat-Amory.

27 Controversial commentator and godfather of Josephine Cochrane, AC's daughter (*b.* 1997).

28 Conservative MP for Rutland and Melton.

29 Circa 1998, before Osborne or Cameron were elected to Parliament.

30 Chancellor from 1990 to 1993 in John Major's government.

31 Cabinet minister in John Major's government.

Hague's[32] father. I think we still have pictures of them with Josephine as a baby.)

I suppose DC doesn't want to hark back to the grouse moor image days of Macmillan[33] or to be seen out on the hills with a powerful rifle. But apparently he's a very good shot; Bruce was with him once when he got a left and a right.

Anyway, he says that recently he fancied a bit of shooting and so took his twelve bore out into a wood near his home and bagged a couple of pigeons. It must have been quite a sight – he said that the wood had to be surrounded by coppers with guns. Whether that was to protect the ramblers from the PM or the PM from the ramblers wasn't clear. Anyway, he misses shooting/killing things. It's changed days if a lad from a council hoose like me can go deer stalking but the Old Etonian PM can't!

Next day, at his speech in Edinburgh, Ruth Davidson[34] kept asking me in front of everyone if I'd enjoyed my dinner with DC. Stupid bugger. Is she pissed off she wasn't there? I have grave reservations about that lady. She's good on telly but crap everywhere else. Is that all that matters now? She really needs someone at her side to tell her what to do and how to behave but she's surrounded herself with kids who just do what they're told. Mind you, who would do it? There would be no rush and the MSPs don't like her. Make McLetchie[35] do it.

---

32 Former Foreign Secretary William Hague was then Leader of the Opposition.

33 Harold Macmillan, Conservative Prime Minister from 1957 to 1963.

34 Leader of the Scottish Tories since November 2011.

35 David McLetchie, former Scottish Tory leader.

2 MARCH

Lib Dem conference in Inverness. Total rubbish, even if there are three or four Cabinet ministers there. Introduced myself to Clegg.[36] Very cold fish. Bruce Anderson is right about him – he is not British at all; he's a European! Danny,[37] on the other hand, was very pally and says the *Telegraph* is the only Scottish paper that knows what it's doing. Quite right. And Simon and I had a beer with Vince Cable;[38] he appears to be a human being.

Very good dinner with Tavish.[39] He's a bit of a hothead but he'd be good running something big. Wasted in the Scottish Parliament. He says that Linda Fabiani[40] told him that the senior Nats are furious with Eck for cosying up to Rupert Murdoch. Why Fandabidosi would confide in Tav is unclear; mind you, perhaps she's lonely and wants a friend. Lib Dems and Willie Rennie[41] are quite right to keep banging on about Rupe. Rank-and-file Nats hate him. When I kid the Nat backbenchers about it, Alex Neil[42] makes a joke, but the younger ones just sit there, saying nothing and looking furious.

---

36 Nick Clegg, Lib Dem leader since 2007 and Deputy Prime Minister since 2010.

37 Danny Alexander, Chief Secretary to the Treasury.

38 Lib Dem Secretary of State for Business, Innovation and Skills since 2010.

39 Tavish Scott, MSP for Shetland Islands and former leader of Scottish Lib Dems.

40 SNP MSP for East Kilbride.

41 Leader of the Scottish Lib Dems.

42 SNP MSP for Airdrie and Shotts.

4 MARCH

Had to have lunch sitting at the bar in the White Heather Club[43] as there were no tables in the restaurant, which makes a change as all those cheapskate MSPs usually eat chips in the canteen. Can they use knives and forks? Anyway, even Eck couldn't get a table. I offered him my seat and, never one to miss a chance, he said: 'I'm usually quite good at taking Tory seats.' Not bad, I suppose, for him.

Next time I saw him in White Heather, he was there with Joan McAlpine[44] and two others – one woman and one of his spads – showing solidarity, I suppose, while she was under attack over her stupid 'Union is like an abusive marriage' article. For a clever lady, she's thick as mince.

11 MARCH

Another night of plotting in the Commons. Met Mundell in the Central Lobby and off to the Pugin Room again. Very funny that Tom Strathclyde[45] could only join us as a guest, as Pugin is reserved for MPs or peers who used to be MPs. I love all these quaint Westminster rules.

Tom, who has survived his 'outing' over his liaison with his former secretary, took me for dinner in the Peers' Dining Room. Very nice of him but the food was pretty school dinner-ish and

---

43 Subsidised restaurant in the Scottish Parliament.

44 Former journalist, elected SNP MSP in 2011, and special advisor to Alex Salmond.

45 Lord Strathclyde, former leader of the House of Lords.

he dished up only 'très ordinaire' House of Lords vin rouge. He is very unhappy about the Lib Dems' plans for Lords' reform. Interestingly, Paddy Pantsdown[46] was at the next table with an attractive young lady. His daughter? Niece?

Highlight of the evening was seeing Betty Boothroyd.[47] I made a big fuss of her, which didn't seem to please Tom. Then headed off to the Strangers' – Kremlin – which was full of pissed Jock MPs, including Jim Murphy, who, as a non-toper, was completely sober. Jim was very friendly and says he's up for a fight with the Nats. I didn't stay long and beetled off to the Caley.[48]

14 MARCH

Wrote scathing attack on Labour over their useless attitude on minimum pricing of alcohol. Lib Dems and Tories are now backing it, leaving Labour isolated. Nicola Sturgeon[49] has wisely stuck to her guns over the years and all those defeats, and has let the rest come to her. Although they have no alternative, Jackie Baillie[50] has refused to give way. Johann Lamont[51] should sack her. Mind you, I think that's the plan anyway. As Paul Sinclair[52] told

---

46 Paddy Ashdown, former leader of the Lib Dems.

47 Baroness Boothroyd, Commons Speaker from 1992 to 2000.

48 Caledonian Club.

49 Then Deputy First Minister.

50 Labour MSP and shadow Health Secretary.

51 Then leader of Scottish Labour.

52 Spokesman for Johann Lamont, former advisor to Gordon Brown at No. 10.

me later, 'We'll give her enough rope to hang herself.' I like Sinky but I wonder if he's as good as he thinks he is.

15 MARCH

Terrible hammering for Labour in the debate on minimum pricing. More praise from me for Nicola. She's getting worried. 'Will I be getting a "doing" next week?' she asks. I told her she can't have three days' running of praise. But although she's a dyed-in-the-wool old-fashioned leftie, I really rate Nicola. She is a very good, determined politician but gets an easy ride. Labour's Baillie is useless and Tories like Mary Scanlon[53] aren't really Tories at all. Mary just wants to spend more money. And, anyway, Simon Johnson's brilliant story about the LIT cover-up[54] allows me to get back to Nat bashing.

Bruce Crawford[55] was his usual friendly, affable self when I met him at the Irish 'embassy' party for Paddy's Day – until, that is, I told him that he was getting a personal bashing the next day following Simon's tale. He got quite huffy. It turns out that he's just another prejudiced, cynical Nat – no different from the rest – just as Jenny has always said. This referendum is really showing them for what they are. Still, I do think there's a human being lurking inside old Brucie!

---

53 Conservative MSP for Highlands and Islands region.

54 Johnson used the Freedom of Information Act to force the SNP to reveal the cost of its proposed local income tax.

55 SNP MSP for Stirling.

The Presiding Officer[56] was there as well. God, how could they have this Fife wifie as their figurehead? She really is dreadful. Oh, all right to have a blether with, but a frontline politician? Gimme a break.

Ian Rankin agreed to judge the Tartan Bollocks.[57] Hmmm, not sure if it's a good idea. We'll have to think some more on this.

16 MARCH

Jenny Marra,[58] the good-looking Dundee lassie who's clearly overly ambitious, was up in the Media Tower – again – making sure that she gets her name into *The Courier* with young David Clegg.[59] She told me she liked my piece of the previous week, in which I'd had a real go at Johann Lamont. She'd better watch herself, saying things like that in semi-public areas. Labour had made sure it was her who welcomed Ed Miliband when he arrived to speak at their Dundee conference. Beauty and the Beast? Miliband's pals apparently say he was permanently wounded when John Humphrys asked him if he was too ugly to be Prime Minister.

Later that same day, that strange bloke Graeme Pearson,[60] the ex-senior copper, said he'd liked what I'd written about Jackie Baillie! Christ, is there no loyalty amongst politicians? What a shower.

---

56 Tricia Marwick, the SNP MSP elected Presiding Officer in May 2011.

57 The annual award given to the Scottish political journalist responsible for the year's most implausible story.

58 Labour MSP for North East Scotland.

59 The then political editor of *The Courier*.

60 Labour MSP for South Scotland.

17 MARCH

Good Morning Scotland and the general class of BBC interviewers are pretty dire, although Isabel Fraser[61] and Gary Robertson[62] are probably exceptions to that rule. Best of all is Glen Campbell.[63] Why he stays up here with these pygmies is beyond me.

In general, BBC Scotland is stuffed with people whose default position is left, left, Nat, Nat, left. But not very discerning left, either. They're just not very bright. And they'd get away with their bias if they were just, well, better at what they do. *GMS*, in particular, is crap. Even Nicola is pissed off with it and tells me she switches to the *Today* programme as soon as she can every morning!

19 MARCH

Received an email from Michael Forsyth.[64] He says he's giving up the deputy chairmanship of something or other to concentrate on different things. I've no idea what he's been doing, except make lots of money, so maybe he reckons he's made enough. I doubt if Cameron will make much use of him, in spite of Michael always trying to give the impression that he has the ear of Downing Street. He might well be right a lot of the time but I think everyone thinks he's too much of a loose cannon. And it's hard to forget that he was in charge when the Tories lost every single one

---

61 BBC Scotland journalist.

62 Ditto.

63 Ditto.

64 Scottish Office Minister in John Major's government.

of their seats in Scotland. He says that wasn't his fault and that it was John Major's for not making him Scottish Secretary earlier! He'd probably be best to concentrate on his salmon fishing, which for a wee boy of modest background from Arbroath he can now afford to do all over the world. Good for him!

20 MARCH

Downing Street rang to say that they're having that meeting with editors, after all, when DC is up this week for the Tory conference. Only thing is, they're having it in Glasgow, on Friday lunchtime, while I'm in Troon.[65] Typical; I'm the one who suggested it, but I won't be there. Andrew Dunlop told them I wouldn't be there but my new best friend – not – Craig Oliver told the press office to proceed anyway. Bugger them! Maybe they think they can count on me whatever. Hmmm, we shall see. I suspect it will be a ten-minute run round the table, instead of the relaxed affair Blair used to have.

Eck getting into all sorts of trouble over his über-loyalty to the Queen. His party members won't like it – they're all republicans. But, mind you, they don't like Rupert Murdoch either and Eck loves him, too. And Angus Brendan[66] made a pig's ear out of attacking the Lib Dems over Orkney and Shetland. Andrew Neil[67] thinks he's won a watch but it goes to show that if you

---

65 The Scottish Conservative conference was being held in Troon.

66 Angus Brendan MacNeil, SNP MP for the Western Isles.

67 MacNeil told Andrew Neil on the BBC's *Daily Politics* programme that Shetland and Orkney could remain part of the UK after independence.

tackle the Nats on issues other than macro-economics, they come unstuck. And how.

21 MARCH

Mundell phoned with funny news that they've finally got agreement with Eck's lot on the Scotland Bill. He says that at the end of the negotiations, the only thing the Nats wanted to talk about was not corporation tax, not excise duty ... but dental hygienists. The Nats insisted that the regulations governing them must be handled in Edinburgh, not London. That was their big issue. I can't believe that's the whole story but it's a bit of a hoot, nevertheless.

I always feel like a spare prick on Budget Day now, thanks to devolution. However, Osborne looked good and his Budget seemed to have hit all the right targets. Good speech, too. Miliband's nose job looks terrible. Oh yes, and Hezza is back in some role or other that I couldn't quite grasp. Must get him out for lunch or dinner ASAP.

I got it totally wrong, as everyone focuses on the Granny Tax, the fact that OAPs' earnings allowance is frozen. This is tripe; it turns out that OAPs might lose £83 per year! We have got to shift the emphasis from OAPs to younger people; the elderly get far too much already. I don't claim free bus travel but I haven't yet handed back my £200 winter heating thingy! It comes in handy for paying the El Vinos Christmas champagne bill. Hypocrisy or what?

23 MARCH

Troon for the Tories. Andrew Dunlop and David Mundell have invited me to conference dinner but it doesn't look like DC is coming. However, because they know I'm pissed off about not getting to the editors' meeting, Ramsay Jones[68] says Oliver is offering me what they call 'face time' with the PM. Jesus. Am I supposed to swoon? They're really not a patch on the Blair operation.

The dinner was quite interesting. Rory Stewart MP[69] was a very good speaker – but he looks a bit, well, driven. Painfully thin. Amazing performance. However, there's something otherworldly about him. And you sort of get the feeling that something tragic is about to happen to him. Funny.

Sat with Dunlop, who is really putting himself about and kept asking me if I still thought that Cameron should launch his own referendum if Eck continues to stall. I said I thought he should, to which Dunlop said, 'Good.' This means that DC is definitely going to do it. Christ, what a story.

Dunlop asks me who he should see on Labour's side, who was close to Johann, so I told him to get hold of Margaret Curran through her Tory pal Mark Menzies,[70] that bloke from Ayrshire who sits for a Cumbria seat, as well as Paul Sinclair. And he asks what to do about Michael Forsyth. What indeed! He is also going to have a go at getting John McGlynn[71] back into the fold. John

---

68 Special advisor to the PM on Scotland, formerly Scottish Conservatives' chief spin doctor.

69 Conservative MP for Penrith and the Border.

70 Conservative MP for Fylde in Lancashire.

71 Tory donor who founded the Airlink Group of car parks. He declared his intention to vote Yes days before the referendum.

is in the huff and wants a cuddle and Eck is being very nice to him, so Dunlop, who's had business dealings with John, is going to get him back for the Tories. I'm not sure he's worth the effort.

Dunlop has already seen COSLA[72] – turns out that Nats are about to take it over. But interestingly, although they disagree with the coalition's welfare reforms, they all agree that something drastic needs to be done, especially in Scotland.

Mike Crow[73] was there, wearing his RBS hat. The Scottish Tories treated him shamefully, especially that idiot Fulton[74] and the other one, Kynoch.[75] They were both wandering about the conference hotel – like ghosts at the feast. Couple of numpties. The Scottish Tories still can't find a chairman. Useless. Had a drink with James Stewart,[76] the new treasurer. He doesn't seem to know a lot about politics.

24 MARCH

DC made a good speech, bollocking the Scottish Tories for being useless, but most of them didn't know they'd been bollocked. Then he buggered off to Glasgow to see the editors. I phoned Angus Macleod[77] afterwards, who is making a bit of a meal of being

---

72 The Convention of Scottish Local Authorities.

73 Michael Crow, former journalist and director of communications for the Scottish Conservatives.

74 Andrew Fulton, chairman of the Scottish Conservatives from 2008 to 2011.

75 George Kynoch, deputy chairman of the Scottish Conservatives from 2008 to 2012.

76 James Stewart is a director of a London-based private equity firm.

77 *Times* political journalist (*d.* October 2014).

'acting unpaid' Scottish editor of *The Times*. Poor old Magnus[78] having been sacked by that idiot Harding,[79] who can't be long for this world.

Anyway, Angus was with Andy Harries[80] of *The Sun* and they seemed impressed by DC. 'He gets Scotland,' says Macleod, which appears to surprise them. Told Dunlop the verdict from the editors, which he thinks is good news. Mind you, I wouldn't bank on the positive vibes lasting very long if I were them.

My *Telegraph* fringe debate was a huge success. McLetchie and Fergusson[81] were pretty good and there were some constructive contributions from the floor. There must have been about 150 in the room and as many locked out. Every drop of wine drunk and every canapé scoffed. Political party delegates are like locusts when there are freebies about! Still, well worth it. Pity I can't do any more – the budget's run out, apparently.

Back in the conference proper there was a very strange ceremony where the Tories launched their Friends of the Union campaign, complete with an English woman, who was also a Muslim and from Yorkshire,[82] an Ulsterman[83] and a Welshwoman.[84] Not very impressive, I'm afraid. They still look odd and old, or at least they have a large crust of elderly people at the top and

78 Magnus Linklater, former Scottish editor of *The Times* and former editor of *The Scotsman*.

79 James Harding, the editor of *The Times* from 2007 to 2012, now head of BBC News.

80 Later to become editor of the *Scottish Daily Mail*.

81 Alex Fergusson, Conservative MSP and former Presiding Officer of the Scottish Parliament.

82 Conservative peer and the then party chairman Baroness Warsi.

83 Former Ulster Unionist leader David Trimble.

84 The then Welsh Secretary, Cheryl Gillan.

then, at the bottom, they have quite a few swivel-eyed, studenty types – not all Scots – but precious little in between. They don't seem to have any thirty-, forty- and fifty-somethings. And that's their biggest trouble.

However, Ruth's speech the next day was pretty good. And she is a toughie, although I still can't make up my mind about her. I want her to be good because the Union campaign needs the Tories, if only for their money. The others won't join in until after the May elections. But Labour would rather attack the Tories and although Willie Rennie is brilliant – by far the best in Scotland – he hasn't got a party, or many supporters.

25 MARCH

Listened to the appalling Derek Bateman's[85] 'news' programme in the car on the drive back from Troon. He really is the Nats' 'Leader at Large'. He spent the whole programme monstering the story Tavish gave us about how Shetland and Orkney wanted to keep their oil if Eck wins his referendum. This is the only mention that BBC Scotland have made of this story – not a word about it all week. Apparently, Bateman's show is being dropped. I don't like to see hacks booted out but he has been treading on thin ice for years. Labour got him sacked from *GMS* for being too pro-Nat.

Message on the mobile to ring Dunlop. He wants to know how I think the conference went. It would be easy and glib to say, 'Bunch of old people, whom nobody likes, meet in small

---

85   BBC Radio Scotland presenter.

seaside resort miles from anywhere.' But that's too harsh – they are trying. The trouble is I'm not sure the voters are ever going to like them again. The May elections aren't likely to bring them much good news.

Iain Martin[86] phoned in great glee to say that Andrew Neil had Mundell on his show and asked him, 'Why are the Scottish Tories so useless?' But it's dead easy to take the piss like that. And not especially clever. But Iain worships at the Neil shrine, so there's no point arguing with him.

26 MARCH

DC in the brown stuff over massive cash-for-access allegations. He's been stupid and arrogant and has had to publish all the names of everyone he's had a biscuit with. Don't they have anyone on 'banana-skin watch' at No. 10? Clearly not. Our dinner at the Peat Inn will have to come out. So what? I suppose the taxpayer paid for it but I paid my own hotel bill and bought Dunlop two drinks – decent malt, although I can't remember which one.

27 MARCH

Had lunch with Boothman.[87] He's not a hack any more and not even a suit. He's a bureaucrat.

---

86 Scottish-born journalist and author, former editor of *The Scotsman* and *Scotland on Sunday*.
87 John Boothman, head of news at BBC Scotland.

Rob Gibson MSP[88] moaned to me that his letter to the editor about Tavish's Shetland story was answered by me and not Tony Gallagher.[89] I told him that he wasn't important enough for the main edition. Christ, he's very lucky to be an MSP. Sixty grand a year for a wannabe like that. Do me a favour!

Kevin Pringle is emerging as a total shit. Told *The Herald* about our Salmond and the millionaire tea party story,[90] when he knew it was only us and the *Mail* that had it. Needless to say, idiotic *Herald* news desk didn't want it. But then they saw our paper and, boy, did they want it then.

28 MARCH

Yet again no mention of an anti-Nat story on the Beeb. It is a total bloody disgrace. The trouble is that although they have oodles of staff, none of them appear to do any reporting; they're all presenters or producers. If these were anti-Tory or anti-Labour stories that we were breaking, they'd be all over them. On the other hand, they didn't do the Henry McLeish stuff,[91] which was a 'storm in a teacup', according to their political editor Brian Taylor. Maybe they're just rubbish! They don't go through the normal routine of following up proper stories. And as for STV? Don't make me

---

88 SNP MSP for Caithness, Sutherland and Ross.

89 Then editor of the *Daily Telegraph*.

90 Alex Salmond hosted lottery winners Colin and Chris Weir at his official residence and then received two half-million-pound donations.

91 The offices expenses 'muddle' that led to the downfall of Labour First Minister Henry McLeish after a year in the job.

laugh – as they say themselves, their news bulletins are the 'murders and fitba programmes'. That's all they cover.

Sinclair eventually came up with the goods as a follow-up, with a reference, under ministerial guidance rules, to Elish,[92] as former Lord Advocate, who is now Parliament's complaints officer, about Eck's tea party. But we had to tell them exactly how to do it. Jesus, what a shower.

29 MARCH

Although my piece made it plain that I thought DC was up to his oxters in the brown stuff over the cash-for-access stuff, the cybernats[93] went apoplectic about me saying that Salmond was guilty too. They all think the Weirs should sue me. For what, pray?

Another load of nonsense at FMQs from Eck but clear signs that Lamont and Davidson have got his measure. They looked like they might be co-operating but I don't think they are. I wish they would. Tricia Marwick allows Eck to attack Labour for losing the election last year and then blasts the Tories for DC's handling of the threatened fuel strike.[94] What's either of them got to do with the responsibilities of the First Minister of Scotland?

By the way, I think all that nonsense about stocking up in case of a petrol shortage after the strike was deliberate by DC's lot; they just overdid it.

---

92 Dame Elish Angiolini was Scotland's first female Lord Advocate, serving from 2006 to 2011.

93 Anonymous nationalists who vent their spleen online.

94 An Easter strike by fuel tanker drivers was eventually ruled out by the Unite union.

Poor old Mike Russell.[95] I think he's in big trouble. His Curriculum for Excellence[96] is hated by teachers: private schools are refusing to do it, some state schools too. Now a new survey says that fourteen-year-olds can't add up. Scottish education is in a shocking state. I like Mike; he's arrogant – incredibly so – although Jenny hates him. But he has a brain and he could be good news, but I fear he's doomed. And lots of his own party hate him, too, from his days as general secretary. And although he said in 2007 that he was burying the hatchet and wiping the slate clean, John Swinney[97] will NEVER forgive him for that article which said it was 'time for the men in kilts' to tell John to resign as leader. It's a tough old life. Astonishingly, although I bashed Mike in my column, he sent me a not altogether huffy email. Strange bloke.

Lunch on the Terrace, amazing weather. Eck was in the restaurant – he always is on a Thursday, although I didn't recognise his guests. He looks hellish – overweight and puffy. I'll be surprised if he lasts until October 2014. He eats too much, probably too late at night, and loves his red infuriator, which, of course, doesn't make him a bad person. Who would take over and would they have a chance of winning the referendum without Eck? I don't think the voters like Nicola all that much; she still has that Wee Nippy reputation, which is undeserved, but she'd be a shoo-in with the party.

---

95 Scottish Education Minister.

96 Derided Scottish education reform.

97 Scottish Finance Minister who led the SNP in opposition from 2000 to 2004.

I don't think John would stand, what with Elizabeth's[98] illness, but I think Mike would, out of sheer vanity, and would get clobbered. I think Alex Neil should stand. He's a very good minister and has increasing support. I don't think for a second that he'd win but he would do well, which would stand him in good stead in the party.

1 APRIL

Eighteenth anniversary of my return to Scotland and THIRTY-EIGHTH since I first went to Fleet Street. Christ, what an old bugger! I can't believe I'm still working and will have to keep on working, for ever, it would seem. Still, great weekend in Yorkshire to see Ally, Sue and the fabulous Fergus.[99] Josephine and Harriet[100] were great. Lovely to have my family all together and now Tina[101] is coming up on Friday.

2 APRIL

Cameron is in all sorts of shit, at least according to the hacks. I'm not sure it's all that bad, in spite of an incredible piece by Iain (Martin) in the *Telegraph* predicting doom and gloom. Sure, they've made major balls-ups over Budget and petrol but they'll

---

98 Elizabeth Quigley, BBC journalist and wife of John Swinney, had been diagnosed with multiple sclerosis.

99 AC's son Alasdair (*b.* 1978) and his wife Sue and son Fergus (*b.* 2011).

100 AC's youngest daughter, Harriet (*b.* 2000).

101 AC's eldest daughter, Catriona (*b.* 1974).

get over it and, anyway, Labour are crap. I think it's a temporary blip. We'll see. Mind you, the only thing I'm concerned about is whether any of this is damaging the referendum chances. I don't care about anything else.

Dunlop was up today and offered me – very generously – a slot at 5 p.m. I said I couldn't make that, but he said that was it. Bugger him. He needs me more than I need him, so he can stew. And, anyway, when I had a drink with Sinky [Paul Sinclair] on the way home, it was clear that he was one of the people seeing Dunlop. And it was me who told Dunlop to see Sinky in the first place. Ditto Margaret Curran. I must give her a ring to see how the land lies.

Sinky's great rival – Rami[102] – lobbed us a good-ish story about a cybernat council candidate[103] attacking Catholics. Nats have suspended him pro tem. They'll have to expel him if the tweets are genuine. They are a desperate bunch, those cybernats, and spell big trouble for Eck, I'm pleased to say.

But the Nats worked fast to try to shut down the tale about them allowing anonymous responses to their consultation period (over what question should be on the ballot paper). But not fast enough to stop us writing about it.[104]

Gerry Hassan's[105] transcript of his interview with me arrived. God knows what he's going to do with it, although it read all

---

102 Rami Okasha, Scottish Labour's head of communications until October 2012.

103 Lyall Duff, SNP candidate for North Lanarkshire Council, resigned from the party on 12 April 2012.

104 The SNP was accused of trying to rig the consultation when it emerged that people could respond anonymously as many times as they liked. The party later agreed to exclude anonymous responses.

105 Scottish writer and commentator. He interviewed AC for his PhD thesis.

right, especially what I said about education. At least I thought so.

3 APRIL

Nats in trouble over their Catholic-hating candidate. They can't stop him being a candidate, as nominations have closed. All they can do, presumably, is tell people not to vote for him. Those who live by the web shall die by the web. Serves them bloody well right. But they clearly hope this story will go away.

Tory press launch of their local election campaign was a total farce. Turned out to be a photo-call only. A complete waste of my time.

Incredible that the *Record*, which had the anti-Catholic candidate story, hardly used a word of it. That paper is fast becoming a joke. Still, the BBC is eventually following up the story. Amazing that an organisation with so many staff takes so long to get to grips with stories. The contrast with the London operation is stark.

I'm glad that others are doing this story, as it was beginning to look like us versus the Nats. That is a far from ideal situation.

4 APRIL

Michael Moore on *GMS* to report that 75 per cent of respondents to his consultation process want only one question and an early referendum. He did very well, stuck to his guns doggedly and kept hammering home the same point. He was quite gentle with poor old Bruce Crawford over his balls-up of the SNP consultation and those anonymous replies. Moore said there was no need to submit his replies to independent analysis as he didn't have the problems that Bruce had. And, interestingly, the Nats didn't put anyone up for the programme – they're in enough brown stuff.

The trouble with Crawford is that he's just too honest and straightforward for this process and admitted lots of things he shouldn't have; the Nats would have been better getting someone much more slippery for such work. Alex Neil could do it brilliantly but I bet Eck doesn't want him in such a crucial role. The upshot will be that the Nats will produce their consultation at the end of May and that will, surprise, surprise, say let's have two questions in 2014. Then we'll have a stand-off and it will be down to an eyeball contest between Eck and DC/Moore, which was always going to be the case.

I've always said that a compromise will be reached on the timing but NOT on the number of questions. The rest is just hot air.

4 APRIL

Just about to leave when the editor's secretary sent me Peter Murrell's[106] letter complaining about our coverage of the sectarian candidate's story. It's a bit all over the place but it took me over an hour to draft a reply. Pete, who is a nice bloke and an exceptionally good chief executive, is trying to suggest that Eck can't sack this bloke because of the SNP's disciplinary process. What rubbish. It just shows how embarrassed they are about the man

---

106 Chief executive of the SNP and husband of Nicola Sturgeon.

– who called Catholic midwives who didn't want to supervise abortions 'money-grabbing old witches'. Alex has been creeping to the Catholic Church, ever since the days of Tom Winning,[107] who was more than a bit of a Nat himself, and now the Church is demanding that this bloke be expelled. Quite right, too. I shall have to reply to Murrell tomorrow. I just hope it doesn't bugger up my trip to Angus. Mind you, that's a hotbed of bloody Nats.

The Nats have obviously decided to take me on. I got a letter from the Weirs – lottery winners – earlier, complaining about what I had written about their tea party with Eck. It looked suspiciously like a put-up job by Nat HQ. Still, it all takes time. I'm very pleased that they're getting annoyed. I just hope that London don't start panicking!

Funnily enough, I haven't had a blether with Murrell since Simon and I took him and Nicola for a champagne supper at that brilliant restaurant in Perth to celebrate their wedding a couple of years ago. It cost a bloody fortune, as none of us stinted on the claret, and both Mr and Mrs seemed to know their way around a wine list. A bit like Eck, actually, as I've found out in the past when he's been a guest – that two-bottler in Rules[108] a few years ago, for instance. That's one good thing about the Nats, they like their red infuriator. Most Labourites couldn't tell good wine from Irn Bru.

---

107 Leader of Scotland's Roman Catholics (*d.* 2001).
108 Restaurant in Maiden Lane, London.

5 APRIL

Angus Tartan Day dinner went very well. My speech seemed to be a big hit; lots of political jokes and maybe Angus isn't so full of Nats after all. Good hotel – the Golf in Carnoustie – but very mediocre food. And they'll need to give it a lick of paint if they want another Open.

6 APRIL

Another letter to Tony Gallagher from Murrell, which has also been passed to me to deal with. I gave it pretty short shrift; I would guess that Murrell will get fed up moaning to Tony G only for him to refer everything to me.

Spoke to Iain M, who's on his way up – he says that lots of senior Tories think that his piece attacking DC was brilliant. Typical Tory backstabbing. What a shower.

Mike Russell in more brown stuff for saying that Scotland needs to be 'liberated' from the English. What absolute crap – he has lost it. Jenny gave him a thorough kicking in her *Sunday Times* column, and Iain McMillan[109] of the CBI wrote to congratulate her. Quite right, too.

7 APRIL

We had a house full of English anti-'liberators' – Tina and Mitch.[110] Great stuff. They seem very happy, which is a relief.

---

109 Director of Scotland's CBI from 1995 to 2014.

110 Michael 'Mitch' Mitchelson, partner of Catriona Cochrane.

Both Ally and Tina happy, and doing well both professionally and in their relationships, is great. Granny[111] here for Easter, too. She's looking fantastic. Happy Easter altogether. So far! Could do with winning the Lottery. Granny's bought loads of tickets.

8 APRIL

Canongate Kirk with Granny. Neil Gardner is a great minister but his style and the whole service is incredibly high. It's not the Queen's Kirk and he's not her Chaplain Royal for nothing! Not my cup of tea at all, and not Granny's either. Mind you, they do Communion very well; at least they make it feel like it means something. But I still can't partake. I just don't believe enough.

9 APRIL

First proper day of holiday. Saw Tina and Mitch off, after minor panic over a lost satnav. Took Granny home and back to empty house, or at least just us lot. Was about to go for a walk in the Botanics when there was a heavy shower but luckily BBC Parliament was replaying its 1992 election programme. Absolutely brilliant. This was my last hurrah at a proper election as political editor of a proper paper – the *Mail on Sunday*. Great memories, although I was pissed off Major won. I wanted him to lose, because he'd beaten Hezza. I spent £60,000 of Lord Rothermere's[112]

---

111 Elizabeth 'Betty' Cochrane, AC's mother (*b.* 1925).

112 The third Viscount Rothermere, chairman of the Daily Mail and General Trust (*d.* 1998).

money on polls with NOP, all of which proved to be hopelessly wrong. I always thought JM was crap and '97 proved that.

Peter Kellner[113] and Tony King[114] were the experts – plus John Curtice[115] with hair (what a shock) – and were saying that if only Labour had John Smith,[116] they'd have won – at least according to a Gallup poll the week before the election. I'm not so sure. I had lunch with Hezza in Mijanou in Ebury Street on the day of John's shadow Budget and he arrived with a great grin on his face, saying: 'Tax, tax, tax – we've won, thanks to John Smith.' And so it proved. But Kinnock[117] was the main reason, I reckon. They could never have won with him. And there were several shots of his speeches. Bloody awful. It was Tina who said after watching the Sheffield rally[118] that they'd never win with that sort of boasting. Very perceptive.

There was a very interesting sequence, too, from Northern Ireland which showed that at the 1992 general election all the Sinn Fein candidates, including Gerry Adams[119] in West Belfast, had lost to the SDLP.[120] But instead of bolstering them, first Major and then Blair – egged on by the bloody Yanks – decided to back the gunmen and over the years they undermined the SDLP and

---

113 Political analyst and president of YouGov.

114 Anthony King, professor of British government at Essex University.

115 Leading psephologist and professor of politics at Strathclyde University.

116 Former leader of the Labour Party (d. 1994).

117 Neil Kinnock, leader of the Labour Party from 1983 to 1992.

118 Kinnock's triumphalism in the Sheffield Arena a week before the 1992 general election is thought to have damaged his chance of victory.

119 Sinn Fein president.

120 The Social Democratic and Labour Party of Northern Ireland.

consistently doffed their caps to the Shinners. And look what happened: the IRA killers now rule the roost and the SDLP are nowhere. We have peace – of a sort – but at what price!

Oh yes, and I see that the Nats have finally expelled Bill Walker;[121] not for beating up his three wives but for not telling them that he had! They really are the most hilarious party on God's earth. And yet people vote for them. Run an independent country? They couldn't run a piss-up.

10 APRIL

And now the Nats have decided to get that headcase Lyall Duff to write, threatening to sue over my commentaries calling him 'sectarian' and a 'bigot'. As I'm supposed to be on holiday, I asked Simon to send Richard Murray, the office lawyer, the SNP statement suspending him and saying his comments were unacceptable, the RC statement demanding his expulsion, a copy of the horrible man's offensive tweets and a copy of the front pages from the local papers. I spoke to Richard, who agreed there's no case to answer, and will write back saying 'fair comment'. Good. I doubt they'll go away, though. Next stop – PCC. Ho, hum.

I subsequently discovered that Duff is alleging that we found out about his comments by hacking into his computer. This is outrageous. He said what he said on public social media sites. Unfortunately, the office – via Murray, the lawyer, and Ben

---

121 Former SNP MSP for Dunfermline who was convicted of twenty-three charges of domestic abuse in 2013 and jailed for a year.

Brogan,[122] the deputy editor, are trying to play it cool – and are waiting until tomorrow to sort him out. This man, and the Nats who are backing him, have to be crushed. And quick.

10 APRIL

Brogan and the lawyer don't think we should do anything about Duff's allegations – they are shitting themselves in case his hacking accusations get wider coverage. What idiots. They don't want to do any more but this is important and we must crush it quickly. I have demanded sight of their response to the allegations of 'hacking' first thing Wednesday; it had better be good.

11 APRIL

Brogan phoned and said again that he didn't think we should do any more. Christ! You'd think we were guilty. I said that Duff was a sectarian bigot and a liar and we must send a stiff lawyer's letter. Brogan still humming and hawing but I insisted. Several hours later he phoned to say they'd send a letter and I got an email copy. At last!

We took Harriet to Strathallan for her Scottish orchestra 'camp'.[123] I met Paul Gilbride[124] with his daughter – she is in the orchestra too, clarinet – and H phoned Jenny later to say that

---

122 Then deputy editor at the *Daily Telegraph*.

123 National Children's Orchestra of Scotland.

124 Political reporter on the *Scottish Daily Express*.

they were now best pals. That's good. I like Paul and he's had a terrible time with his wife's long illness and eventual death.

Very funny watching the news of DC's visit to Indonesia. It's an almost exact re-run of Maggie's to the same countries – Malaysia and Singapore, too – that I did all those years ago (how many? – must check). And when she got to Indonesia she said how nice it was to be in Malaysia (which we'd just left). Denis[125] dug her in the ribs and whispered, 'Indonesia, darling' and, as a reward, she gave him a look that would have curdled milk. There's gratitude for you. It was here that they made us all wear Batik shirts for a walkabout next day and they gave Denis one that would have fitted Cyril Smith.[126] Gordon Greig[127] of the *Mail* and Tony Smith[128] of the *Star* were on that trip – both dead now. So was James MacManus,[129] who thankfully is still going strong – just about.

12 APRIL

Poor old John McLellan (or is it McLelland?)[130] has been sacked as editor in chief of *The Scotsman*. Everyone at Magnus Linklater's drinks party expresses great grief about it. I'm sorry for someone losing his job but, Christ, McLellan has had a bloody good innings at pretty good money without ever showing himself to be

---

125 Denis Thatcher.

126 Gargantuan Liberal MP for Rochdale (*d.* 2010).

127 Political editor of the *Daily Mail* (*d.* 1995).

128 Political editor of the *Daily Star* (*d.* 1996).

129 Journalist and author.

130 John McLellan, editor of *The Scotsman* from 2009 to 2012.

any good, other than many years ago at the *Evening News*. Average at *SoS* and the same at *Scotsman*. Sure, they're cutting back like mad, but they never seem to get the front of the paper right, which is what makes people buy the bloody thing. And McLellan always seemed to be more interested in being on the PCC and 'being' an editor, rather than editing a newspaper. Ho, hum – he'd probably say worse things about me. But of course, Johnston Press are a bunch of idiots, who paid too much for the title and will never, ever get it back. They will now probably bring up some numbskull from the *Scunthorpe Bugle*, or whatever, to edit from Embra. More disaster looms, I'm glad to say. Only hope is for DC Thomson to buy the whole shooting match … but they'll wait a while until the price drops, thanks to this latest nonsense.

I think I'll ask for another reporter. We can't fail against this lot of numpties.

13 APRIL

Anguished emails from Iain Gale,[131] saying that they need another title for this magazine whose board I'm supposed to be on. They've now decided that the 'Edinburgh Arts Review' won't work, as they want to broaden its scope and coverage. I suggested Gazette or Scottish Gazette, Richard Holloway[132] suggested the Review and they've lit upon the Summerhall Review as

---

131 Scottish journalist, author and publisher of short-lived arts magazine.

132 Former Episcopalian Bishop of Edinburgh.

the winner! I think Summerhall is the base of Prof. McDowell,[133] the man with the money who's backing the thing. It's difficult to disagree with Trevor Royle,[134] who, after that first shambolic board meeting, intoned, 'It's doomed, doomed.' Cast of thousands on the board, some of us know what we're talking about, others clearly haven't a clue. Richard Holloway, as ever, looking very pleased with himself and patrician. Still, he's basically a good chap and he *is* a cut above the common herd. Still, I'll find his weak link one of these days.

Alan Taylor[135] is one of the board members, too, and Iain wants us to find a regular subject on which we can disagree every issue. Oh God, this sounds all very boring, not to mention amateur night out.

13 APRIL

That sectarian bigot has been allowed to resign by the Nats – that can be the only conclusion to be drawn from their ten days of silence and not expelling him. Nobody will believe me when I say this, but I really cannot think of a scummier bunch than the Nats at present. They throw out Bill Walker – deservedly – not for beating up his three wives but for not telling the SNP that he beat them up. As the man himself said: Nobody asked me if I beat up my wives, so how could I admit it?

---

133 Robert McDowell, the investor behind the Summerhall arts complex in Edinburgh.

134 Military historian and journalist.

135 Scottish journalist and author.

And with Duff, any decent party faced with his disgusting conduct would have been itching to expel him and urge people not to vote for him. But no, they hum and haw, concentrate on issuing threats to us and then afford a worm like this the dignity of being able to resign. What a bloody shower. I wonder what John Swinney really thinks of his party? Does he believe that any means justify the end he's looking for? He never used to be able to stand Eck; can he really be happy to throw in his lot with him now?

14 APRIL

Eck's gone nuts about way over the top *Economist* article.[136] Of course it's a piece of crude propaganda but it is merely the other side of the coin, where Eck waxes lyrical about how there'll be free beer for the workers in his Nat Nirvana. The fact that all of the leading Nats piled in on the *Economist* front, with tweets and emails, shows how rattled they are generally and how fearful they are about the result; the longer they wait, the worse it's getting for them. I think the strategy was to prove how good they were at running Scotland and hope that the voters get sick of a Tory PM. But the person they're getting sick of is Eck. Everyone – even the haverers on BBC Scotland's Sunday morning programme – reckon that Salmond over-cooked his stuff about *The Economist*.

Sure, the 'Skintland' map and front page are sixth-form – if that – humour but the leader and article inside are perfectly balanced. But if anyone doesn't back Eck, he and his acolytes scream blue murder.

---

136 *The Economist*, 14–20 April 2012.

15 APRIL

Eck will be furious that the Scottish Sundays seem to have ignored the Skintland story today. And he'll probably blame Kevin Pringle for that failure. Mad Angus of Moray[137] was emailing all yesterday with outraged quotes. Still, he has more problems with the *Sunday Herald* splash, saying that the multiple wife-beater Bill Walker has also been accused of raping someone. What will Eck do now? If the accusation is true, he'll probably castigate Walker – not for the rape, but for not admitting that he's a rapist when he was interviewed as a prospective Nat candidate!

They really are hilarious but at the root of their problem is the fact that it's very much a one-man band. Oh sure, they have competent ministers, like Swinney, Sturgeon and Neil, but as far as we can see, it's still Eck who decides everything. His high-and-mighty behaviour isn't winning him any friends. He sits on Mount Olympus – or in his case the mill at Strichen – and pretends to be above all these problems about sectarian candidates, like Duff, and wife beaters, like Walker, and refuses to say anything. It's not good enough: Cameron has had to confront, comment on and sack his trouble-makers; and Miliband and Lamont had to speak up over the madman from Falkirk, Eric Joyce.[138] Why does Eck think he can continue to get away with being so aloof? After all, his party is the ultimate democracy. It is one man, one vote. And he's the one man with the one vote!

Simon says they're due to debate membership of NATO at

---

137 SNP MP Angus Robertson.

138 Labour MP for Falkirk, who was convicted of assaulting four people in a House of Commons bar in February 2012.

their executive meeting soon. That will be interesting. Hope they decide to stay out – it's easier to attack them that way.

DC is due up this week. Christ, I hope there are no more balls-ups. They appear very accident prone and there seems to be a U-turn every day or so. That Oliver bloke is getting all the blame now, just as I predicted when I met him. Useless.

16 APRIL

Harriet was in great form last night when we saw her after her concert in Perth. The music was very good, although the Poulenc thingy for two pianos was too much for me. However, Josephine and Jenny said the pianists were great. So what do I know?

The Nats are actually pretending to have a debate on NATO. I wish them well, really, I do. But I hope they realise that if Eck has decided on membership – which I think he has – then that will be it, no matter what the great unwashed think.

17 APRIL

Wind farms could easily be the nemesis for the Nats: there is a helluva groundswell building against them, and south of the border they're apparently not giving any more licences. There's a big protest march to Holyrood next week but Donald Trump's[139] involvement is not helping. The Tories should get stuck in here. If

---

139 The US tycoon sued the Scottish government over its plans to build an offshore wind farm close to his Scottish golf course. He lost the case in February 2014.

they attack wind farms and the arse Russell is making of education, who knows, the world might beat a path to their door. Maybe!

Hammered the Nats on their phoney NATO stuff[140] and got herogram from Adam Ingram,[141] ex-Defence Minister.

18 APRIL

Alan Taylor and I have agreed to bash each other on private schools for Gale's mag and Jenny is going to write a piece, too, on funding for kids' orchestra, so that's all right. Eventually, I persuaded Iain G that I can't write about ballet. Christ, what a job!

Bloody Scotland Bill[142] got its Holyrood blessing. Load of absolute tosh – pure appeasement of the Nats. Gave everyone a kicking and felt better.

The wife-beating alleged rapist and ex-Nat turned up and got a monstering from the hacks. He's finished now – I don't know why he doesn't just accept it and piss off somewhere.

Interesting blether in the street with George Reid,[143] ex-Nat Presiding Officer. He said that if he was Cameron he'd just hold the referendum himself and bugger Alex. Had a chat with Jackson Carlaw[144] in the bar. That's what he's advocating, too. I think it will happen that way.

---

140 Salmond planned to abandon opposition to NATO membership.

141 Labour Defence Minister from 2001 to 2007.

142 This set out amendments to the Scotland Act 1998, with the aim of devolving further powers to Scotland.

143 Presiding Officer from 2003 to 2007.

144 Conservative MSP and deputy party leader.

DC up tomorrow but no word from Dunlop. Still, in his absence I told Ramsay Jones to bang the drum on wind farms and schools. After forty-odd years, the Scottish Tories are deciding to be different. He said he was going to a meeting and would bring it up.

19 APRIL

DC here – or there, somewhere in the west where some dairy owners have lobbed him some dosh. Otherwise, only pitched up at winnable Tory seats but did focus in his speech on wind farms and schools. Funny that!

Bruce Crawford was very pleased that I was nice to him. He shouldn't be.

Salmond got a complete drubbing on lies about inward investment and also about NATO. There is no doubt in my mind that the unanimity behind Eck is beginning to fade. Alex Neil is asking what I thought about FMQs[145] – clearly worried that things are going awry and not happy with the NATO stuff; Neil would be on the side of the rank and file – in other words, against Eck. I told him to keep quiet and that I'd run his campaign for leader. He laughed. But I like Alex Neil. Wonder if I can ever get someone like him out for dinner? And what about Nicola? John?

I do think that maybe – just maybe – the worm, or worms, may be turning. I must keep picking at the scab. Who knows what

---

145 First Minister's Questions, held every Thursday in the Scottish Parliament.

we might find? The NATO debate – if it is a debate and not just some stunt by Mad Angus of Moray – could easily be the catalyst for dissent. They've just about put up with the Queen. But now they've got to accept NATO, too. We'll see.

Simon didn't win political reporter prize.[146] Told him he wouldn't. Absolutely ridiculous that the best journalist in terms of unearthing things doesn't get the prize when a lot of numpties do. Let us give them hell! I have tried – again – to raise Gallagher. I never worked for an editor who was so hard to get hold of. Christ, even Sir Peregrine[147] was easy to reach; ditto Charles Moore; Derek Jameson,[148] Nick Lloyd[149] etc. Will Lewis[150] – too easy! Why this should be, I have no idea. But I want him to take Simon for lunch.

21 APRIL

Harriet twenty-eighth out of 150-odd at primary school cross-country race at Kirkcaldy High School, Broon's[151] alma mater. It must have been très swish at one time; getting very seedy now. Still, H and her pals did well. And H is a star.

---

146 At the Scottish Press Awards.

147 Sir Peregrine Worsthorne was editor of the *Sunday Telegraph* from 1986 to 1989.

148 Editor of the *Daily Express* from 1977 to 1980 (*d.* 2012).

149 Editor of the *Daily Express* from 1986 to 1995.

150 Editor of the *Daily Telegraph* from 2006 to 2009.

151 Gordon Brown, Labour PM from 2007 to 2010.

22 APRIL

Frans's[152] 75th birthday party at the Kinloch House. Absolutely brilliant lunch and J drove home, thank God. Unfortunately, everyone there read the *Telegraph* and I got lumbered – shouldn't say that – with having to address the Stirling Tories in the autumn and also to write a piece on gardening leave. Christ! When will I manage?

Mail on Sunday has really tough piece from Cameron about Eck bullying all the businessmen. Absolutely true but none of them will shop him publicly.

23 APRIL

Wind farms getting to be THE subject. Eck put out a mass of figures showing what a boon they are, which proves that he's worried about the whole issue.

At last had a blether with Dunlop but as he clearly now thinks he knows everything, I doubt if No. 10 will have much use for me now. It's the usual practice – get everything you know out of Cochrane, adapt and adopt it as your own and, hey, you are the masters now. Still, we'll see. And at least they're being more aggressive towards Eck, which is what I've always said they should be.

All-party pro-Union campaign to begin at the end of May/June. Big licks, big names and crash bang wallop. I reminded Dunlop

---

152 Frans ten Bos, Dutchman who played rugby for Scotland and a friend from the Angus glens.

that it must be done in June as Scotland goes on holiday in July. Said he'd be up next week. We shall see.

Andrew was very funny about Sinclair, whom he saw a couple of weeks ago. He said that he'd been warned that Paul has a dark side. How droll; there are lots of people still looking for Sinky's lighter side! Still, Paul will love that. He likes being thought of as a bit of a shit. All spin doctors do. Twits.

Iain M was on radio news at ten havering a complete load of bollocks about the crisis that Cameron is in and all because Nadine Dorries[153] said he didn't know the price of a loaf/eggs/whatever. Jesus, what a lot of crap. We've had crises before – Falklands, Black Wednesday, terrorist attacks etc. – and this is a crisis in Scotland with Salmond and the Nats. Everything else is bloody fluff.

24 APRIL

Election expert announced that the referendum must have only one question. Excellent. Needless to say, daft old Henry McLeish disagrees. How come the worst and stupidest politician Scotland has ever produced is still listened to … except he's not, apart from by the Nats and the Beeb.

What a day! Wrote a column about Edinburgh Airport, hoping that it doesn't turn into an even bigger shopping centre, then did a leader on Eck and Trump, and then the big one broke! Just as I thought, Salmond's squalid association with Rupert Murdoch

---

153   Conservative MP for Mid Bedfordshire.

has jumped up and bit him in the arse. Astonishing Leveson evidence shows that Eck was hawking his backside around Murdoch executives to get *The Sun* on side for the 2011 election in exchange for his support for their purchase of BSkyB.

As usual, on TV he answered questions he wasn't asked – namely that he hadn't been in touch with Jeremy Hunt[154] – but nobody said he had been; merely that he'd made himself available to support the Murdoch bid. It could be that the Murdoch comms bloke[155] is over-egging the pudding but we're getting mighty close to Eck now. I reckon we'll get a body – his – and long before the referendum, too. The man is a shyster. This one has a way to go.

Iain is on the phone – demanding credit for tipping me off about the Salmond thing. In a way, he did, but Labour were well on the case, unlike the Tories who were miles behind. They are just not up to the job, I'm afraid. Poor Mike Tait[156] is completely out of his depth and the kindergarten leadership team are actually hopeless. Iain is having a good run, which is good for his bank balance.

Can't wait until tomorrow. Must speak to as many Nats as possible. They won't like this Murdoch stuff. They've held the line so far and there's been no public criticism, but that surely cannot last. Or can it? The only problem for Wednesday is that that idiot Trump is in town, when the only story now is Murdoch. Mustn't let Trump distract us from the real job of nailing Eck down.

---

154 Conservative MP for South West Surrey and the then Culture Minister.

155 News Corp's European head of public affairs Fred Michel, whose email suggested Salmond's advisor had agreed to call the Culture Secretary about BSkyB.

156 Director of media for the Scottish Conservatives.

25 APRIL

Labour, Tories and the Lib Dems totally useless in failing to force Salmond to make a statement on his sucking up to Murdoch. He has now changed his tune and far from saying he hadn't lobbied Hunt, he now says he would have if he'd been asked. He's getting away with everything thanks to the stunning incompetence of the opposition.

Even Paul Grice[157] is astonished that the opposition parties haven't banded together to demand a statement from Eck. He thinks that even the daft Fifer[158] couldn't have turned down a joint request. But they didn't do it, so Eck goes on his merry way. Tavish is furious that they didn't force this one. The trouble is that, much as I hate it, this isn't really a parliament; it's a meeting of people who're very grateful they've got a £60,000-a-year job.

Went to Canongate Kirk for the memorial service of Sir James Cayzer.[159] Everyone who's anyone – apart from me – was there. Spoke briefly to Archie Stirling[160] and Julia Ogilvy[161] and Henrietta[162] but had to rush back to the day job – keep bashing the Nats.

---

157 Clerk and chief executive of the Scottish Parliament.

158 Presiding Officer Tricia Marwick.

159 Shipping heir and bon vivant (*d.* 2012).

160 Stirling landowner who set up his own political party Scottish Voice (2007–12) to defend the Union.

161 Wife of James Ogilvy, only son of the late Sir Angus Ogilvy and Princess Alexandra, the Queen's cousin.

162 Henrietta Cayzer, wife of Nigel, Sir James's heir.

26 APRIL

As predicted, Eck was as oily as ever, refused to make a statement and, with a Presiding Officer like Tricia, all we got was FMQs. I phoned Sinky to tell him to get Johann to use a few pars of Oborne's[163] piece in the *Telegraph* about the number of investigations mounted against Murdoch. It sums everything up. She did it – magnificently – and the sight of all those Nats looking very uncomfortable was wonderful.

I had a few words with Alex Neil afterwards and while he was trying to insist that Eck had won the exchanges, he agreed that Johann had been doing well until she asked too many questions and lost the initiative. I kept on and on at him and it's clear he's totally pissed off with Eck. Wrote a column trying to drive wedges between Eck and his Cabinet. I know they hate this. But they hold the line. Bastards!

27 APRIL

To London for the Scottish Ballet. Wonderful, wonderful show.

Had an argument with Simon before I left – telling him to write a story based on Nicola's angry argument with the Beeb over Rupert Murdoch. He wasn't keen but we got there in the end and he wrote a smashing story. He does listen, even though it sometimes sounds like he isn't. It is obvious that Wee Nippy hates all of this scummy stuff.

---

163 Peter Oborne, *Daily Telegraph* columnist.

Fantastic lunch with MM [Murdoch MacLennan].[164] He is very worried about the Union, especially after having dinner with Sly Bailey[165] on Wednesday night. She thinks that Eck is the funniest, most charismatic politician she's ever met, especially as Eck kept her amused with his Sean Connery[166] impersonations! This is his party trick, mocking his greatest supporter. Jesus, is that what it takes to get the *Record* on side? Eck pretending to be Shir Shaun! And what would the great man think if he knew Eck was taking the piss?

MM wants to meet some of the Labour people so I'm going to wheel Margaret Curran into his orbit.

28 APRIL

Back to Edinburgh. Plane late. God, I hate flying. But I did have a good chat with Christopher Thomson,[167] who was on the same plane. He was appalled by the Sly Bailey story and clearly hates Eck. Excellent. Interestingly, he said that *The Scotsman* and *Herald* would merge their back office functions within a year, just keeping separate editorial teams. Very good goss.

29 APRIL

Fantastic story in the *Sunday Mail* – for once – that Jack

---

164 Chief executive of Telegraph Media Group.

165 Then chief executive of Trinity Mirror, publisher of the *Daily Record*.

166 The tax-exile actor is a lifelong Scottish Nationalist.

167 Joint managing director of DC Thomson.

McConnell's[168] phone was hacked by the *News of the World*. I assumed it was something to do with his dalliance but it seems to be something to do with his children.[169] Whatever, it's outrageous and more trouble for Eck.

Totally ludicrous Scottish Politics Show.[170] Completely useless bunch of idiots. Interview with Cardinal O'Brien,[171] who wrecks his argument – such as it was – by saying that Cameron is 'immoral'. The man is no intellectual but this was even worse than usual. Not a patch on Tom Winning. What a wonderful man he was, a real muscular Christian. BBC Scotland were left to their own devices today, because of local elections; this was the worst political programme I have ever seen. Must have been organised by the Little Sisters of the Poor. Why does Isabel Fraser have anything to do with it? Christ, it was very bad.

Had a blether with Andrew Neil, to keep him on the case re: Eck, but he's aware of what's going on, which is more than most of the south of the border TV and radio presenters.

1 MAY

Just when I thought that the Rupert Murdoch stuff was going away, along comes the Commons Select Culture Committee to lambast Rupert and tell Eck to have a Scottish Parliament

---

168 Labour First Minister of Scotland from 2001 to 2007.

169 Hannah and Mark McConnell.

170 The BBC's *Sunday Politics Scotland*.

171 Keith O'Brien, the then leader of Scotland's Roman Catholics and Britain's most senior Catholic. He was forced to resign in February 2013 over allegations of sexual misconduct.

investigation. And, of course, we also had that Joan McAlpine saying in her newspaper column that she, too, had been hacked, because she had to claim that it was all Labour's fault. I'm beginning to think that the Labour Party is right and that far from banning her from writing this tripe, she should be encouraged to carry on as it damages the Nats with every instalment.

Wonderful stuff and no Pringle to dig them out of a hole. Why not? Where is Kevin? Is he disagreeing with Eck? Is he really ill? Boothman says he's been told he is getting time off to prepare for his wedding. Really? Doesn't sound like Eck. Had a word with Nicola's man – Noel[172] – to tell him that she should put clear blue water between her and her boss. He responded and I think agreed with me but maybe not. He is a good, wily operator. Gives nothing away.

Dunlop is coming up on the 10th. I asked him if he wanted lunch in the Parliament. He jumped at it when I told him Eck was usually there, too, on Thursdays, and told him he could eyeball the enemy. Should I introduce them? Interesting.

2 MAY

Eck got away with it again today, even though he talked the most complete bilge imaginable about Rupert Murdoch and hacking. Needless to say, BBC Scotland swallowed the lot – all that guff about forty of Strathclyde's finest investigating things.[173] What

---

172 Noel Dolan, special advisor to Nicola Sturgeon.

173 Salmond said a Strathclyde Police special unit was investigating allegations of criminality in Scotland related to phone hacking.

about Scotland Yard's investigation? Hadn't they heard of that? Brian Taylor just takes the easy line. And he's an Arab,[174] too, so I can't really bash him.

Later, I had a very interesting conversation with John Swinney in the bar. He was taking the piss about how bad the opposition is; the Nats are all extremely cocky, and with good reason. God, it will be wonderful when they fall. John said that if all the opposition parties had demanded that Eck answer an 'urgent question' last week there was no way that Tricia Marwick could have refused it. Or at least John says it would have been very difficult for her to turn down all the parties. Mind you, I as good as wrote that in my column. I suspect that John might have liked that. When he was leader he always thought that the Salmond-ites were undermining him – which they were – but he's been über-loyal since he stood down and Eck came back. He says he's started with a clean slate again. There will be a blood-letting all right when Eck fails. It's what keeps me going. Please God, spare Eck until that great day!

But first things first. Let's hope the Nats don't win everything tomorrow in the local elections. There's a limit as to how much I can take of their successes.

Had a blether with Margo MacDonald,[175] who's now at home after crap NHS treatment for her infection; she seems to be on the road to recovery thanks to them eventually deciding that she needed a pacemaker to help her circulation. She says she's coming back next week. I hope that's not too soon.

---

174 A Dundee United supporter, as AC is.

175 Independent MSP, former member of the SNP.

3 MAY

Voted early, although could hardly get in the polling station for bloody Nats loitering at the gate. They recognised me and we exchanged some banter. As it was polling day, and there were witnesses present, we both had to behave. It won't always be so polite.

4 MAY

What a glorious day. We have to be grateful for small mercies and although the Nats won seats all over the place, they flopped – at least by comparison with what they'd hoped for. I'm sure the more sensible ones didn't think they'd do as well as they did in 2011[176] but given the high they've been on for the last year, it was great to see the reverses rolling in. Glasgow – thumped; Edinburgh – beaten into second place and generally forced back to where they always are, at about one-third of the popular vote. By the way, that word 'popular' is a misnomer, as the turn-out was pathetic. Not as low as I'd thought it might be, but still hopeless.[177]

The Lib Dems were all but wiped out and the Tories were useless. I thought Jackson Carlaw looked very unhappy on the telly. He thinks he would have made a better show of it than Ruth and I think he's probably right. She is a disaster.

---

176 When they won an overall majority in the Scottish Parliament elections.

177 The turn-out was 39.7 per cent, according to the Electoral Commission.

5 MAY

I tuned in, by accident, to the Derek Bateman bilge on BBC Scotland. What absolute rubbish. It is like a parallel universe; they had Joyce McMillan[178] (who regards herself as the Mother of Devolution) and Peter Lynch[179] (Nat-leaning academic from Stirling University) on, wittering about how the result now means that Labour will have to go for devo max.[180] What tripe – it means the absolute opposite. Eck gets nowt now, absolutely nothing. Labour has re-learned how to fight and will grow in strength. Johann can go to town now. But she has to extend her influence beyond Glasgow, which was a sensational result, and poor Nicola looked extremely pissed off.

Oh sure, the Nats took Dundee, which everyone will hold against me. But so what, I once voted twice for them in one day: at the 1970 general election I voted Nat in Dundee East, then I got the train through to Perth and voted for them again! They lost in both!

6 MAY

All the party leaders are on *Sunday Politics*; Eck still denying everything and insisting that it all went to plan. Nobody believes him and Isabel Fraser, again, failed to nail him. Johann was modesty personified. She's becoming a real star. I hope

---

178 Theatre critic and columnist on *The Scotsman*.

179 Dr Peter Lynch, senior lecturer in politics at Stirling University.

180 Shorthand for full fiscal autonomy.

she doesn't let it go to her head. I don't think it will. Prof Jim Mitchell[181] made a bit of an arse of himself; he's too Nat for his own good.

Spoke to Dunlop and tried to urge him to pre-empt Eck's launch but he says the Unionist campaign is not ready and won't be ready until sometime in June. Pity. We should be keeping Eck on the back foot. I hope things are not slipping.

7 MAY

Matt Bayley, the *Telegraph* news editor, didn't tell me about a story from the Defence Secretary[182] about cuts in the army in Scotland. Thankfully, I spotted it on their news list and managed, with a bit of help from Brigadier George Lowder[183] and Andrew Og-Wedd,[184] to get a better story out of it.[185]

More trouble for the Tories, I fear, but why should I worry; they have all those expert special advisors, don't they? Like hell they do. Hammond's quotes make him sound like he's been captured by the bad boys at the MoD, the heirs to Mike Jackson,[186] who want to extinguish everything that smacks of tradition and history. Well, they'll get into trouble on this one from the Nats

---

181 James Mitchell, professor of public policy at Edinburgh University.

182 Philip Hammond, Defence Minister from 2011 to 2014.

183 Then commander of 51 (Scottish) Brigade, the second most senior soldier in Scotland.

184 Lt Col. Sir Andrew Ogilvy-Wedderburn, former commanding officer of the Black Watch.

185 Philip Hammond planned to scrap the names and cap badges of Scotland's historic regiments.

186 General Sir Michael Jackson, the former Chief of the General Staff (2003–6) who oversaw the restructuring of the regiment system.

and I certainly ain't defending them. You cannot abolish names like the Black Watch and get away with it.

On my way to bed I saw the announcement that Labour and the Nats are to join forces to run Edinburgh Council. I don't like the look of that one. I suspect we'll get more madness like congestion charging and trams. I smell trouble – big trouble. Daft old Ruth appeals to the Lib Dems to join the Scottish Tories or face oblivion. If I were them, I'd opt for oblivion. There's not a lot of difference between that and joining up with her party. And that millionaire nutty Dutchman, Peter de Vink,[187] has sided with the Nats to run Midlothian. Christ, what a country. If we get ever get any money, we're out of here. Pronto.

Had to send a bit of an apology to Tanya[188] for being so anti-Hollande's[189] victory. But he'll be useless and take the easy way out. The only good thing is that the euro's crashing. Pity I'm skint, so can't take advantage and start buying some! Ho, hum.

Dunlop texted to find out the date of the SNP national council. I suppose that's what I am now – just the message laddie! Serves me right.

8 MAY

My story about Hammond abolishing the cap badges has taken off – massive follow-ups everywhere. Needless to say, the main

---

187 Independent councillor, former Conservative.

188 Tatiana Sévenier, Harriet Cochrane's French godmother.

189 Francois Hollande won the French presidential election on 6 May 2012.

edition didn't use our version, so missed the main point, and then Deerin[190] commissioned a piece for op-ed, again without telling me. Thought about complaining to Gallagher but he doesn't pay any attention anyway. Waste of time. Anyway, Jim Murphy did a good comment piece, or at least his spad did! Put Jim's picture on the front; circulation slumped, I told him.

9 MAY

This cap badge tale just rolls on and on. Huge follow-ups everywhere. Maybe I should have put my own by-line on the tale in the first place. The Tories are getting a right bashing.

10 MAY

Yet again, the cap badge story is everywhere. Told Dunlop that they've got to sort it out. I said he should get Cameron involved and eventually Ramsay Jones phoned. He's actually doing a better job in London than he did up here. We agreed a form of words to indicate that they're halfway to a U-turn. Mind you, I'm getting a bit tired of this story – we've kept it going all week, which is very good. Salmond piling in too, and he even called me 'Alan' when I passed him in the corridor tonight! Jesus.

Did my stint at the Ramsay Garden seminar.[191] Not a brilliant speech by me; bit of a hangover, I fear. Still, they seemed to like

---

190 Chris Deerin, then comment editor of the *Daily Telegraph*.

191 Political salon in Edinburgh, established by the late Michael Shea (*d.* 2009), a former press secretary to the Queen.

it. And needless to say, Magnus (Linklater) just had to say how much better Angus (Macleod) was than me. I shouldn't get narked but that did irritate me, probably because Angus was very good. Lots of worthies there. Don't know who gets onto that mailing list. Mona[192] very friendly – lovely lady, as is Lady Robertson,[193] Malcolm's[194] mither. They gave me a bottle of whisky, but gave Angus a book token as he's off the booze. I'd rather have had the book token; I've got so much bloody whisky!

Must get some euros tomorrow, the rate is going up again!

11 MAY

Watched Rebekah Brooks[195] at Leveson. Although the *Sun* lot have got us all into this mess, it is an outrage the way the questioning is going. Leveson and his QC were pounding her about why she told Ed Balls[196] to sack that Haringey social worker woman[197] who was responsible for that Baby P[198] cruelty case. Why shouldn't the bloody *Sun* tell a minister to sack someone?

---

192 Michael Shea's widow, who took over the running of the seminars.

193 Sandra, wife of George Robertson.

194 Son of George Robertson.

195 Former CEO of News International and editor of *The Sun* and the *News of the World*.

196 Labour's Children's Secretary from 2007 to 2010 and shadow Chancellor since 2010.

197 Sharon Shoesmith, Haringey Council's former chief of child protection. She went on to win compensation, said to be in the region of £600,000, against Haringey Council for unfair dismissal which had been prompted by Ed Balls (the then Children's Minister)'s interference in 2008.

198 Peter Connelly, one-year-old killed by his mother, her boyfriend and her boyfriend's brother in 2007.

That's what papers are for. But you can see the way this thing is going – protect all officialdom forever from any kind of criticism. We deserve a kicking and we'll probably get one but this is going much too far. We are heading for a shackled press and a secret society. That really would suit officialdom and the politicians. Terrible.

Phoned Iain M and said all of this above about Leveson to him. He agreed and said he was going on *Newsnight* to discuss it. I hope he has a go on this issue.

Watched Iain on *Newsnight* and he did have a go. First class. But he needs someone to teach him how to speak. He keeps gulping and swallowing his words. It's hard to make out what he's saying. Wish it was me on the telly. But then they don't want some ancient Jock from Edinburgh. More's the pity.

Mind you, it must be excruciating for Cameron to see himself pilloried in that way, signing all his emails 'Lots of love'. What an absolute prat. He's going to get a terrible hammering on this and quite right, too. And why has he still not sacked Hunt? The longer he holds out, the worse it gets for him.

Not a cheep on the army cap badges. But we'll keep going.

Went to the Usher Hall with Jenny for the last RSNO[199] concert with Stéphane.[200] Great night and we weren't in the VIP room. Thank God, the wine in there is always execrable, but all the freeloaders looked down their noses at us as we passed in the corridor. It's not even as if it's their money that they're spending

---

199 Royal Scottish National Orchestra.

200 Stéphane Denève, music director of the RSNO from 2005 to 2012.

in supporting the RSNO – it's their companies', just like me!
Mind you, at least Norman Lessels[201] spends his own money in
supporting them and he'd rather be outside with us than in the
VIP reception. I liked most of the programme, except that mel-
ange by MacMillan[202] at the start. All over the place it was, but at
least it was called Britannia, which must have annoyed intensely
our wonderful Culture Minister, Fiona Hyslop.[203] What she
knows about culture you could write on a postage stamp, unless
of course there were accordions and fiddles involved.

12 MAY

To the Cayzers for tea and dinner with the girls, who were admired
by all for their poise and, well, for just being wonderful. Jenny,
too, looked gorgeous. Nice crowd but only one Viscount, one
Viscountess and one Countess. Poor show! Nigel and Henrietta
were in great form – it was H's birthday – and made everyone
very welcome. They are great hosts. The wine, even though Nigel
doesn't drink now, was out of this world. What a treat to stay over
at Thricpley[204] – lovely house, full of servants.

13 MAY

To Belmont Arms pub, which Nigel has bought, for the Red

---

201 Edinburgh arts patron.
202 James MacMillan, internationally acclaimed Scottish composer.
203 Appointed Minister for Culture in 2011.
204 In Newtyle, Angus.

Cross lunch. All Angus there. Great fun, apart from not drinking because of the car. Jenny and the girls had gone back to Edinburgh, lucky them. The speech by Sarah Bradford[205] went on far too long, although it was nice to blether with her at the table. She's interviewed everyone, including Denis Healey,[206] who she said was 'very naughty'. And how.

14 MAY

Gave Hammond another kicking. This man is a positive menace. Asked a simple question by Jim Murphy, he refused to say he'd keep the cap badges and/or names. Christ, why can't Downing Street get a grip? What's the point in co-ordinating policies that affect the Union if they can't sort this one out? All he has to say is that the famous names will live on and everything will calm down. Jesus, I'm beginning to think that DC's critics are right. There is no control at the centre. Ramsay Jones tries hard but is very low in the pecking order. Don't know what influence Dunlop has. All he keeps saying is: 'This is very high on our radar.' Really? It doesn't show.

15 MAY

The Nats will love my column. And now they've got Fatty Fraser[207] in *The Courier* saying that the Union is finished. Peter's gone mad.

---

205 Royal biographer.

206 Lord Healey, former Labour Chancellor.

207 Lord Fraser, former Lord Advocate and Conservative politician (*d.* 2013).

Saw Fiona, his very nice wife, at the Red Cross 'do' and she didn't seem too pleased when I asked where he was. She said: 'Well, you know he can't stand for very long, nowadays.' Not a happy lady, if you ask me.

Tried to find our stuff online, only to discover that 'Scotland' has been abolished. Phoned the news desk to get them to sort it. They said they will. Hmmm, we shall see. I think I'll tell Brogan to chase it up, nevertheless.

Texted Tom Strathclyde to voice my fury at Hammond. He replied within minutes to say he'd be seeing him at Cabinet and urged me to complain to No. 10. Yeehaa.

Had a bit of a spat with Brogan, who sent me a paean of praise about Hammond and said – incredibly – that this was all about the Scots being conditioned to raising their hackles about anything and everything said by an Englishman. I texted him back to say this was absolute bollocks. Really, what a total idiot and to think that he spent most of his career on the *Glasgow Herald*! He really is just a suit – completely useless – and his columns read like PR hand-outs. Jesus. On any paper with an ounce of nous about politics, he'd be no. 3 in the lobby.

It seems that Kevin Pringle is going to run the Nats' 'Freedom' campaign, or whatever they plan to call it. Dunlop said he'd heard that rumour, too. Oh sure, Kevin's denying it. But nobody believes him.

Online people have reconstituted 'Scotland' in our web edition after all my complaints. Very nice of them.

Had a long chat with Fraser Nelson[208] at the *Speccy* and tried

---

208 Editor of *The Spectator*.

to interest him in Hammond's House of Horror. No luck. At least not yet. It's become the Beltway's Organ of Choice under Fraser, which is a surprise. Very metropolitan is his *Speccy*.

16 MAY

Dunnit! Gotcha! Whatever. After a phone call from Jim Murphy, who told me that rumours suggested a U-turn by Hammond was on the cards, Simon got a phone call from the Def. Sec's spad, who confirmed that the abolition of the names and cap badges had been called off. Great stuff. Crowed a bit to London about our – repeat OUR – victory and texted Gallagher to tell him. Total silence by return. Still, what do I care? WE WON. And the main edition did at least use the bloody story.

Tipped off young Cleggie about our success at 9.30 p.m. Should have had time enough for him and *The Courier* to catch up.

Dunlop rang and was pleased to hear the news, although it was clear he knew it was coming, and agreed that there needs to be more co-ordination to make sure that policies fit in with our aim of saving the Union.

He was puzzled that some people are annoyed at Cameron saying he'd live with the 2014 referendum date. The only people annoyed are those who haven't been listening to Cameron. It's the number of questions that matter most – much more than important than the timing.

17 MAY

Got a nice text from Tom Strathclyde congratulating us after I told him of our triumph over Hammond: 'Great stuff, well done and thank goodness!' What loyalty. And Ramsay Jones texted to say that Cameron and Davidson had forced Hammond's cave-in. Rubbish. I did it.

Mustn't get carried away. Be careful.

Herald had a stupid splash saying Cameron will go along with autumn 2014. Yes ... and? Mind you, Ruth got bashed by Eck for opposing it when everyone knows that DC's always been prepared to do that and has actually told everyone – editors, pol. eds, even Eck – that he'd give in on that.

No wonder *The Herald*, along with *The Scotsman*, is the only paper to see a drop in sales in April. And now Currie[209] is off, having handed in his notice. Poor Robbie[210] – he's the best pol. ed. they've never had but they'll never give it to him. Idiots.

Dreadful FMQs – not a line in it, although Sinky thought that Johann was brilliant. Back to the drawing board, old boy. Ruth D tried too hard to flog that dead horse of Eck's being hacked ... or not. Got nowhere.

Mind you, I wrote her up a bit for her part in the victory over Hammond. Whether she deserved it or not, I'm not sure.

Had lunch in the White Heather Club, after having a glass of champers with Aus and Simon to celebrate our triumph and also to toast Margo's return. Unfortunately, she's on so many pills

---

209 Brian Currie, political editor of Glasgow's *Herald* from 2009 to 2012.
210 Robbie Dinwoodie, chief Scottish political correspondent at *The Herald*.

that she couldn't have any. Says she takes thirty-nine tablets a day! Made sure we weren't sitting next to Eck but maybe I should have insisted on being there as Joan McAlpine was his guest – again – and got a terrible bollocking from old Tricia for missing her question slot for the umpteenth time. Very embarrassing but, Christ, the corridor went mad, whooping and hollering to do her in and filching menus from the restaurant to work out what she was eating/drinking. Everyone hates her but I don't. She is arrogant and refuses to accept that she's a nobody. Good for her. She won't content herself with being a backbencher. If only she'd pace herself, she'd be a brilliant asset. It's all come too quickly for her. Still, what do I care?

18 MAY

Emailed Scotland Office first thing to see if I could have a blether, off the record, with Michael Moore. They didn't get back to me until 4 p.m., by which time I'd written the bloody column. Typical. Still, I spoke to Dunlop at No. 10 and he gave me a very careful, but quite stylish, view of things. Didn't tell me anything I didn't know, of course, and wouldn't tell me who is to lead the big Unionist campaign, which is to be launched in the middle of June. But it is pretty clear that they've got someone. Reid? Darling? One of those, I'll bet. It has to be Labour. They'd better tell me first or there will be trouble. Or, better still, I should find out through my own devices.

Sue Cameron[211] rang after I'd emailed her about her *Telegraph*

---

211 *Daily Telegraph* columnist.

column on the dearth of special advisors at No. 10. She didn't seem to know that there were only two: old Patrick Rock[212] and Dunlop. She's very good on mandarin stuff; I shall keep in touch with her.

20 MAY

What a day! Michael Moore phoned and we had an excellent blether. He gave me more than Dunlop did, including the fact that Darling is to run the Union campaign. Great stuff. He'll be good, very good, and the Nats know that. I spoke to several others – Margaret Curran, Paul Sinclair included – and everyone seems to know that Darling was going to do it. So why couldn't Dunlop tell me? We won't get very far if he plays secret squirrel all the time. Still, if Moore is happy to talk, so much the better.

Then the sky fell on us, with the news that Megrahi[213] has finally died. Auslan's backgrounders were all in and I just lobbed in a commentary, insisting that Salmond was not in cahoots with Brown/Blair/whoever over the release.[214] Nobody believes me in London, of course. They're all experts down there.

---

212 Deputy head of Cameron's policy unit until his resignation in February 2014. He was arrested in March 2014 on suspicion of child pornography offences and was charged in June 2014.

213 Abdelbaset al-Megrahi, the Lockerbie bomber who was released from a Scottish jail on compassionate grounds in 2009 when thought to have only months to live.

214 There had been claims that Megrahi's release was linked to trade deals with Libya.

· 21 MAY ·

Spent most of the day in our office in the *Scotsman* building; much better there. However, I called in first to the Parliament to discover that someone has objected to me sticking bits of paper on the window and – incredibly – to having things on the window ledge, so everything had been dumped on my desk. Really, this is the biggest bunch of jobsworths I have ever clapped eyes on. A media office that is literally stuffed with people who do bugger all, but take all week to do it. A massive security staff that protects a bunch of useless politicians and arguably the ugliest building in Britain ... and for what? It is massively overstaffed and completely useless. For instance, it takes three security checks just to get in the building and when I forgot my pass the other day, they took great pleasure in treating me like some complete stranger, even though I've been in the bloody building – and the one before this – every day since the thing started in 1999.

I really must must must spend much less time there. It drives me potty.

One good thing was that I finally caught up with Darling. He phoned and we're having lunch in a couple of weeks. Murdoch (MacLennan) says he's seeing him and Maggie[215] sometime in July. Alistair was very friendly and, who knows, I hope I might not need Dunlop much longer, if both Moore and Darling are on tap. He's playing things much too close to his chest for my liking and, anyway, he's too much of a Tory.

I arranged to see Douglas Connell of Turcan Connell, big-time

---

215 Alistair's wife.

solicitors, later this week. I don't know why, but I think he may turn out to be very useful one of these days. He's always very friendly and supportive any time I meet him. Who knows? He might be able to galvanise the industrial/commercial/business community into some kind of action against Eck. Frankly, they're a bunch of wasters and chancers.

Interesting to note that Guido Fawkes's[216] column in the *Star on Sunday* is focusing on Eck and Joanie. This is bound to start that hare running.

22 MAY

Absolutely incredible report from a training scheme run by Arnold Clark motoring group which says what most people believe, namely that kids are coming out of school and these completely useless 'further education' colleges unfit for anything that might make them a living. Everyone has piled in, although Simon and *The Scotsman* were the only ones to get the story. Boothman of the BBC is furious that they didn't have the tale.

But there's nothing new here; it's been going on for years under every government, including the Tories. It's mad but people like Willie Rennie have decided to attack the messenger and stick up for young people. This is a completely cynical exercise on his part; as a Lib Dem he's got to keep on side with someone, so I suppose he thinks he can suck up to the teenagers by saying they're not all bad. Rubbish, of course.

---

216 The political blogger Paul Staines.

There's to be a 'summit' on Wednesday to tackle the problem. What a total waste of time, especially as the Nats have Angela Constance,[217] arguably, the worst minister since Fiona Hyslop, as their lead minister. She's useless but I'm not sure if anyone can sort it as the damage has all been done – the worst of it in the '60s and '70s – and now the products of that crap education system are in charge of the asylum. What a state.

Joanie's column in the *Record* was a hoot and drops the Nats further in the shit. The *Record*'s eejit editor thinks that it's smashing and says he's going to keep it because Labour keep demanding that he scrap it. Little does he know, but Labour think that it's a great column – for them!

23 MAY

Lovely weather at last. Played tennis – yes, really – with Jenny after I'd dropped off the girls. She's getting a bit too good, but of course I'm not moving as fast as I used to.

Deadly dull day but then I discovered that the Nats are not going to have their NATO debate at the national council next month and have postponed it until their October conference, when the 'men in kilts' will surely savage it.

I commiserated with poor old Angus Robertson, who is a strange fish really. I call him all the names under the sun but he keeps coming back for more and insists on being friendly. Very unnerving! Eck has obviously closed down the debate on NATO

---

217 The SNP's Minister for Youth Employment.

as it was leading to discussion within the ranks of the SNP and that would never do. Angus always looks very lonely.

Also NATO annoys the Greens and Eck wants them to sign up to this rubbish about a joint campaign on independence, which is launched on Friday. Patrick Harvie[218] is playing hard to get; Jesus – tiny party says bugger off to giant party and giant party shits itself. Some coalition, Eck!

Great night at St George's,[219] where Josie should have won in charity debating contest but her adult choice of subject – rape – might have been a bit too fruity. Went to Fontana afterwards for pizza and were joined by Josie Inwood.[220] Great girl; we're really blessed with our neighbours.

24 MAY

Had a coffee with Mr Connell. Nice guy, very sharp, knows everybody, represents most of them. Pretty self-assured, as well he might be; says that the biggest trouble isn't necessarily independence but the Scotland Act, which, as Forsyth always said, is a time bomb of tax rises. People with money are already beginning to shift southwards, even before the referendum. Douglas is a solid Unionist and pretty disparaging about the likes of Angus Grossart,[221] Peter de Vink etc. but, like the rest, won't stick his head above the parapet. Not yet, not ever maybe.

---

218 The leader of the Scottish Greens.

219 Edinburgh girls' school.

220 Neighbour.

221 Sir Angus Grossart, Scottish businessman and patron of the arts.

FMQs pretty useless, except that Eck kept having a go at Darling, which must show he's worried and will start attacking him. That's good, because Brown tried that and Darling more than survived. Ruth had a good joke – saying that the cinema where Eck launches his campaign on Friday is also showing *The Dictator* and *Dark Shadows*.

Still, best of all was a Darling-commissioned poll which showed that the Nats are still stuck on 30-odd per cent, and half their own supporters don't want independence. Eck and his celeb friends will try to rubbish it tomorrow but as hardly any of them live in Scotland, we shouldn't worry over-much about that.

Good start by Darling and I hear that the money's rolling in. Excellent.

Can't wait to see Eck's launch, which the Greens are now moaning about and Margo MacDonald says she's not going to attend because of a hospital appointment. Oh yeah?

25 MAY

What a load of tartan cobblers that Yes launch was. Five hundred people talking and singing to themselves. Nothing coherent, nothing common to all, just this nonsense about freedom! Patrick Harvie will regret getting involved with this. But, Jesus, Brian Cox[222] ain't going to convert anyone. He was positively scary. Hannibal Lecter has nothing on him. I can't believe that that's the best they can offer. They must have something up their sleeves. It

---

222 Actor and outspoken supporter of Scottish nationalism.

was so bad, it had me thinking that maybe they've already given up on winning on one question and will now redouble their efforts at getting the second question.

Got the usual sneering treatment from Andrew Wilson[223] and Duncan Hamilton.[224] God, I've never known two people more pleased with themselves. Wilson wore jeans to show he was on a day off. If for no other reason than to wipe the self-satisfied smirks off their faces, I want independence to bomb. Strangely, on this one I find myself on the same side as many, many Nats.

Darling was pleased at how bad it was and so was Moore. And Andrew Dunlop phoned to see what I thought. We must not get complacent. That would be fatal. I feel strangely worried, as if something's going to happen. How come the Nats were so bad? Very odd.

Interesting. I met Andy Wightman[225] when I was on the way to join Jenny at the Grange (watching the cricket). He hadn't been at the launch but as a good Nat (although not, I don't think, SNP – he's probably more of a Green than that) he watched it online and thought it was rubbish, too. He was very disappointed and wondered why it had been so bad. What the hell happened?

---

223 Former SNP MSP.

224 Former SNP MSP.

225 Author, campaigner for land reform.

26 MAY

Didn't see all the papers but the *Mail* gave Eck a real doing –
The Great Dictator. A bit strong, but then again, we ain't pissing
about. This is war. Simon was out with Stuart Nicolson,[226] one
of the Nat spads, who was horrified. Excellent.

27 MAY

Jesus, what absolute and complete crap in the Scottish Sundays,
which were fed and bought the Nat line that they're after Labour
voters in the campaign. Of course they bloody well are – and
Tories and Lib Dems. How else do they think they can win? And,
oh yes, they've got Jeane Freeman[227] now on their side. Christ,
that should scare the shit out of everyone. Ridiculous. How can
someone like Eddie Barnes[228] write such garbage? Still, their circulation is dropping like a stone, so who cares?

28 MAY

Good news about Tom Farmer[229] stepping back a bit from the
Nats; at least he doesn't support separation. But much better news

---

226 SNP head of communications and former journalist.

227 Member of Women for Independence and former aide to Labour First Minister Jack
McConnell.

228 Political editor of *Scotland on Sunday*, appointed head of communications for the Scottish
Conservatives in January 2014.

229 Scottish businessman and philanthropist.

is that Simon J spotted that an alleged tweet from Seb Coe,[230] which bashed the Scots, was a phoney and that Field Marshal Robertson (aka Angus Robertson MP) had re-tweeted it to all 4,000 of his followers.

Mundell rang to ask if I'd give a speech that Ruth Davidson is making the once-over. I said that if I could do it for the PM, I could do it for her. As long as we keep schtum about it. It was actually not at all bad. I made a couple of minor suggestions, mostly about her noising up the Nat backbenchers, most of whom want a simple Yes/No question. They must know that Alex is preparing to sell them down the river by insisting that there's a second question on devo max, which he thinks he could win.

29 MAY

Appalling – or at least revealing – insight into how Big Brother Nats would order the broadcasters after separation,[231] with the most telling comment coming from Marco Biagi.[232] 'Too much redundant British news,' he said. That said it all. Mind you, their criticisms of *Good Morning Scotland* were at least valid. The programme is dire. And it's nothing to do with money.

Told Paxman that the Nats had claimed he gets paid as much as the whole *GMS* budget and asked how he could live on so little! Very grumpy reply.

---

230 Lord Coe, chairman of London 2012.

231 The SNP announced plans to replace the BBC with a Scottish Broadcasting Service.

232 SNP MSP for Edinburgh Central.

30 MAY

Began walking to work, then it started to rain and then Simon phoned to say Glesca polis had lifted Coulson.[233] I knew it would happen sooner or later. Auslan's not well but he said he'd persevere. Hope he's OK.

News broke that Coulson had been arrested and charged with perjury just in time for *News at Ten*. Who says Strathclyde's finest are poor at PR? Mind you, the Nats probably ordered them to get it on the telly just to show how good *their* cops are. I'm not joking either.

Nat Fraser[234] found guilty for the second time. There never seems to be much evidence against him, at least from what I can see, but I think that juries just don't like him and decide to lock him up. There will be another appeal, I bet.

Hilarious debate on the Queen at Holyrood. Masses of hypocritical Nats paying tribute to the royalty they want rid of. Had a bit of fun with Shona Robison,[235] who couldn't hide her hypocrisy and was giggling at all the gushing speeches. But she's a pretty over-promoted lady and owes everything she has to her friendship with Nicola, who at least could see the humour in what was going on. Robison is married to that other Nat with a good conceit of himself, Stewart whatsisname.[236] Between them

---

233 Andy Coulson, former communications director for Cameron, former editor of the *News of the World*, arrested by Strathclyde Police and charged with perjury in the trial of Tommy Sheridan (see note 235).

234 He was first convicted of killing his wife Arlene, who disappeared in 1998, in 2003 but had his conviction quashed in 2011. Following the retrial, in 2012, he was sentenced to a minimum of seventeen years.

235 Minister for Commonwealth Games, Sport, Equalities and Pensioners' Rights.

236 Stewart Hosie, SNP MP for Dundee East.

in salaries and exes they could well be pulling in a good quarter of a million in taxpayers' loot. Nice work if you can get it. And you can get it if you creep.

At least Roseanna[237] was frank – she said she had to vote for Salmond's motion. She's a minister and if she didn't vote for it she'd be out on her ear. She has many faults Roseanna, but she's honest. And can laugh at herself, unlike Robison.

Very interesting gossip about Andrew Wilson. Apparently, he's being seconded from the Royal Bank of Scotland to WPP, the giant PR firm, for eighteen months, so I told Dunlop at No. 10 to watch out for WPP suddenly helping the Salmond cause. However, there's more to this than meets the eye. Apparently, Wilson's boss is a rabid Unionist who intends to begin an RBS effort in that direction by making subtle anti-Nat noises, asking difficult questions, but also making it clear that Salmond can't answer them. RBS won't come out, we're told, as overtly anti-Nat but it will be pretty obvious that they don't want independence. Given the bloody bankrolling they've had from the British taxpayer, it would be outrageous if they did anything else.

I had a laugh with Alex Neil, the housing and infrastructure minister, over his interview with *Holyrood* magazine. I told him that it was full of code that I hadn't quite cracked yet but that I was working on it. He doesn't like Salmond or Swinney and I think he fancies himself as leader and FM. He might just be quite good at it, too.

And he remains a Fundie.[238]

---

237 Roseanna Cunningham, Minister for Community Safety and Legal Affairs.

238 The fundamentalists were hardcore nationalists who opposed devolution and believed in holding out for full independence.

31 MAY

Alex's worst ever day, I'm glad to say, at FMQs. He was totally, wonderfully, marvellously useless. Johann Lamont skewered him good and proper and on one of his pet subjects – the Bank of England and the Monetary Policy Committee. Why didn't Ruth and Willie Rennie keep up the pressure? It could have been brilliant. Ruth went on a good subject but doesn't know how to ask questions and Willie was just, well, havering about joint police forces, which nobody gives a damn about.

Nicola was very good in her summing up and I've given her a glowing write-up in comparison to Salmond's car crash. Hope it causes trouble but I doubt if it will. Even I think it's a bit too juvenile. Still, one must try.

Then went to the opera – *Tosca* – with the Hoopers.[239] Great night out. Very dramatic production. I think I really love opera like this, Italian opera. Will refuse to go to *The Magic Flute* in the autumn, however. Don't like it, which probably makes me a philistine.

1 JUNE

Bugger all to write about, so began preparing for the Jubilee Party for Inverleith Row/Howard Place. Fetched tables from Edinburgh Academy with Josie Inwood.

---

239 Ian and Julie, next-door neighbours.

2 JUNE

Set up our bit of the party, and prepared to repel boarders should the Eildon Street lot encroach on our area of the park. Josie made sure they didn't get too near by lawnmowing a huge square for croquet. And I laid out a course for a slow bike race. Made huge mound of cucumber sandwiches but managed to burn the sausage rolls – they're still just about edible.

Everyone started to turn up just after 3 p.m. and the party was judged a roaring success. Masses of Union Jacks, including my waistcoat, and the wind-up gramophone was a huge hit. Very cold, but the rain stayed off and everyone had a great time. Harriet bombed about on bikes and Josephine looked really grown-up … and very beautiful.

3 JUNE

Dropped off the girls at the station for their London train and then drove up to Dundee to take Granny to the kirk. Interesting service, which included a baptism for people who had clearly never been in a church before. But it went off quite well, in spite of the mother looking frightful in an 'aff the shidder' creation. The wee minister did extremely well.

Had lunch with Granny in the Woodlands and then I went up to the Glen to stay with Mary and Martin.[240] Brilliant weekend with lots of walks. Saw what Jamie[241] is doing to Glenuig

---

240 Mary and Martin Friedrich, old friends from Glen Prosen, where AC used to rent a cottage, Glenuig.

241 Jamie Stormonth Darling, Glen Prosen landowner and laird of Glenuig.

– not sure it will work – and I think I got it out of my system. Went up to the top of the Glen and was amazed at what the new owner is doing. Had a barbecue with Hector and Jeannie[242] and saw what they plan for Spott.

4 JUNE

Up Cat Law for the great beacon party.[243] Fantastic numbers, mostly decent people but the inevitable Angus farming fraternity included. Met Og-Wed's new lady. Very nice but shy. Very clear night until forty-five minutes before light-up, when a huge cloud came over and dropped buckets of rain on us. Still, everyone had plenty of warming liquids, which was just as well as it was very cold.

Had a good blether with Lord (Charlie) Lyell[244] and met his new heir – it is not Andrew Gifford,[245] it's his big brother.

5 JUNE

Gave Eck a real monstering over his idea of replacing the Union Jack with the Lion Rampant. He must be thoroughly pissed off with all that red, white and blue, and his mouthpiece – wee Joanie – echoed those thoughts in her *Record* column. Funny

---

242 Hector and Jeannie MacLean, lairds of the other side of Glen Prosen.

243 For the Queen's Diamond Jubilee.

244 Angus landowner and former Conservative whip in the House of Lords. One of the ninety-two hereditary peers elected to remain in the House.

245 Lib Dem donor and lobbyist and cousin of Lord Lyell.

that. Over 200 angry Nat protests about my column on the website. Excellent.

6 JUNE

Had lunch with Alistair Darling in Centotre. First class but very fiery spicy sausages. He is in good heart and confident of seeing off Eck. Says that the money is rolling in but that not everyone will stick their heads above the parapet, although some might. Got the impression that the Union launch won't now be until the end of June. But he agrees that the Queen's celebrations have done us a whole lot of good.

He's off to the Hay Book Festival and says his book[246] is doing well, thanks to all the interviews he's doing on the Euro crisis. Very gloomy about our economic prospects and confirms what everyone knows, that the financial services industry in Edinburgh and those, like lawyers, who serviced them are contracting massively. He cannot see much light ahead and bad economic news must mean – surely – that voters will stick with the UK. And he thinks that Tesco Bank is unlikely ever to be much of a goer, especially with the new man at Tesco[247] looking to concentrate on core business. There goes another of Eck's big hopes.

He was also very interesting about the Calman Commission[248] and the Scotland Act. When it was proposed by Wendy

---

246 *Back from the Brink: 1,000 Days at No. 11.*

247 Philip Clarke, CEO of Tesco from 2011 to 2014.

248 Review of Scottish devolution, convened by Sir Kenneth Calman, published its findings in 2009.

Alexander,[249] the idea in London, in agreeing to it, was that it would be a 'long grass' type project and could be kicked there. The Labour Cabinet – Broon and him especially – hoped that if the Tories won in 2010 that would be the last we'd hear of it. Unfortunately, the Tories didn't win outright and the bloody Lib Dems, as well as daft Annabel Goldie,[250] got the tax proposals inserted into the recommendations and thus into the subsequent Act, along with all the other devolved nonsense, such as air rifles.

This is basically the opinion I got from Cameron when I talked to him at Bruce Anderson's 60th birthday party in Victoria in the autumn of 2009. He shrugged his shoulders and made it clear that he was very reluctant to have anything to do with Calman, but with Labour and the Lib Dems insisting that they'd implement it, and Goldie pressing him to say the same, he went along with it. Stupid bugger. The whole thing was a farce from start to finish … but I've got to watch myself as MM was a member of the commission.

Darling confirmed the view, expressed recently, that the Revenue might well refuse to collect the new Scottish taxes if they are too different from the English ones and if it makes their lives more complicated. And he was also supportive of the Douglas Connell view that it will make people decide where to have their domicile – depending on the tax rate. But he was also of the view that there aren't enough high taxpayers in Scotland from whom to raise much money.

249 Leader of Scottish Labour from 2007 to 2008. Sister of Labour MP and shadow Foreign Secretary Douglas Alexander.

250 MSP and leader of the Scottish Conservatives from 2005 to 2011.

Michael Forsyth is trying to get hold of me; I bet he has pronounced views on it. In fact, when he finally got through to me all he wanted was my advice about how he should perform and what he should say on *Question Time*. I should charge a consultancy fee; after all, what did old Mikey ever do for me?

Bloody awful weather. Where is flaming June?

7 JUNE

Salmond not good – again – but Ruth Davidson was absolutely awful. She is totally and utterly useless and so are her team. They haven't a bloody clue but she is the problem – big problem. Not up to the job, as Attlee[251] would say, and I suspect that some hacks will start asking questions. Mundell said he knew she wasn't cutting the mustard, after I'd phoned to tell him the bad news. But he claims they've got someone lined up to help her. Christ, they need it. They're all just bairns in her office and I suspect the Tory MSPs ain't helping her.

But then Swinney glibly announced a new tax-gathering body. He's decided that if HMRC won't collect his higher taxes then he'll set up a new body to do it instead. And he claims that this will save money. Oh, sure. And this is only from the stupid Scotland Act – never mind independence. Connell was dead right. What a frightful mess and all because of an accidental whim by Wendy, which Broon took up, then the Lib Dems, then daft Bella[252] and

---

251 The reason Clement Attlee, post-war Labour Prime Minister from 1945 to 1951, gave to the MP for Dagenham, John Parker, when he sacked him from the government in 1946.

252 Annabel Goldie.

finally Cameron. What a shambles.

Girls watching what could have been a good programme about William,[253] except that it's full of 'royal corrs' and they're all make-up artists, especially that clown from the *Mail* who, I will bet, has never met anyone who even knows anyone who might have met Wills. How do I know? Because we used to do that ourselves on the *Express* to keep Mad Evie[254] happy.

7 JUNE

Very interesting goss from Campbell Gunn.[255] He was phoned by Stuart Nicolson and told how Eck's tips at the races at Musselburgh had won him and Kevin Pringle £1,600 and he put it into his *Sunday Post* diary. Unfortunately, not many people had read it and the red tops only picked up the story on Wednesday. Incredibly, however, they agreed to hold it until after FMQs on Thursday because Eck was afraid that this betting coup could be used against him. Incredible that he asked them to hold the tale. What's he worried about? Even more incredible that they agreed.

8 JUNE

Times have a splash written by Hamish Macdonell[256] saying that after a No vote all income tax collection will be devolved to

---

253 Prince William.

254 Eve Pollard, editor of the *Sunday Express* from 1991 to 1994.

255 Then political editor of the *Sunday Post*; appointed special advisor to Alex Salmond in 2013.

256 Political journalist.

Scotland. What a load of tripe, I thought. I confirmed with both Mundell and Dunlop at No. 10 that the story is bollocks, and then it dawned on me. Of course, he'd got it from Danny Alexander, who was up in Scotland dishing out money for broadband. And, of course, the Lib Dems are daft on giving more tax-raising powers to Holyrood. It is complete crap and will lead to an exodus of people who earn more than normal.

The Scotsman has written up Swinney's announcement on replacing stamp duty[257] as if he's doing us all a favour. Their splash was by-lined Tom Peterkin[258] but when I berated Tom – unfairly – he confessed that his copy had been changed. Christ, no wonder that paper is going under.

I have got to get out of this bloody country. Wrote my denunciation of the Scotland Act and felt better. Doubt if anyone, other than the likes of Frans ten Bos, will take much notice. So what, I'm right. Unfortunately, I couldn't get Douglas Connell to give me a quote; he was off making a speech, funnily enough warning people about the dangers of the Scotland Act!

Strange thing is Connell often has daft Jim Mather[259] at his seminars, selling the Nat line, with the aid of his whiteboards and picture shows. Jim appears nice on the outside but there's a hard streak there. How else could he be a millionaire?

Funniest example ever was when Jenny, the girls and I turned up in the Loch Ailort Hotel for a weekend with Steel[260] and

---

257 With a land and building transactions tax.

258 Political editor of *The Scotsman* and *Scotland on Sunday*; champion piper.

259 Former SNP MSP for Argyll and Bute.

260 Brian Steel, retired journalist.

Dow.[261] I told Mather I'd be there on the Friday night and, sure enough, he turned up wearing those funny tight cycling breeks and he fished out of his pocket £2.87 in change, which was the exact price of a pint of Guinness. Tight-fisted creep.

Dunlop texted to ask how I thought Ruth had done at FMQs and I gave him the truth – both barrels – and told him to read my column. Didn't hear another word from him. Amongst all his other worries, Cameron must know that he's backed a real dodo in Ruth. I wonder if Dunlop has the balls to tell him that.

Then poor old Michael Tait came in to seek my advice about Ruth. They're clearly worried and the poor lad is completely out of his depth, as is she. I didn't tell him that Mundell is looking for a heavyweight to run her office but I did tell him that I had been consulted on her Union speech last week. He got the impression that I was being constructive and I'm not all that sure that's what I am being. I am very reluctant to dish out any more free advice. But I feel sorry for Tait; he is clearly under the lash.

Boothman phoned to say that the Beeb had a good story for Sunday's *Politics* show, which reveals that the Union Jack is much more popular than the Saltire. Great stuff. And the Olympic torch is attracting huge crowds all over Scotland; the Nats will be furious. They hate the Games, because they're British and in London.

---

261 Alan Dow, semi-retired journalist.

9 JUNE

Fantastic ceremony at Glasgow Cathedral, where General Euan Loudon,[262] dressed in his best uniform, organised a fabulous laying up of the colours of the Royal High Fusiliers with HRH the Duke of York and a nice wee reception at Glasgow City Chambers. Excellent stuff.

10 JUNE

More trouble for the Nats. The Greens say they're pulling out of Eck's Yes campaign because they now realise – as they always should have – that it's nothing but a Nat front organisation. And John McGlynn, who is in the huff with the Tories, says he's backing the Nats over having a second question. The Nats will live to regret getting John on side: he needs a lot of attention and is very demanding. More trouble than he's worth, frankly. It would appear that Dunlop failed to keep hold of him. Still, he won't be missed.

11 JUNE

I have never seen a bigger pack of lies than Gordon Brown at Leveson, saying that Whelan[263] and McBride,[264] his thuggish spin doctors, were instructed to, at all times, operate through

---

262 Former head of the army in Scotland, producer of the Edinburgh Military Tattoo, and appointed chief executive of the St Andrews Links Trust in 2010.

263 Charlie Whelan.

264 Damian McBride.

the civil service head of their information department. What complete and utter LIES. For God's sake, even on the pettiest levels, they ran the show. Charlie told me that it was he, Charlie Whelan, who ordered Alistair Darling to shave off his pointy little beard, on Gordon's instructions, when Darling came into the Cabinet for the first time.

And it is entirely laughable for Broon to say that he didn't attempt to undermine Blair, using the likes of Whelan and McBride; he did nothing BUT undermine Blair. He has not enhanced his reputation with this crap. If anything, I have even less respect for him now than I had before he gave evidence. He really is a pathetic individual and the worst thing is that everyone knows when he's at it – he gives that phoney little smile. God knows why that nice wife of his sticks by him. She deserves better.

My piece about supporting England for the very first time was in the Notebook section and I got monstered by both Scottish and English Nats for my troubles. I watched the match with Simon and got very confused; must admit that it wasn't very comfortable backing bloody England. I don't know if I can keep this up.

Then dinner with the John Smith Memorial Trust[265] people; very good and much better than last year. Elizabeth,[266] John's widow, and the girls made me very welcome. Sat beside Jean Urquhart,[267] who I like even though she's still an unreconstructed

---

265 Set up in the name of the former Labour leader, to nurture young leaders.

266 Lady Smith.

267 Then SNP MSP for Highlands and Islands; became an independent in October 2012, after the SNP changed its NATO policy.

Nat. She's a human being and will calm down eventually. On the other side was the MacLaren of MacLaren,[268] a clan chief and former press attaché in the Moscow embassy, where he had a reputation for being a bit of a prat. But he's quite a nice guy now, even if he's half a Nat.

12 JUNE

John Swinney is in trouble for saying that Scotland's banks would be run by England's FSA. They really don't want independence, do they? At least not as anyone would understand the term. Everything seems to be just a variant of what we've got already. However, once they got that they'd keep pushing for more and more and more.

13 JUNE

To London for dinner with Murdoch MacLennan and Margaret Curran in the Goring. A great night. She brought Gordon Banks[269] with her, a real star who impressed Murdoch mightily. She is a toughie but he is a smashing operator – a great campaigner and number cruncher and credited with winning the Glenrothes by-election and with helping Labour retain Glasgow. But he does say that the Nats machine is incredibly slick – hand-held computers, feeding into the main one back at HQ, which allows them

---

268 Donald MacLaren, stood as an independent against Gordon Brown in Kirkcaldy and Cowdenbeath in 2010.
269 Labour MP for Ochil and South Perthshire.

to know precisely who to target. Labour is not nearly so good, he says, but they're getting there slowly.

Salmond at Leveson charmed the pants off the learned judge and lobbed in a lollipop for the hacks about his bank account being hacked THIRTEEN years ago, though he's only now decided to tell the world about it. And guess what? The entire Scottish press corps bought it. What a complete bunch of dupes.

14 JUNE

Back to Edinburgh, where I find I'm in trouble over allegations that I swore at the security men after I couldn't get out of the building on Monday night. I had to tell MacLeod[270] in the press office that I apologised if I caused any offence. The classic non-apology apology. But, as I say all the time, I've got to spend less time in that bloody Parliament building. Drives me nuts.

18 JUNE

Lunch with deputy German ambassador and Wolfgang,[271] the German consul. The former seemed to have made up his mind before arriving. It's amazing how often people manage to fit their national stereotypes. Arrogant and completely sure of himself and his country. This guy fitted the bill exactly, or maybe he was play-acting. But anyway, once he'd calmed down and got all his

---

270 Eric MacLeod, head of media relations in the Scottish Parliament.
271 Wolfgang Mossinger.

German shit out of his system, he was quite sharp and he confirmed many things – to wit, the Germans believe that Scotland will have to apply to join the EU; that there will have to be borders – immigration, customs and Shengen types. He also believes that a different kind of UK would not necessarily keep its place on the UN Security Council.

Very hurried lunch and pretty poor, sweet Mosel wine. A couple of lame jokes about Alsace wine (French or German) and about how they lost the war. I don't know why they bothered with me. Or maybe I did convince them that there ain't gonna be no independence, which disappoints our EU friends.

19–21 JUNE

Life is boring without Eck. He's off on a jolly to the States to see that *Brave* movie, which he could have seen here a couple of weeks ago. But he is nothing if not an international statesman. Bugger all happening here.

Nicola did FMQs and was not very good; in fact, she was pretty poor, at least by her standards. She is a very competent minister and a good debater but has been used to getting her own way for too long. I think she got a bit of a doing from Johann Lamont but our work experience girl thought the opposite, which just goes to show how little we so-called experts know about anything.

Ridiculous announcement by the Nats: that they're bringing forward work on the A9 'dualling'. What a load of old bollocks, which of course most of the hacks have swallowed. The work still won't be finished until 2025, another thirteen years, for God's sake! And why is it taking so long? Maybe a conversation I had with Fergus Ewing,[272] the junior minister in that department, a few years ago provides the answer. He said: 'I don't want the A9 dualled. All we'd get then is lots of people from the Central Belt moving to the north and none of them will vote SNP!' Now that's what I call pragmatism.

Made the farewell speech for Brian Currie's last night on *The Herald*. He's a good hack is Currie, but he knows as much about politics as the average guy on the street, which is not much. However, he knows how to play the game, which is something that Robbie doesn't. And although Currie likes a good drink – a very good drink – he doesn't ever show it and never really starts until he's finished work.

I bought Robbie a consolation lunch at Iggs and he's very unhappy, but at least with Magnus Gardham, who got Currie's job, he's now got a civilised boss/colleague. But I suspect he'll get fired.

Thank God there's only one week to go of this awful place.

Interesting exchange with Dunlop at Downing Street. I sent him a text saying that Cameron is making an arse of things, and instead of waiting for days for a response, I got one almost immediately, asking me if I meant generally or only in relation to Scotland. As he hasn't said a word on Scotland for weeks, they must know I don't mean that. I told Dunlop that he looks as if he's on his own, which is the impression that's being given. Stupid arguments with the French[273] and getting involved in silly

---

272 SNP MSP for Inverness and Nairn.

273 The PM annoyed the French by saying he'd roll out the red carpet to their top-rate tax exiles.

grandstanding with the Argies.[274] What the hell's wrong with the guy?

Needless to say, Iain M said, 'I told you so', which in a manner of speaking I suppose he did. But Iain thinks it will all end in disaster, whereas I think things will recover.

Iain said he'd had dinner with Andy Coulson last night and feels sorry for him. Oh, do me a favour!

24 JUNE

Mundell phoned me early to say, 'We've taken some of your advice.' As I'm always giving them advice, I said, 'Which bit?' They've appointed John McLellan, ex-*Scotsman* editor, as Ruth's new something or other – campaign or communications director. They'll be well matched, those two. She's a thrawn wee bugger and he's a bit of a toughie, or at least likes to give that impression. It's a pretty good appointment, although I'm not sure if either of them has much judgement. Still, he knows the hacks and at least gives the impression of carrying a bit of weight.

25 JUNE

The Save the Union or Better Together campaign launched at Napier, the same place Eck used to stage his spectaculars. However, this time there were no free bacon rolls and instead there

---

274 He confronted the Argentine President over her country's continued claim to the Falkland Islands.

were long queues for coffee. Still, Darling did well and proved that he'll be quite an operator even if the Nats are planning a long campaign of denigration against him, blaming him for the recession. I'm not sure that it will work as Darling appears to be the only one who emerged from the ashes of the Labour government with any shred of a reputation left.

It was quite a good launch, though nothing spectacular, and they had ordinary people instead of phoney celebs. But Charlie Kennedy[275] didn't show – said his parents are ill. Charlie is a brilliant performer and campaigner but he is totally unreliable. They'll have to ditch him, which Ramsay Jones tells me is what's going to happen.

27 JUNE

Reviewed Gen. Andrew Mackay's[276] book.[277] God, it was hard going but managed to do it. Jenny was talking to another general, Mark Strudwick,[278] who says that Mackay is deeply unpopular and too self-centred. It's amazing how all those generals hate each other. The wee fat brigadier I met at the Glasgow Cathedral event says the same about Andrew. Too clever by half, is the general conclusion, which is about the worst anyone can say about him.

---

275 Former leader of the Lib Dems; MP for Ross, Skye and Lochaber.

276 Former General Officer Commanding 2nd Division and Governor of Edinburgh Castle.

277 *Behavioural Conflict: Why Understanding People and Their Motives Will Prove Decisive in Future Conflict* (co-writer Steve Tatham).

278 Former General Officer Commanding Scotland and Governor of Edinburgh Castle.

28 JUNE

Eck at his very worst at FMQs, actually pretending to be God. 'Set my people free' he would say to Cameron if he met him – that's what he told one of his creepy crawly backbenchers. Jesus, what a total shit. However, Johann took the piss quite mercilessly and everyone – including many of the Nats – hooted with laughter. Bruce Crawford was one of them and I mentioned that in my column; poor Bruce will be mortified that his human and not Nat side was showing. Ruth showed definite signs of improvement with her question – maybe McLellan is having an impact already.

29 JUNE

We were badly scooped by *The Sun* and *Mail* about Linda Fabiani complaining about there being too many Union Jacks and red, white and blue balloons on the tables in the canteen. However, we did the story again and I monstered the Nats in my column. It really is outrageous that anyone, but anyone, pays any attention to Linda. Always seeking reassurance. Eck simply had to sack her.[279]

But what a bunch of total creeps the Parliament authorities are to remove all the balloons and kowtow like that. That's what I wrote in my column but I might have to apologise; it appears that it was the canteen staff and not the Parliament who gave in.

But it's the Parliament that looks stupid; they should be aware of that. And if they complain I shall tell them that.

---

279 She was replaced as Culture Minister in 2009.

John Swinney sent quite a good piece, over laying into the banks for their latest outrages, and he is absolutely right – they are a total disgrace. And to think that those buggers have been lording it over everyone else in Edinburgh for years. They are low-life scum for the most part and John was right to have a go. Unfortunately, he couldn't resist playing the Nat by bashing Labour for not keeping a lid on RBS and HBOS, forgetting that he and Eck were encouraging them in their excesses, and for pretending that the whole thing wasn't a Scottish problem. Not much it ain't!

London are doing an army cuts story which doesn't seem to be much different from the ones they've done before. Ramsay Jones says he'll fill me in next week and Andrew Dunlop says that No. 10 has worked really hard on it to make sure it's not a gift for Eck. Sounds like the suggestions from London that 2 Scots is to get whacked and 5 Scots turned into the TA might yet be wide of the mark. Dunlop suggests a Monday get-together. Interesting.

He says he sat next to Murdoch MacL at the Downing Street lunch on Wednesday and says everything went well. I asked about DC and he says that he was in good form and that he gets quite aerated on the subject of the Union. I'm beginning to think that it's about the only thing he's calling correctly just now. But I still think he'll come good in the end.

30 JUNE

Drove to Wetherby in preparation for Harriet's concert[280] in York the next day. Stayed in Mercure on the outskirts. Quite a nice hotel, marred only slightly by a real 'muck 'n' brass' northern wedding, full of fat burds with tattoos. We found a fantastic pub for a meal and really liked Wetherby. On Sunday morning there were people out on the town's streets, cleaning up – with yellow vests declaring that they were volunteers. Wonderful but can't imagine that happening in Scotland. People don't now do anything for themselves and expect the council or the government to do everything.

1 JULY

Gave Ben[281] a ring to say that one of these days we'd be blagging a bed off him and Liza, once Harriet goes to Chetham's.[282] He says he lives about an hour from Manchester, which isn't too bad.

He says the *Telegraph* have got it wrong over the regiments to be axed and also says, as I thought, that Hammond is nothing more than an accountant. Absolutely dreadful piece by Charles Moore in Saturday's *Telegraph* – he's bought, in its entirety, the whole Hammond line. Quite awful and I never thought I'd ever write that about a Moore piece. Ben says No. 10 and MoD totally useless on the regiments; he says he's also been telling them to brief me in advance to make sure they get a better press. They've

---

280 With the National Children's Orchestra.

281 Ben Wallace, Conservative MP for Wyre and Preston North.

282 The music school in Manchester where Harriet had just been offered a place.

refused, as Dunlop and Ramsay Jones made clear when I spoke to them on Friday. Oh well, maybe I can have some fun after all.

Ben is clearly still enjoying working with Ken Clarke,[283] as I knew he would. I hope that their camaraderie means that Ben will get a job at the next reshuffle and I also hope that working with Ken knocks all those daft right-wing edges off him.

Simon phoned to say that Isabel Fraser had given that eejit Blair Jenkins[284] a tremendously easy ride on *Sunday Politics*, while laying into Richard Baker.[285] What's got into the wummin? Two separate emails and texts from others saying exactly the same as Simon.

2 JULY

I was on *GMS* and, predictably, they tried to do a number – attacking Cameron over Europe and equating it with Salmond over referendums. It was total bollocks and when Gary Robertson asked what was the difference between Eck's multi-option plan and Cameron's, I said that I'd read DC's piece three times and I hadn't heard the word 'multi-option' until the BBC researcher phoned me to set me up for the programme.

At that Robertson said: 'Right we'll leave it there!' What twits, amateur twits, too.

Had a quick blether with Dunlop at Centotre. Didn't get much out of him and he wouldn't tell me about the regimental cuts

---

283 Former Conservative minister and MP for Rushcliffe, Nottinghamshire, since 1970.

284 Appointed chief executive of the Yes campaign in June 2012.

285 Labour MSP for the North East Scotland region.

although, like Ben, he says that the *Telegraph* story last week was wrong. He says that Ramsay Jones will tell me. Really? The announcement is coming on Thursday, so unless they tell me on Wednesday they can get stuffed about my giving them a fair hearing. They are taking a bit too much for granted. But at least Dunlop conceded that I'm the most important opinion former. We'll see.

Lunch at the New Club with David (Earl of) Airlie.[286] Just happened to meet him in the loo. He's in Edinburgh all week because Ginny[287] is on duty as lady-in-waiting for the Queen at Holyroodhouse. He says that the Knights of the Thistle[288] are giving the Queen lunch in the Signet Library as a change from her giving them all lunch. Prince William, who is the Earl of Strathearn in Scotland, is being made a KT. David is boss of KTs and is rumoured to have blocked Catholics.

David was in good form, for someone of eighty-six, and looks great. One of the reasons must be that he doesn't eat or drink much. He had a plate of soup and then club paté – two starters – and then a small glass of claret. He says that Ginny is not too bad, healthwise, but is still on steroids for that mystery ailment she had a few years ago and still doesn't feel right. But she's a real trouper and she'll manage this week all right.

He was a bit worried about his son Bruce, who is in hospital in London. David says that he's OK, as long as someone from

---

286 Scottish peer with estate in Angus.

287 Lady Airlie.

288 The Most Ancient and Most Noble Order of the Thistle, founded in 1687.

the family is with him. As a result, David (Ogilvy) was off to see him.

We talked about this bloke who's spending all that money at the top of Glen Prosen and David says he's going to take a drive up there to have a look. The Earl was very interesting about wind turbines. He said the energy companies had a look at the left side of Glen Clova but that they didn't come back with an offer, which stood to make him around £300,000. He says he's totally opposed to them but then said that the trustees – those who are supposed to ensure there's enough money to go to the next generation – would have supported the turbines. And so the Bonnie Earl not wanting them wouldn't have made a great deal of difference, now would it?

He talked quite a lot about how, when he was twenty-six, he decided that, unlike his predecessors, he had better make some money and so he got a job at Schroders. After two years, he had progressed to assistant manager, which his father didn't think was up to much. But anyway, he ended up as chairman. However, he said he didn't make anything like as much money in financial services as people do now. Mind you, I think that everyone suspects it was Ginny who brought the money into that family. Theirs must be one of the few castles – Cortachy, which is beautiful – that has central heating. Still, the Airlies are fantastic, lovely people and I really miss them, now that we're not up at Glenuig.

Andrew Campbell was at the table, too. He is New Club secretary and a retired Black Watch colonel. He'd sent me a copy of a speech his Aussie brother-in-law is making about Scottish independence. It is brilliant stuff and as well as keeping it on file for myself, I sent a copy to Simon and to Dunlop. Andrew C was very funny about the new minister at Alyth – it's another relation of his who was in the East Neuk of Fife but had to leave because he was having an affair with a woman who was not his wife. That's Neil Gardner's[289] old parish. I told them both that Neil's services are a bit too 'high' for my liking, although Andrew said that at least his sermons are short.

Wasn't going to write a column but then Salmond put out a statement monstering Cameron for his referendum plans. I had to write something. It was so two-faced. But at least Eck and Labour are right – the Tories are all over the place on Europe.

3 JULY

Bugger all happening, so went off up town to meet Josephine. Then all hell broke loose. Two Tornadoes crashed off Wick and then this amazing stuff happened re: Barclays. First, the Crown Office announced that, after all, they had been investigating crooked behaviour at the Scottish banks, which killed the piece I had commissioned by Alistair Bonnington,[290] but then, even more astonishing, Bob Diamond's[291] statement came out, which said that the Labour government had colluded with the Bank of England to give Barclays permission to fiddle Libor.

Alistair Darling looked under huge pressure when asked about

---

289 Minister at Canongate Kirk in the Royal Mile.

290 Solicitor-advocate.

291 Barclays' chief executive resigned that day over the manipulation of interest rates.

it on *Channel 4 News* but I don't think he had any part in it. But this puts Labour right in the stew, though it is only Diamond's word for it.

I asked Ramsay Jones if, as Dunlop said, I'd be getting something on the regiment cuts today – which is what he told me last Friday – and I got a snotty 'no promises' reply. I sent him an even snottier reply and then late on I got a text saying he'd ring me on Wednesday morning. We shall see what we shall see.

I have started packing for France, which the girls think is funny. But someone's got to do it. Can't wait. I'm desperate to get away from this bloody rain.

4 JULY

At last! Ramsay Jones eventually rang me with a comprehensive rundown on what the regimental cuts will be, including a pretty neat way of making sure that the Jocks will be as badly off as the English county regiments – cutting most of the battalions down to 450 men apiece and making the poor old Argylls some sort of ceremonial-only company strength lot of 120 to 150.

Still, it looked a pretty neat solution.

5 JULY

Total disaster! Ramsay Jones has got it completely wrong. And he got it wrong the wrong way round! He couldn't run a raffle, that bloke. The truth is even better than he briefed. The Scottish battalions are going to be kept just about intact, with the spare bods from the Argylls being used to bring the other battalions up to their establishment strengths. Christ, this is the biggest balls-up I have ever been involved in! It wasn't just me, either. Maddog[292] on *The Scotsman* got the same load of nonsense, too.

I fired off angry texts and emails to Jones and Dunlop, and gave Mundell a complete chapter and verse about how useless No. 10 is. Iain Martin has been right all along – they are totally crap. One of the troubles is that Dunlop, having made a few bob, clearly doesn't want to get his hands dirty by doing any briefing of the hacks, and they've decided to leave that scruffy stuff to Ramsay. But he's an idiot – has anyone ever considered that fact? He was got rid of from Holyrood because he was no good, and so what do the Tories do? Instead of paying him off, they send him to Downing Street. Incompetence is thus rewarded by significant promotion.

I was going to write to Cameron, but what's the point? He'd probably never see the letter. Instead, I shall fill Bruce's boots with how crap is the press operation at No. 10, so that at least he might tell Ed Llewellyn[293] about it. And Mundell says he's going to have a go at Dunlop.

Mind you, Mundell had been in Scotland all day Thursday and he hadn't even read the *Telegraph*. This lot are doomed, or at least they deserve to be. Useless, totally useless – from top to bottom.

I'm not sure what to do. Should I insist that Ramsay Jones is moved? Or should I just say that I shall no longer take any

---

292 David Maddox, *The Scotsman*'s Westminster editor.
293 Chief of staff at No. 10.

briefings or comments from him? It's all pointless, of course, the damage has been done. But vengeance shall be mine!

God, when do I get away on holiday? I cannot wait.

6 JULY

Still furious about Ramsay Jones and am still firing off memos and texts to No. 10.

Took Josephine through to Dundee to see Granny. The Ferry[294] looked great; the sun was even shining, which is something we haven't seen in Edinburgh for weeks. Granny was in good form. We had a wander around all the charity shops and then went into Vissochi's for coffee and bacon rolls. But first of all, I took Jose to see my old council hoose in Douglas. Someone has obviously bought it and has done it up a bit; there's quite a posh car sitting outside.

John McLellan rang and it's obvious that he has been designated as the peacemaker between me and No. 10. He wants to have a meeting but as we're both away on holiday at the same time it will have to wait until August. I gave him the gist of my complaints and told him what a complete idiot Jones is and how Dunlop needs a kick up the arse, too.

I texted Mundell and thanked him for his efforts but said that Jones was no longer wanted as any kind of information giver for the *Telegraph*. Total war. He replied that he'd had a word with Dunlop, too. Oh sure!

---

294 Broughty Ferry.

Ben Wallace phoned after I got back; I was actually in Tesco buying cat food. He came over all pompous about how he knew everything about the regiment cuts because his former army boss was now some high-up bod at MoD, and that not just Ramsay but Downing Street knew nothing. None of them were in the loop, he says. What the hell is going on? How can the PM not know what the MoD is doing? I think Ben is talking bollocks and told him so. Result? He sent me a huffy text.

Had a word with Iain M, who says Ben is in a bit of a state just now as there is a reshuffle on the way and he's hoping that his loyal service with Ken Clarke will mean that there's a ministerial job for him in it. I hope he gets one – but not a 'too hard' one.

I sent Ben a placatory text but I doubt if it will do much good. I must ring Bruce before we go on holiday. Must.

We got Harry back last night after her week away with the children's orchestra. Gosh, we miss her when she's not here. It will be terrible when she goes to Chetham's.

Andy Murray won at the Wimbledon semi-final, although Jenny and Jose were supporting the Frenchman, Tsonga. That means I'll have to work on Sunday, when the final is on. Bugger.

8 JULY

Poor old Andy Murray, he lost and became a bit of a hero with the English, instead of their arch-enemy, because he burst into tears. Funny race. Still, at least it spared me from working; I'm so desperate to get away on holiday that I can't be bothered.

9 JULY

That's it! We're off. Two days with Ali[295] in Twickers and then la belle France. Great stuff. Asked Aus to mind the fort.

30 JULY

Hame again. Left Reims this morning at nine and got back to Edinburgh about 10.30 p.m. Knackered.

31 JULY

DC was in Glasgow and Fife today – to what end I wasn't entirely clear. No access for the hacks, no questions and no real idea why he was here. Still, he put out a statement demanding action from Eck on the referendum, which will be studiously ignored; at least it gave us a page lead.

However, I blew my top when the DC statement was issued by Ramsay Jones. I texted both Dunlop and Mundell to ask them if they thought I was kidding when I said we were having no more dealings with Ramsay. Dunlop, as usual, ignored my message, which leads me to the conclusion that I'm going to ignore him from here on in, but at least a panicky Mundell phoned to say he hadn't realised that Jones was putting out the statement.

Then Clark Dunn[296] from the Scotland Office put out the exact same statement, which was fine, and then shortly thereafter I got

---

295 Alison Hjul, Jenny's sister.
296 Chief press officer at the Scotland Office.

this grovelling text from Jones, offering profuse apologies as well as lunch. I am inclined to reject both but I'm not very good at maintaining these vendettas, so I'm not sure how this will work out.

1 AUGUST

Eck and the Nats are behaving disgracefully over the Olympics, as well they might, as they're turning out to be a brilliant Brit-fest. Eck cannot even say the words British or Team GB and it must be totally sickening for him. However, I think somebody in the Nat bunker is having second thoughts because Shona Robison's statements (she's taken over from Eck in London) are now mentioning Team GB. Maybe they've decided that ignoring things is working against them. And let's face it, Shona is not allowed to think for herself, so someone must be pulling the strings.

I monstered Eck in my *Telegraph* column and was astounded to see more than 500 Nat blogs in reply, all anti of course. One Canadian reader emailed me to say how much like the Nazis they all appeared. His description, not mine. God, the 2014 Commonwealth Games will be like Berlin in 1936 – again, my Canadian friend's description – if Eck and his pals get their way. Surely they're not that stupid.

6 AUGUST

Sport, sport, sport, all we get is sport. But my God aren't the Olympics wonderful! Great Brit news. The Commons Select Committee came up with a report that confirmed that Holyrood doesn't have the powers to hold a referendum off its own bat. No surprise there and no surprise, either, that this committee should have said it. Even a black-hearted Unionist like this one can't help but view them as hopelessly biased, although biased in the right direction. And if Eck has any complaints he should blame himself for failing to get the twenty-one or so MPs he said he'd get in 2010; that's why there's only one Nat[297] – and a completely hopeless one – on that committee.

John McLellan rang to invite me for lunch. I suspect this is more Ramsay Jones fall-out. I'm looking forward to working with John; at least he should be a bit more professional. But he'll get a shock with the standard of the idiots he's got to work with. The young lad in the Tory press office – Adam something or other[298] – grinned as we walked out of Holyrood tonight, saying: 'I hear you're having trouble with Ramsay Jones. Everyone could hear you shouting at Mundell over it.' Oops! I should make sure the door is closed.

Remembered to get El Vinos to send Tina some fizz for her birthday – her 38th, if I'm not mistaken – and Beryl emailed me to say that in future she would remind me when her birthday comes round. Good idea but I have three daughters, all born in August. Expensive month!

297 Dr Eilidh Whiteford, MP for Banff and Buchan.
298 Adam Morris.

7 AUGUST

A triumph! Boris Johnson[299] has answered my complaint about Jenny's Scottish fiver being rejected by a London bus driver and has instructed London Transport to accept what he calls 'Scottish legal tender'. On that, sadly, he's wrong – they're not really legal tender – but it's the thought that counts and I did a page lead on it. The girls were impressed by my amazing influence with the Mayor of London, although they pretended they weren't.

8 AUGUST

My Boris story has taken off a bit and I did both BBC Radio and STV 'slots', but I wish I hadn't said that bit about Boris being bonkers. That was very ungrateful of me and ungracious. But imagine his finger on the trigger! It's a very metropolitan thing to think that Boris is great. The rest of the country thinks he's barmy.

Iain M has a lead story in the Speccy about the effect of the Olympics on Eck. He's a duplicitous wee bugger, as usual, not telling me he was writing it until after he'd written it, and nicking some of my lines; still, I suppose he's got to make a living and I can't expect everyone to stand aside and let me be the only commentator from north of the border.

But I still think he's a sneaky wee bastard, especially as he's blagging a weekend off us from Saturday.

I stupidly sent emails to Brogan and Gallagher to say that I

299 Mayor of London since 2008.

had written the Olympics stuff first. They won't pay a blind bit of notice and it's now easier to get a response from the Queen (or Boris) than it is from Gallagher.

Had a few phone calls and Simon says there's a lot on Twitter about Isabel Fraser and Ian Davidson's[300] clash on *Newsnicht*.[301] Watched it on iPlayer and I think Issy made an arse of herself. As I said before, what's wrong with that wummin? She used to be so good and sensible; i.e. anti-Nat. Wrote a column bashing her, which won't make me popular.

9 AUGUST

Sang 'Happy Birthday' to Tina on the phone, who reminded me that she's thirty-eight not eight; as if I needed reminding how old I am!

Had a coffee with the lady from Scottish Ballet and told her she'll be lucky if she gets much money out of us this year. She seems a bit of a pro and has lots of good ideas. As long as Murdoch supports them, she'll be all right.

Lunch with Malcolm Robertson. He was paying, which I couldn't really understand until he asked me to get the *Telegraph* to take a table at an SCDI[302] event at the Caledonian Club in London. I'm pretty sure we'll do it, except that it's John Swinney speaking, so Murdoch might jib at that. However, I shall sell

---

300 Labour MP for Glasgow South West.

301 Scottish bit of *Newsnight*. The clash was over legal issues surrounding the independence referendum and Davidson labelled the programme 'Newsnat' for its alleged bias.

302 Scottish Council for Development and Industry.

it as a good chance for people to really challenge Swinney's prospectus. We shall see.

Malcolm hates devolution, even if his father helped to invent it, and he told me that over dinner with Andrew Wilson. The latter said that there didn't need to be a referendum and all that's needed is for Holyrood to be granted many more powers and that would do. Oh, sure that would do – for now! Wilson's pretty close to Eck and the mood is growing that that's all he wants. If that's so, and I think it might well be, then it's all the more reason for DC to call that referendum so that we can smash Eck once and for all.

Interestingly, Iain M, who sees a lot of Wilson, says the same about Andrew's view. Hmmm.

Isabel Fraser rang me to complain bitterly about my column, which was not unexpected, but she appeared to think that she was immune from criticism, my having praised her in the past. The plain fact is that in several interviews recently she has simply come over as much too pro-Nat. People, and not just me, cite a patsy interview she did with Eck and a terrible doing she gave that numptie Labour man – wotsisname[303] – that even Boothman admitted was 'not one of her best'.

She'll never forgive me on this one and we were pals, all of which is unfortunate. And, when she was giving me a hard time, I didn't even cast up her accusation, from the last time I was on her Sunday programme, that I was a Tory. But, then, everyone at BBC Scotland reckons that anyone who deviates from the Nat line is a Tory. They had better get used to the fact that all of

---

303 Richard Baker (see note 287).

the political establishment, except the Nat bit, think that Pacific Quay[304] is now a hotbed of Nats.

Strangely enough, Ian Davidson rang me, too, to complain. He said that I'd accused him of subtlety – the last thing you'd ever accuse this man of. His gripe was my comments about the Scottish Select Committee's attack on Frank Mulholland.[305] Most of Scottish Labour reckon Frank is an out-and-out Nat and that he'd do anything to please Eck. I'm bound to say that Frank, whom I like, doesn't really give the impression of being terribly independent of the Nat hierarchy and there are lots of moans about him; Labour, for instance, made it clear – to me at least – that there was no way he would have got the Lord Advocate's job if they'd won in 2011.

Davidson said he was no part of any larger conspiracy. Hmmm, we shall see.

My story about the backing Boris is giving to my campaign to have Scottish pound notes more widely accepted in London has taken off; it's a cracker, even though the girls sneered at me when I first wrote to the Mayor. However, I reckon that – secretly – they're quite pleased.

10 AUGUST

Had a drink with McLellan who says that McLetchie is close to death's door. Great pity. He was the Tories' best man in Scotland. John is a bit perplexed about working for the Tories, as well he

---

304 BBC Scotland HQ in Glasgow.

305 Mulholland was appointed Lord Advocate in 2011.

might be. He had five minutes with DC on his appointment and was told, 'Don't worry about policies – get a message over.'

He's rightly suspicious of MSPs – especially Liz Smith[306] and Jackson Carlaw – but thinks Murdo[307] is behaving. I reckon that's about right. We didn't really sort the Ramsay Jones thing; however, I did say that I can't maintain vendettas.

13 AUGUST

Had a day at the Book Festival and was delighted to see the Great Broon in such sparkling form – jokey and self-deprecating. Astonishing. And smashing attack on fiscal autonomy. But the *Scotsman* story saying that he wants to be back as the boss of the anti-Nat campaign is the usual tripe. He can make a few speeches but that's it. He'd be a useless leader; he can't work with anybody and he and Darling would be at each other's throats.

Useless dinner with Crow and a bunch of RBS dunderheids. Why do I go to these bloody awful events with thick bankers?

14 AUGUST

Stupidly agreed to go on 5 Live to talk about the Olympics and was monstered by that cretin Martin Hannan.[308] I should have hung up after the first exchange as it was clear this was going to be

---

306 Scottish Conservatives' education spokesman.

307 Murdo Fraser, beaten by Ruth Davidson in the leadership contest.

308 Scottish sports journalist.

a shouting match, but I persevered until that numbskull called me a 'fascist Tory git'. I hung up immediately and almost straight away the idiot began ringing to try to apologise; again I hung up. Then, clearly going for his five minutes of fame, he got All Media Scotland[309] (All Media ScotNat more like) to ring to say he'd posted an apology and would I accept it. I said: 'I'm not interested. The man's an arse.' Needless to say, they didn't post the last bit.

Interestingly, Simon Pia[310] told me that Hannan had been effectively banned by BBC Scotland for going nuts on one of their programmes. But, more interestingly, he also said that the Nats were putting up Hannan for broadcasting. Must try to check that through FOI.[311]

Anwar's[312] story about his daughter being rejected by Dundee in favour of fee-paying English students worked a treat. And it's not just Dundee – Glasgow and Edinburgh too. Great splash. Must get stuck into Mike Russell.

15 AUGUST

No reaction from our opposition papers to the students story and, needless to say, not a mention of it on BBC Scotland. It really is the worst station on God's earth.

Another day at the Book Festival but it's getting to be too much of a *Guardian* fest. Don't think I'll do much more.

---

309 Scottish website.

310 Journalist, former spin doctor for Wendy Alexander.

311 Freedom of Information.

312 Local newsagent.

I gave Russell a real going-over and was prepared to give him right of reply if he asked for it. Not a cheep, which suggests that the Nats know we've got them bang to rights. Still, hardly any follow-ups. Tiny one in *The Courier*, even though I tipped them off about the story. *Mail* at least did a page lead.

16 AUGUST

I think this will be my last day at the Book Festival. *Guardian* writers being interviewed by *Guardian* book editors. Jesus, what a bunch. Need some fresh air.

That bloody Hannan thing keeps rumbling on, with people bringing it up all the time. I'm going to continue ignoring it. He clearly thinks he's a bit of a star and the Nats keep saying I'm a fascist. I shall ignore them, too. But it's not a nice accusation.

17 AUGUST

At last. The *Mail* has splashed the university clearance thing and called it an exclusive. Cheeky buggers. And Tom P says that *The Scotsman* is finally writing the tale. How their education reporter got away with knocking it down all that time is beyond me.

Roddy Forsyth[313] came up with the suggestion that Rangers and Celtic had been lobbying the PM, through the Scottish Tory hierarchy, to save the Gers and get both Old Firm clubs into English Premier. Sounded far-fetched but Mundell lied to me about

---

313 *Daily Telegraph* sports writer.

Douglas Smith,[314] the alleged contact, not working for Cameron and now I discover that he is! Why tell fibs?

Had a chat with Michael Moore, who confirmed my worst fears that he and Labour are shitting themselves about Eck. They're terrified that if they do anything to pre-empt or even take charge of the situation, Eck will cut up rough and say 'it's the English Tories calling the shots'. However, their way means that Eck calls all the shots. We are playing his game. It is a pathetic situation but I don't suppose there is any way that DC can do this on his own. He must take Moore, but especially Labour, with him.

I spoke to Margaret Curran and she's as 'wet' as the rest of them. Do nothing seems to be all they can think of; I must poke them all in the eye with a sharp stick at the weekend. Mundell is up for the fray but he doesn't count for a lot, although he's a good minister.

I also spoke to Bruce Crawford in the canteen. He's had a terrible summer, poor chap. He had to fly back from Bali after his mother died suddenly. Bloody shame.

18 AUGUST

Absolute drivel, elegant drivel perhaps but still complete drivel, from Jonathan Freedland[315] in *The Guardian* today about independence, devo max or whatever. Let's just give Eck what he wants – much more powers – and all will be well; stunningly

---

314 Westminster lobbyist and Conservative spin doctor.
315 Journalist, writes novels under the pseudonym Sam Bourne.

naïve rubbish from one of those English writers who drive me mad every August when they tell us what's best for us.

20 AUGUST

Strange morning. Texted Alistair Darling to see if he fancied a lunch and he texted back immediately saying that he did and that he liked my column this morning. Liked my column? What, the one that bashed the Scottish Labour Party for their policy of appeasement? What strange people. Still, I've heard that Darling is a bit more hard-nosed than the bulk of Scottish Labour. They really are pathetic about their 'let's not annoy Eck' policy.

Had lunch with Craig Harrow[316] of the Scottish Lib Dems. Extremely interesting. He said that there are moves afoot to shift George Osborne from his position as chairman of the Cabinet committee on the constitution and replace him with Danny Alexander. That would make a lot of sense. It would stop the Nats attacking Osborne as the English Chancellor setting the policies for Scotland and would end the conflict of interest between Darling and Osborne. They agree on the Union but disagree violently on the economy.

I'm sure that Harrow wants me to write that story to give it a bit of life but what the hell – it's worth a punt and it's better than a lot of the other rubbish that's around at present. He also says that the Lib Dems think there should be another minister at the

---

316 Convenor of the Scottish Lib Dems and director of Better Together.

Scotland Office and that it should be a Tory. I phoned Ben Wallace but he's clearly still in the huff and didn't answer, so I didn't propose him for the job. I'm not sure if he'd want it as he and Mundell hate each other so much.

Much more interesting was his suggestion that Michael Moore should be replaced by Alistair Carmichael,[317] who is currently Chief Whip, in about a year's time. Very keen that I shouldn't write the tale, at least not yet. I shall keep it up my sleeve for the moment. Carmichael would be a brilliant bruiser against Eck but perhaps it's better to hold him in reserve for a bit. He would be good though. But they really are a bunch of shits to be talking about dumping Moore. I wonder if this is Better Together – the thing that Darling heads – talking or just the Lib Dems.

21 AUGUST

I think Mike Russell must have had a nervous breakdown ... he's acting very strangely, calling a group of distinguished academics who've been assembled by Jim Wallace[318] to have a look at the second-question thing a 'kangaroo court'. Needless to say, he tried to retract it later. They really are a shocking bunch, those Nats.

And he's put pressure on the principal of Dundee University, who's convenor of the Scottish universities, to write me a letter complaining about our stories saying that clearing is now loaded in favour of those who pay. I refused to accept his letter,

317 Lib Dem MP for Orkney and Shetland.
318 Lord Wallace, Lib Dem leader in the House of Lords and Advocate General for Scotland. Former MSP.

as written, because he said there had been a 'misunderstanding'. And his amended letter wasn't much better, so I rejected that, too.

The whole of Scotland is in thrall to those buggers; it's appalling. BBC Scotland is getting worse by the day. I went onto BBC Ulster to talk about our stories about clearing; they seemed to see it as a story. But still not a cheep on BBC Scotland. Incredible. Also, the education corrs of *The Herald* and *Scotsman* are completely in the pocket of Russell. Patsies!

Met Sinclair in the street and he said he'd complained to Boothman at the Beeb about the bias on *GMS*. They had Robbie Dinwoodie and Campbell Gunn – both Nats – discussing the second-question stuff and guess what? They both said the Nats were correct.

Finally managed to get hold of Ben Wallace: he says he would resign rather than take a job in the Scotland Office. He still hates Mundell and, anyway, he claims that he has two or three job offers that would give him a comfortable living, especially as MPs' pay and expenses are truly shocking.

22 AUGUST

Three wise men[319] pronounce on the 'question' for the referendum and get it hopelessly wrong, because they leave out the words 'United Kingdom' or 'leave the United Kingdom'. Needless to say, the Nats are euphoric about this omission. Why do we Unionists

---

319 The expert panel considering the wording of the referendum question consisted of Prof. Stewart Sutherland, Dr Matt Qvortrup and Ron Gould.

have to play fair all the time? However, there's still time to sort it through the Electoral Commission but this is a bad miss. I told David McLetchie that the parties who commissioned these three should ask for their money back.

23 AUGUST

Salmond in all sorts of trouble over homosexual marriage and was picketed by Catholic activists. He doesn't like this sort of thing at all, of that I'm sure, but he's being goaded by Nicola Sturgeon and 'liberal' opinion, but I'm certain he's not happy with any of it. But the Catholic church is making a complete hash of it.

Had a three-hour medical. Everything in working order but, still, a bit scary. Simply must lose weight – am going to try for one and a half stone by Christmas and the same again by next summer. I'm determined to have a go but it means a drastic reduction in red wine.

Another loaded – in favour of the Nats – discussion on *GMS*, featuring Peter Lynch, ostensibly a neutral academic from Stirling but in reality a raving Nat.

24 AUGUST

Did a bit of body swerve and headed up the Glen for the weekend, now that the girls have gone south. Marvellous to be here and had a great night at Mary and Martin's with most of the Glenners in attendance.

25 AUGUST

Josephine's 15th birthday but I can't phone her because there's no signal up here. Amazing, she went up to London on her own on the train from Twickers yesterday. She really has led a sheltered life.

Brilliant tea party at Fred's Cottage with Jeannie Mackie[320] and David Leigh.[321] Superb couple. David is one of the best journalists anywhere but completely unassuming and simply a great bloke. He's desperate to retire, get a nice package and just chill out. But Rusbridger[322] wants him to hold his hand until he packs up. Difficult.

As if that wasn't enough, then went to Hector and Jeannie MacLean's barbecue hut for more food and drink. Stuffed and exhausted we staggered back to Mary and Martin's at 10.30 p.m.

26 AUGUST

Jenny and Josie back from London, Harriet in Dorset on an orchestra course. It was great to get home.

27 AUGUST

The independent schools' lot put out the exam results figures. Completely useless and the boss, John Edward, chose this very day to bugger off; his office say he's at a meeting. Oh sure, on a

---

320 Criminal defence barrister at Doughty Street Chambers.

321 *Guardian* investigative journalist.

322 Alan Rusbridger, *Guardian* editor.

bank holiday! They really are idiots pandering to *The Scotsman* and *Herald*, whose education corrs hate private schools, and ignoring *The Times* and *Telegraph*, whose readers send their kids (or their grandkids) to them and who are interested in reading the figures. Another totally useless public body, except that it's a private one!

Gen. Andrew Mackay tipped me off that Alex Salmond had been booed when he turned up at the Tattoo and so I checked with Brig. Mel Jameson, who said he'd check. Mel is a great bloke who ran the Tattoo for years and said that, as Lord Lieutenant of Perthshire, he had banned Eck from the dais when the Queen granted city status to Perth and so Eck didn't turn up. Amazing, somebody who actually stands up to the First Minister. Watch your back, Mel!

However, when Mel rang back he said that it was only a few people who'd booed Eck, so no story. Pity. Another day, perhaps.

28 AUGUST

Wrote a column bashing Labour and the Tories for being invisible all summer; it was a bit of a make-weight but it seems to have struck a chord and, needless to say, the Nats thought it was brilliant.

Had an interesting conversation with Kevin Pringle. Eck couldn't go to Orkney because someone in his family is ill; it could only have been his wife, Moira, but they're very leery of admitting it. Eventually agreed a form of words about 'family illness' with him, but they're exceedingly touchy when it comes to anything to do with Mrs Salmond.

29 AUGUST

Lunch with Darling at Centotre; he's not a toper and that suits me at present, with my trying to stay off the red infuriator. Mind you, seventy-five quid for two courses each and it doesn't feel like I've eaten a morsel. He was fascinating, as usual. Looked great – he's had two weeks on Lewis and the weather, unlike for the rest of us, has been very good.

He says that there really should be an agreement by the end of October over how many questions there will be on the referendum ballot paper, but he doubts if it will happen as Eck will find an excuse to play it long as he's desperate for a second question. Eck will produce thousands of people from his consultation process saying that they want a second question, but everyone knows that that's baloney; one of them is Martin Sime at the SCVO[323] and he has been well and truly exposed for the Nat supporter he is.

Alistair very chipper about the Unionist prospects, as distinct from March, when he was pretty gloomy about things.

All the signs and the polls and the focus groups are now pointing in the direction of a handsome victory, but he's not complacent and he's definitely not aiming to play the Olympics card, or at least not too often or too hard.

Although he's a bit more robust than Scottish Labour about keeping the pressure on Salmond, he says that Westminster holding the referendum is very much a last resort – once every other avenue has been exhausted and Eck continues to be bolshie. However, the prevailing view is that Salmond is desperate for a deal.

---

323 Scottish Council of Voluntary Organisations.

Alistair says 'it's all about him saving face, now' and Clark Dunn, at the Scotland Office, says that the word they're picking up suggests that Eck may well accept there will be only one question on independence in the official referendum, but that he will hold a second referendum on extra powers. He can only hold a referendum on separation if Westminster allows it, but they might be able to hold his poll on extra powers under the existing powers of the Scottish Parliament. I've 'flown' it as a column but I'm not sure if I believe it.

It's all about Eck pulling a rabbit out of the hat at his Perth conference in mid-October – the number of people backing the second question, for instance, which they'll make sure is massively in favour.

Darling was very interested when I told him how good Broon was at the Book Festival last week, and says that he'll be getting back to normal now that all the pressure's off. He says that Gordon is good at set-piece speeches but was no good at PMQs and didn't enjoy it, whereas it's clear that Cameron does like it and is good at it.

He says that Downing Street was a terrible place to be when Gordon was preparing for PMQs on a Wednesday. There would be papers everywhere and every conceivable question would be thrown at him. Nothing would get done for half of Tuesday and all morning Wednesday while he got ready for the weekly session. 'Gordon kept practising his lines over and over again and even if they didn't work, he'd still use them.' The rest of Wednesday was then invariably taken up with inquests after PMQs.

Alistair wasn't much taken with the idea of moving Osborne out of that Cabinet committee chairmanship job on the constitution: 'He's got much more clout than Danny. Nobody really takes him all that seriously.' Interestingly, at least as far as I was concerned, Alistair seems to have time for GO. 'He's much nicer privately than he appears in public and he's much nicer as a person than Cameron.' Very strange.

Darling was also very interesting about the two Eds – Miliband and Balls. 'I told Miliband not to give the other Ed the Treasury job in the shadow Cabinet, which is why he gave it to Alan Johnson.[324] But then Balls got it when Johnson, who didn't know much about economics, had to resign. I don't think Miliband gets much of a look-in on the economy now. He's a difficult man is Balls.' I said I thought Balls's wife[325] was very good but he said: 'I haven't seen much of her this summer.'

He wasn't very enamoured of the current crop of Labour MSPs and said, 'I don't really know who half of them are and I couldn't really name many of the front-bench team'. But he agreed with my piece today that there's no reason why they shouldn't get out into the country to meet people and to press the flesh.

Told Alistair that I'm off south as soon as the girls finish school – Scotland is getting worse with every month that passes. He said his daughter had just got back from Boston and was complaining about how parochial we've become. And, of course, he joined in

---

324 Former Labour Home Secretary.

325 Yvette Cooper, shadow Home Secretary.

the chorus of criticism about BBC Scotland. Does it have a fan anywhere? It really is dire.

He repeated what he'd said at our lunch in June: that the Labour Cabinet only went along with the Calman recommendations because they were sure that the Tories, when they got elected, would kick all that nonsense into touch!

Pretty good speech trailed by Moore's office, putting pressure on Eck to settle on one question, but quite interesting suggestion that they think Eck may accept one question on the ballot paper and then, if he loses, have another referendum on devo max. The Nats think he could probably do this, legally, as it doesn't break up Britain, but I'm not so sure as it's bound to have implications for the rest of the UK.

31 AUGUST

Kevin Pringle has been moved from spad back to the SNP but it's not entirely unexpected and won't make much difference. Eck will still be in charge and Kevin will implement the orders and tell St Andrew's House what to do. Hilarious that Geoff Aberdein[326] is some kind of chief of staff – in other words, he goes for the pizzas!

Labour and Tories decide not to say anything – eejits. But, as ever, Willie Rennie comes to our rescue, saying it's desperation. This is probably not true but it will do for a page lead and allows me to write a column.

---

326 Long-standing member of Salmond's inner circle.

2 SEPTEMBER

Cruel parents that we are, we took Harriet to Chetham's in Manchester. Smashing place and H very brave, braver than me, anyway. She left us all notes inside our books telling us to be adult about everything and keep a stiff upper lip. Jesus, who's the bairn here?

Eck did his legislative statement, which was all mince except for the bills on gay marriage and the referendum. Johann very ordinary and Ruth pretty crap, I'm afraid. The Tories are trying to put pressure on me to be kind to her; well, they can get stuffed.

Bit of a flurry over whether there's a deal on the cards. I don't think so – there are meetings planned but they are a long way from a deal. Sev[327] said there's a deal looming and the normally sane Mags Gardham[328] did too. There isn't, unless Eck caves in. Mundell says he's meeting Bruce Crawford on Thursday, then there will be a meeting with Moore next week and then there's the possibility of a meeting with DC on 24 September. I still can't see a deal but DC must be quicker on his feet on this one; don't let Salmond pull a fast one. If Eck backs down on the second question it's a surrender, not a deal.

Iain says that poor old Ben Wallace has only been offered a job as a junior whip and he's turned it down. I think Ben might as well clear off. He says he's had a couple of offers from outside. I think he'll take one of them. I must phone him.

---

327 Severin Carrell, *The Guardian*'s man in Scotland.

328 Magnus Gardham, political editor of the *Daily Record*.

5 SEPTEMBER

Spoke to Ben, who's very depressed, and Liza[329] is furious that he's not taken the job. Phoned Bruce to get him to tell Mitchell[330] to offer the job again. Iain is furious because he says Bruce only cares about the Tories; partly true but then Iain feels DC has been rotten to Ben.

No. 10 very angry with Ben for turning down that job in the whips' office, so Bruce thinks that it is very unlikely that he'll get another offer. Ben has slunk off north with his tail between his legs … to get another bollocking from Liza, probably.

God, the Tory conference is looking grim – all those right-wing pals of Iain. Must keep away from them.

Eck's reshuffle brought on by Bruce Crawford saying he's had enough.[331] I suppose we have to accept that the reasons are genuine. Nicola is now in charge of the referendum negotiations.

Is there a surrender on the cards? It's beginning to look like it, as the Nats – in the shape of Robbie and Gunn – are now saying that there was never any real demand for a second question; it was only ever a tactic. All the cybernats are saying the same, but as most of them work for Nat ministers at Holyrood – and of course the Odd Couple, aka Wilson and Hamilton – it's what you'd expect. Maybe. Maybe.

Did Radio Ulster – my old pals – and BBC2; Ulstermen much more professional than the Jocks.

---

329 Ben's wife.

330 Andrew Mitchell, the then Chief Whip.

331 He resigned as Cabinet Secretary.

6 SEPTEMBER

Nats seem to be in total retreat over the second question – they know there's no demand for it but they're not conceding, at least not in public. Said a fond farewell to Bruce Crawford and asked him who I can be nice to now; he was the only Nat I was ever nice to.

Ramsay Jones phoned – will they never get the message – to say that Osborne was having a wee blether with the Scottish editors and would I go. I said I wouldn't or rather that I couldn't. He then offered me a phone chat with GO and again I said I wasn't interested.

However, I told Simon to try for a chat with GO and that eejit Jones came back to say that he couldn't 'find a slot' for Simon. Just as well I didn't bother. They really are totally useless. Roden[332] of the *Mail* was also offered a phone chat and he was later told there wasn't one available. Why not piss off the *Mail* and the *Telegraph*? Brilliant people, that lot. They really are.

Macleod of *The Times* said that the forty-five minutes' blether was quite good but that GO's mind seemed to be elsewhere, as well it might be, and that he was a bit flaky on many of the issues. However, he did say that Salmond was now in the negative campaigning business – his best line seems to be reduced to attacking the Tories.

Angus said that the two *Herald* editors – Jonathan Russell and Richard Walker – were a positive embarrassment with their idiotic questions.

---

332 Alan Roden, political editor of the *Scottish Daily Mail*.

But, as Angus says, GO demolished Eck's economic argument good and proper.

CBI buggered up the arrangements for covering the speech. Those hacks that did turn up were segregated at a solitary table and given crap food, Mags of *The Herald* amongst them. Why on earth did he – and they – put up with that treatment?

Ruth a bit better at FMQs. At last. Johann not so good. Eck quite good and it's clear that he's going to keep bashing Labour over their alliance with the Tories because Labour really are shit-scared of this association. What a bunch of fearties. The Tories probably think that I wasn't nasty to Ruth because of all their complaints. They had better learn that I call them as I see them, because if they think that by moaning I'll change tack then they'll have to learn the hard way!

Mundell phoned to ask if I was going to the CBI dinner. I said I hadn't been invited and he said he'd bollock Dunlop for not arranging it. I told him not to bother as after his and Ramsay Jones's total balls-up on the regiments, I'm not sure I want much more to do with that genius.

7 SEPTEMBER

Jim McColl[333] of Clyde Blowers has come out for full independence, or at least the latest version of full independence. Murdoch MacLennan came up with a good quip re: his company name: 'What an appropriate name for a supporter of the wreckers of Scotland!' I'll use it one of these days.

---

333 Scottish businessman.

8 SEPTEMBER

Scotland couldn't beat Serbia in World Cup qualifier. Levein[334] is useless. Sack him now!

9 SEPTEMBER

Harriet's not having a great time in Manchester because of those little buggers she shares a room with. They regard her as the spoiled rich kid and when one of them said that her father was a Polish truck driver, Harriet replied, with perfect candour: 'Oh, our cleaner comes from Poland!' That just confirmed their view of her. So what! She'll see them off in her own time.

11 SEPTEMBER

Fantastic win for Andy Murray in New York. Texted Kevin Pringle and urged them to organise ticker-tape down the Royal Mile for him. Encouraging response.

Idiotic Jeremy Vine[335] trying to goad Nats into making political capital out of Murray's win. Astonishingly, the Nats – Pete Wishart included – didn't rise to the bait. Did a column, praising the Nats! First time for everything. But I also bashed Angus Brendan McNeil for failing to toe the respectable line and said that it was another case of 'post-ceilidh foolishness', which refers to the time he was caught in bed with two burds. Most of the Nats

---

334 Then Scottish coach Craig Levein.

335 BBC Radio 2 presenter.

– Bruce Crawford and Calum Cashley,[336] for instance – thought it was very funny. John Swinney, however, did not.

John Scott, the Deputy Presiding Officer, said he had good news for me: the Ayr Tories want me to speak at their lunch club! I quite like John but I told him that I could do a speech like that every week in life and that, no, I wouldn't be doing Ayr, thank you very much. He said he'd leave it to me to tell them. I wish I hadn't agreed to do that Stirling gig; it sets an awful precedent.

Got a phone call from *Question Time*, sounding me out about doing a programme before the Nat conference in October. I said I'd love to, just as long as I'm not billed as the Tory. The woman in Glasgow insisted that this wouldn't be the case and that she'd get back to me, after she's talked to her editor. That means it probably won't happen. Still, fingers crossed.

Had lunch with Mike Crow, who's really missing politics. Treated dreadfully by those stupid Scottish Tories, including that idiot chairman Andrew Fulton and his numpty deputy Kynoch – still, he's built a conservatory with his pay-off money.

13 SEPTEMBER

Alex Salmond is in real trouble now, thanks to the EU president Barroso[337] saying that all new states had to apply to join the EU. Eck flannelled and havered at FMQs but he is really buggered

---

336 SNP activist.

337 José Manuel Barroso in an interview with the BBC.

with this declaration by so senior a figure. He is getting painted into a corner.

John McLellan, the chief Tory spinner, phoned to ask what I thought about Ruth's performance after FMQs (I'm getting really tired of the Tories asking me this) and I said I wasn't interested in what she had asked – something about the NHS in Ayrshire – and told him that the only thing I was interested in was Europe. Why the Tories didn't go on that is a mystery to me. I wonder if McLellan is up to the job? He has a mountain to climb with that woman, though.

17 SEPTEMBER

Drove to Fealar for my stalking treat. God, what a spot. It really was a good one-hour drive off the Moulin Road, which is itself little more than a track. Fantastic place. Bill Gammell, of Cairn, and Angus MacDonald, a teuchter millionaire, had RUN the last three miles back to the lodge after their stalk; Christ, what have I let myself in for?

18 SEPTEMBER

I fear I was a bit out of it on the hill. Not too bad, at least not until we started tramping through all of those bloody peat bogs. After nearly seven hours I got a shot and killed a stag, but unfortunately, in trying to make sure it was a goner, I shot a hind too. I think that stalker should have known that my stag was down and dead but I shall just have to live with the ignominy of it for ever more. Ho, hum.

19 SEPTEMBER

Completely knackered drive back to Edinburgh but what a great time. How come I know so many rich people when I am so totally skint? Happens all the time.

20 SEPTEMBER

Swinney's draft Budget. Peanuts, frankly, and when I talked to him afterwards it was obvious he was worried about the reaction. He was right to be – he got absolutely slaughtered the next day. Best line came from one of the unions: Swinney is just Osborne in a kilt. He'll hate that.

21 SEPTEMBER

Harriet's coming home but I won't be there to meet her because I agreed to talk to the Stirling Tories. Wish I hadn't. Bloody awful dinner, really bad. But stayed with the Scotts,[338] lovely people, in a massive house which was freezing because they don't know how to work the central heating boiler! Decent wine at dinner and a few drams back at their house, when suddenly Helen shouted, 'What's that?' and we all rushed outside to see this bloody great meteor, or was it a meteorite? Amazing.

Interesting wee blether with Michael Forsyth. He doesn't think much of Dunlop. Does anyone? And he thinks that allowing sixteen-year-olds to vote is wrong. I say it's a bargaining chip but

---

338 Helen Scott is chairman of the Stirling Conservatives.

he says we shouldn't do it as a matter of principle. Quite right, I suppose.

22 SEPTEMBER

Back to Edinburgh for weekend with Harriet, although I hardly saw her – house full of wee girls. H looks to have grown in the last three weeks. We'll see her next weekend, I hope, as well as Ally, Sue and Mighty Fergus! Fantastic.

Did a 'one year on' assessment of Ruth, but it was more about a one year on from Cameron being at Balmoral and finding out that Murdo Fraser wanted to scrap his party. What must the Queen have said to him when she saw my story then in the *Sunday Telegraph*? 'I say, Prime Minister, what's all this about your Scottish party being abolished?[339] Pass the marmalade.' No wonder DC decided to back Ruth.

I was very kind to Ruth; too kind, says Simon. And that's what Raymond Robertson, the former Tory chairman and mediocre minister and MP, said too when I met him with Jackson Carlaw, Ruth's deputy, in the new bar, which I have dubbed The Backsliders. Carlaw's not exactly totally horrible to her, but he's not totally supportive, either.

They are shits, are politicians, and being little more than a sect, the Scottish Tories are worse than most.

Funnily enough, Ruth gave me a cheery wave earlier and said

---

339 Fraser, in his leadership bid for the Scottish Conservatives, proposed disbanding the party and starting a new one.

that I'd been – on the whole – pretty fair to her. I must have done something wrong.

24 SEPTEMBER

Eck's off to the USA for the Ryder Cup jollities and has finally conceded that the second question is never going to be included in the referendum. He admitted it to the Yanks before he bothered telling the Jocks; in fact, he's still not told us! Interestingly, Simon's story about the fact that he's spent nearly £400,000 on piss-ups and dinners since becoming FM is the tale that's really taken off. I do doubt if his total is a great deal more than Jack McConnell's but everyone goes nuts about politicos spending our money on booze and grub.

Mundell thinks that Andrew Mitchell is getting all he deserves in his row with the police. I know Mitchell and I can imagine him swearing like a trooper, but I think the cops are lying through their teeth in respect of him using the 'plebs' word.[340] Why, nowadays, do people believe every word the police say? Especially after Hillsborough. I'm sure they've fitted Mitchell up, but he may still have to resign.

25 SEPTEMBER

Brave and honest policy statement from Johann Lamont.[341] But

---

340 Mitchell allegedly called the Downing Street police 'plebs' for barring his exit through the main gates. He resigned a month later, on 19 October.

341 Lamont said it was time to end the 'something for nothing' culture.

it does presage the end of all the freebies. It has been denounced by *The Sun* but then Andy Nicoll[342] reckons he's the only person in Scotland who pays council tax.

Extremely interesting that the Nats haven't gone hell for leather in attacking her speech. However, I think Nicola, who'll be standing in for Eck at FMQs, won't be able to resist saying either it's the second longest suicide note in history or that it's a lurch to the right. Or both.

26 SEPTEMBER

Very interesting piss-up at Turcan Connell, although absolutely disgusting wine and attended by all of Edinburgh's worst and most self-satisfied, in the shape of lawyers, accountants and estate agents. Douglas gave me a very interesting bit of gen about the cultural offensive that's about to be launched in 2014. Eck's already got Ben Thomson[343] at the Galleries – which are going to have a Famous Scots series throughout 2014; and another Nat sympathiser is due to be appointed, he says, as boss of the National Library.[344] More heroic Scots, perhaps? Mr Connell is just about the shrewdest observer there is in Edinburgh. He says that the business community is nowhere near ready to rally to the Union standard. Pathetic. Left early. Rest of the company extremely boring. They know nothing.

---

342 Political editor of the *Scottish Sun*.

343 Founder of the think tank Reform.

344 James Boyle was appointed chairman of the board of trustees by Culture Minister Fiona Hyslop in October 2012.

Great news about Harriet, thank goodness. She's been elected to something like class rep or class president. And it's been voted on by all her contemporaries. Brilliant. She likes being popular, does H. But then, don't we all? Can't wait to see her this weekend. And Fearless Fergus, too.

Have been to the gym twice this week – don't laugh. And will have another go on Friday. Very knackering. But it might be doing a bit of good. Who knows?

28 SEPTEMBER

Brief sojourn in office and then off to Lancashire! Easy drive down to Hornby to stay with Ben Wallace. Iain warned me that I might be annoyed by his anti-Cameron stance, but then he didn't surprise me at all. He doesn't like DC but he doesn't appear to hate him as much as Iain would like him to, or as much as Iain does.

We had a lovely evening and a nice dinner. Liza is such a star. Very frustrated at being stuck up there when Ben is in London. Clever girl who is doing lots of intricate work for Ben. She should be living in a big city, not this Dead Man's Gulch! During dinner, David Davis[345] phoned for Ben, ostensibly about that BAe deal[346] that they're all fighting. But we decided differently; Jenny dubbed it the Lancashire Hot Plot. Excellent, except that I told Iain. I also told him not to nick it! What a hope.

---

345 Conservative MP and twice a leadership contender.

346 Planned merger between the UK's BAe Systems and the Franco-German Airbus owner EADS. The deal fell apart on 10 October.

Iain was disappointed when I told him that Ben wasn't foaming at the mouth about DC. Really annoyed.

29 SEPTEMBER

Off to Manchester to pick up Harry. She was in great form and clearly popular with the other girls (boys?). Chets is such a doddle to get to, and then we set off for Sheffield. Again – dead easy. Eventually went over Snake Pass. What a drive. Amazing and, incredibly, Ally's turn-off was almost as soon as you get into Sheffield.

He and Sue have a fantastic house but not as fantastic as Fearless Fergus, my grandson. What a boy! Marvellous creature. Played with him all afternoon, then went for a long walk. Then a couple of pints at first-class local, followed by mediocre, I'm afraid, curry. Still, we had a great time watching rubbish *X Factor* on TV.

30 SEPTEMBER

Took the bus into Sheffield city centre, which is the same as every other city centre. But what a lovely city, generally! More fun with Fergus and then off to Manchester, again via Snake Pass, to take Harry back to Chets. She's really growing up fast there, height-wise and maturity too. She couldn't wait to get rid of us when we took her back to school.

1 OCTOBER

Took Granny out for a birthday lunch in Broughty Ferry but got
a telling-off for failing to send her a birthday card. BUT I DID!
However, it didn't arrive. Anyway, we had a nice blether and she
doesn't eat much nowadays – she's a cheap date!

2 OCTOBER

The Nats are really getting into trouble over their freebies.

3 OCTOBER

Instead of hiding, Johann Lamont came out fighting over her
'end the freebies' speech and, for once, we had a decent debate
in the Scottish Parliament. Lamont and Sturgeon were both
good, but I think Lamont was better because the best Sturgeon
could come up with were a lot of insults about Labour joining the Tories.

And, boy, the Nats don't like it up them. After decades of hurl-
ing personal abuse at their opponents, they now scream like stuck
pigs when they get it back. Hugh Henry[347] was denounced for
saying that that Mackay[348] bloke had profited from his kids having free lunches, when other Renfrewshire schools had to pay.

And Roseanna was swearing and shouting afterwards, asking when Labour were going to claim that John Swinney was

347 Labour MSP for Renfrewshire South.
348 Derek Mackay, SNP MSP for Renfrewshire North and West.

benefiting from Liz Quigley's free prescriptions. Answer: they're not and have never intended to. It's really pathetic.

4 OCTOBER

Murdo Fraser collared me in the lobby to say that Ruth D was about to cave in on more powers for Holyrood at an evidence session with a Commons Select Committee. Great story? Well, quite good; but what she's doing is backing the idea of a constitutional convention so that all of the UK will be included in any more devolution. She told me, frankly but off the record, that it is merely a ploy to kick the whole issue into the long grass, which is what McLetchie said too. And Cameron is a party to all of this chicanery. Best news is that we got away with the whole thing. Good exclusive.

A bit cynical but who cares; there's been too much change already.

Another smashing scrap on Lamont's 'end the freebies' agenda at FMQs. Salmond very tough and kept bashing Labour for playing the Tory game, but I think the Nats are beginning to worry as Labour are now looking pretty good. Ruth should have kept on that subject, too, but unfortunately she didn't. As usual!

5 OCTOBER

Birthday. Christ, sixty-three! Loads of smashing prezzies but we can't go out because Jenny has to pick Jose and her pals up from

Merchiston![349] The girls sang wonderful 'Happy Birthday' to me in Chinese! Fantastic. But I missed not having Harry here. Boo hoo.

7 OCTOBER

Off to Brum by plane for the Tory conference. Why do I fly? Tiny FlyBe plane. Grumpy stewardesses. Still, Holiday Inn not far from the station and had an enormous room. Not bad. Conference hall deserted and bunch of animal rights nutters outside shouting 'Tory Scum' – that's normal – but protesting about the badger cull. For Christ's sake, what a load of baloney. The world's gone mad.

There are very few politicians here. Hardly any MPs. Cabinet ministers cocooned away in the upper floors of the Hyatt. Just armies – masses of them – of lobbyists, PR men, hacks and general no-good-niks. They all seem to be making pots of money.

I was invited up to one suite, occupied by Craig Harrow, who's chair of the Scottish Lib Dems, and it was fabulously opulent: wall-to-wall expensive canapés and champagne. Astonishing largesse.

8 OCTOBER

Caught the end of Ruth D's speech at some hole-in-the-corner conference affair and it's clear that she's got her figures about Scotland's scroungers more than a bit wrong. She's getting a

---

349 Merchiston Castle, Edinburgh boys' school.

hammering but is not withdrawing. Good for her. We need to end that bloody consensus where the Tories want to be loved rather than be different.

I then had a full 28-minute grilling from the *Question Time* people to see whether I'd be suitable for next week's programme on the Nats. I'm certain, however, that I didn't appear right-wing enough and I doubt very much if I'll get on.

Went back to the hotel to write what turned out to be a favourable piece about Ruth, had a few zeds and then back to the fray. The Scottish piss-up turned out to be quite good and Cameron made an appearance – and a decent speech.

I then had dinner with Burnside[350] and his guests, including Bill Cash[351] and that Foreign Office minister Hugo Swire[352] – another Old Etonian, of course – but an old mate and quite good, I reckon. Good fun.

9 OCTOBER

Home.

11 OCTOBER

Great announcement by Cameron that special commemorations to mark the start of World War One will be held in September

---

350 David Burnside, Northern Ireland politician and PR man.

351 Eurosceptic Conservative MP.

352 Conservative MP for East Devon.

2014, one month before Eck's vote. Excellent news. Did some radio but, needless to say, the Beeb claimed it was a political move. What a bunch! Still, they're right. It will not help Salmond.

13 OCTOBER

Andrew Mackay phoned with the news that Clive Fairweather[353] had died. Very sad but not unexpected. I wrote a tribute for the *Sunday* after its editor said he wanted one.

15 OCTOBER

Big Day. Cameron and Eck signed what they call the Edinburgh Agreement,[354] with Eck trying to look like a world leader instead of a nonentity. Sev Carrell was nearly arrested for shouting – à la Mitchell – at the police for not letting him through the barrier. Had a nice lunch with Magnus Linklater, who's very relaxed now that he's not the *Times* editor; mind you, he was always (too) relaxed. I wrote a nice piece but London have now lost all interest in the story.

Question Time has finally said that I'm on, on Thursday night. Wow!

16 OCTOBER

Day off – this recess is busier than ever.

---

353 Colonel Fairweather, senior officer in the SAS (1944–2012).

354 This committed to a single-question Yes/No independence referendum by the end of 2014.

17 OCTOBER

London for lunch with MM and made it by the skin of my teeth. Great craic and he's very supportive.

Then down to Eton for debate with Sarwar,[355] Pat Kane[356] and Gerry Hassan from Dundee. Great fun. Really good. Fantastic dinner with Waldegrave[357] in the Provost's House. He didn't remember that I'd once had breakfast in his house, way back in the '80s, when he was appointed Green Minister. He was pleased that I'd reminded him, but what I didn't tell him was that although I was political editor of the *Mail on Sunday* and the meeting was at breakfast time, I didn't even get a cup of coffee from him or his snooty wife.

18 OCTOBER

Up to Glasgow by train and boned up on everything I could think of for *QT*. Programme was from Easterhouse with Sturgeon, Curran, Davidson and Serwotka.[358] Amazing experience and seemed to go all right, although Margaret was dreadful. Everyone called her 'Deep-fried J. K. Rowling'. Not sure if either lady would like that description. Everyone thought I did OK and it was incredible how many people saw it.

---

355 Anas Sarwar, deputy leader of Scottish Labour, MP for Glasgow Central.

356 Nationalist activist, one half of pop duo Hue and Cry.

357 William, now Lord, Waldegrave, former Conservative minister, appointed Provost of Eton College in 2009.

358 Mark Serwotka, general secretary of the Public and Commercial Services Union (trade union for civil servants).

19 OCTOBER

Things are hectic. Straight through to Perth for the SNP conference. Good debate, but daffy-duck resolution on NATO.[359]

22 OCTOBER

Bugger all happening. Labour spin doctors told me they were aghast at how badly Margaret Curran had done on *Question Time*. They said she'd done it twice before and had had massive rehearsals but was still crap.

I told Jean Urquhart that I liked her 'principled' speech at the Nat conference, even if I didn't believe a word of it. She was surprised and said 'really?' as if she didn't believe me. She went off to have her lunch with that other teuchter[360] who spoke against NATO but I decided to leave them alone.

23 OCTOBER

How wrong could I have been? Both Urquhart and Finnie have resigned the Nat whip and old funny-eyes Wilson[361] has told Simon he might be following them.

Great story but it got better, even though I was lying on the dentist's chair by the time it happened, with Eck being proved a huge fibber for telling Andrew Neil that he had sought legal

---

359 The SNP dropped its historic opposition to NATO membership post-independence.

360 Highlands and Islands MSP John Finnie.

361 John Wilson, MSP for Central Scotland.

officers' advice[362] when Nicola had just told the Parliament he hadn't.

Completely stupid Paul Martin[363] called Eck a 'barefaced liar', so that's the worst they can say about him, which is what Patricia Ferguson[364] said when I blethered with her.

24 OCTOBER

Terrible night with toothache and got in very late. Nats are in a state of shock. Fantastic. Wrote what I hoped would be seen as a mischievous piece about Nicola taking all the flak for Eck, even if it turns out that he's on TV after all later tonight. Who cares? *Telegraph* readers don't watch rubbish on STV!

Had a couple of red wines at the Poppy Day event and ended up with Bruce Crawford emptying a glass all over me. Still, it was an old suit and even older shirt and he's a good guy. Brig. David Alltrey[365] was also there and I complained to him that I hadn't been invited to the Tattoo this year. He said he'd sort it.

26 OCTOBER

Poor old Harry is off to Chetham's tomorrow, so that's a big cloud hanging over all of us. Jenny is taking her down and coming back, all in one day.

---

362 Over an independent Scotland's entry to the EU.

363 Labour MSP for Glasgow Provan.

364 Former Labour Culture Minister.

365 Appointed producer of the Edinburgh Military Tattoo in December 2011.

But we went to see Jose playing piano at a church in Morningside. She was brilliant. Very proud of her; she's such a modest lassie, just like her mother.

27 OCTOBER

Jenny and Harry head off, leaving me and Jose on our own. However, Jose went to the pictures with a boy! I pretended that I wasn't listening last night when she was telling Jenny and Harry about it but then I looked up and said 'What's this?' But I was just kidding and anyway she went to see *Skyfall* with a crowd and they went to the morning showing at about 11 a.m.!

28 OCTOBER

Wrote a piece – a bit po-faced – decrying the propensity of politicians to call each other 'liars', 'fascists' etc. But the language is being devalued and, for once, it's not the Nats to blame. Labour are easily the worst.

Went to that RBS piss-up at Mike Crow's behest. Very good, Jenny came too. Hester[366] was a complete wash-out: stayed rooted to the spot and didn't say a word. However, his chairman, Sir Philip Hampton,[367] was brilliant, essentially telling everyone – Swinney was there – that you couldn't have a giant bank like RBS in a wee country like independent Scotland.

---

366 Stephen Hester, RBS CEO from 2008 to 2013.
367 Appointed RBS chairman in 2009.

1 NOVEMBER

Repeated my diatribe about bad language after Johann Lamont called Eck a 'chancer' and Tricia Marwick didn't pull her up, even after she'd issued an edict telling the MSPs to clean up their language.

2 NOVEMBER

Train to Tunbridge Wells to see Tina. Wrote a column linking speeches by Hampton and Jim Wallace, underlining Hampton's warning but having a bit of a go at devo nuts like Jim. What Jim has been doing[368] has of course encouraged Eck. No point denying it.

Had great dinner with Tina and Mitch; they're happy, so I'm very happy. While we were there I got a call from Ben Wallace saying that Alistair McAlpine[369] is being named as a child molester by *Newsnight*. It was a rubbish claim and a rubbish programme. Poor man. I sent a text to Gallagher to tell him how outrageous this was. As usual, no reply, probably because he doesn't know McAlpine – or anyone else for that matter. I sent another to Brogan and at least he replied and agreed that *Newsnight* was well out of order.

---

368 He said he wanted to 'bust the myth' that independence was an extension of devolution. AC described him as an 'enthusiastic player' in the devolution industry.

369 Lord McAlpine, former Conservative Party treasurer, fundraiser and close ally of Thatcher (*d.* 2014).

5 NOVEMBER

Wrote a reasonably positive piece about Ruth D's first year. My heart wasn't really in it but I tried, really tried, to be positive. She should be a hack or broadcaster and would probably do the Tories more good by doing that than as a politician. She has acres to learn and not much time in which to do it, but at least she'll get a lot of TV in the next couple of years, which she is good at.

8 NOVEMBER

Although I keep saying I'm fed up with Europe stories, I couldn't think of anything else to write about than Europe for my Saturday column. Christ, this is getting bloody boring.

11 NOVEMBER

Went to Easter Road as a guest of Margo and Jim Sillars[370] to see Dundee United being robbed by Hibernian, 2–1. Still, Hibs deserved to win as United were useless.

12 NOVEMBER

Wrote a piece agreeing with Eck that everyone has to be positive and behave properly during the referendum debate. I will if you will, Alex!

---

370 Former deputy leader of the SNP, husband of Margo MacDonald.

13 NOVEMBER

Quite interesting debate on freebies, with Alex Neil being his usual outrageous self, but it was quite funny.

BBC absolutely crucified for attacking McAlpine – just as I told Gallagher on the very night it happened.

Went to BMA dinner, where doctors tried to justify their strike plan. What a hope.

15 NOVEMBER

Clive Fairweather's memorial service. Masses of booze, masses of sojers and masses of SAS men. Luckily, I managed to remember to take Jenny's birthday present home. Then General Andrew Mackay 'dropped in' for even more booze – another bottle of whisky bit the dust.

16 NOVEMBER

Felt hellish and played hookey. Painted the door instead. God, I was ill.

17 NOVEMBER

Took Jose and Eva to the rugby. Scotland crap in the first half, good in the second and, of course, lost. Robinson[371] will have to go. He's had long enough now. Nothing's happening.

---

371 Andy Robinson, Scottish head coach. He resigned on 25 November 2012.

But it was great fun with the girls. They were wrapped in Scotland flags. Smashing, apart from tripping up and falling all my length while walking home. Winded and sore knees but otherwise nothing wrong. Sober, too!

18 NOVEMBER

Joined in the bashing of Eck over his lying ways. I see that Ted Brocklebank[372] has a similar piece in the *Mail*. He really does think he's a great politician but actually he did bugger all.

20 NOVEMBER

Contacted Gallagher's secretary – again – to see if he'll have lunch with me before Christmas. She said she'd already emailed me, which she hadn't, to say that his diary is full and that I can have a coffee with him some morning. Don't think I'll bother. Strange bloke, and he's allowed his Wikipedia site to include all that stuff about what a hard man he is. Any normal person would have edited that out.

21 NOVEMBER

Great story from Rupert Soames, brother of Fatty[373] and boss of Aggreko, about how the Nats are bullying businessmen. Phone MM to tell him the good news.

---

372 Former Conservative MSP (2003–11).

373 Sir Nicholas Soames, Conservative MP for Mid Sussex, and Churchill's grandson.

23 NOVEMBER

Total chaos at FMQs. Tricia has thrown McMahon[374] out for challenging the chair, Labour are in a state of absolute ferment, Nats are even more bolshie than ever, the whole place is a disaster. Not that I should care, but I do for some reason. Tricia looks in a terrible state. But, interestingly, so does Nicola. She looks very unhappy with the way Eck is behaving and there was a very revealing blog from one of the cybernats on my website, saying that Nicola looks fed up with Eck's continual lying. I think he's right.

24 NOVEMBER

Old Campbell Gunn, a veteran Nat, agrees that Nicola looks fed up with Eck. 'I wish we could get Nicola as leader. Alex is becoming a liability,' he says. Hmmm. Something's going on. I had a blether with Margo MacDonald, who says that Alex Neil has been telling tales out of school about the mess that Sturgeon left behind at Health. She hasn't taken any big decisions, just kicked everything into the long grass. I wonder if Eck moved her from Health so he could keep an eye on her?

25 NOVEMBER

Harriet home for the weekend but unfortunately she wasn't the centre of attention because Ali was here with Mariella[375] and I

374 Michael McMahon, Labour MSP for Uddingston and Bellshill.
375 Mariella Walker, AC's niece (*b.* 2008).

didn't get nearly enough time to blether with H. M is a great kid but poor Ali is in a bit of pain with her arthritis. Harry looked down in the mouth when she had to get back on the train to Manchester, but at least she grinned at me because of my lack of a front tooth (a crown came out in my porridge).

26 NOVEMBER

Long lunch – too long – with Craig Harrow of the Lib Dems. He says that too many bosses think that independence will never happen and so they are refusing to come out in support of the Union. We shall have to scare the bastards. It's a pity we can't fiddle an opinion poll nowadays; the buggers put all their results online. Cameron and the coalition are planning a New Year offensive and a big poll is underway.

Jenny said one of the St George's dads had been at a London lunch of businessmen where Andrew Marr told them that there wouldn't be independence. So that's all right. Andrew Marr! One of the people who invented all of this devolution crap and was no doubt paid handsomely for his opinion. Course, I'm only jealous.

27 NOVEMBER

Fleet Street getting its knickers in a twist about Leveson. Hilarious. We deserve a kicking and will probably get one.

28 NOVEMBER

Fantastic St Andrew's Night dinner at the National Gallery. God knows why we get invited, as it's for patrons who lob thousands in their direction. Even if I could afford it I wouldn't give them any money; much better to give it to Save the Children or Oxfam. I sat next to a nice, but very pukka, lady who was married to the Turcan bit of Turcan Connell and seemed to be the only Tory in Fife. On my other side was a younger woman who turned out to be Nicky Fairbairn's[376] daughter, although from which wife I didn't ask. She's married to a bloke who bought most of the Gannochy estate in Angus. He was wearing some kind of Mao/Beatles jacket. Making a statement of sorts, I suppose. Ho, hum.

29 NOVEMBER

Leveson at last and didn't the judge do well? I thought so, even if the *Telegraph* line was decidedly anti. I hate being disloyal but the reaction of Fleet Street is completely stupid and Cameron is a twit to suck up and not do the legislation bit. As Clegg said, all of the UK papers signed up to the Irish Ombudsman system, which is underpinned by statute. What's the difference? I wrote a piece backing Eck, which makes a change. But the other parties won't talk to him.

---

376 Sir Nicholas Fairbairn, late Conservative MP for Perth and Kinross (1933–95).

30 NOVEMBER

Jesus, what a load of total and absolute crap in most of the papers, *The Guardian* excepted. Fraser Nelson wrote the worst piece of his life in hailing DC as some form of saviour. Total nonsense. Fraser had said he would never co-operate with any form of legislation and has clearly been seeking martyrdom. Why didn't he set light to himself in Trafalgar Square?

Iain Martin seemed quite sensible about the whole thing, even if he does have to toe the party line, and even Bruce thought Cameron had taken a strange decision.

St Andrew's Night tonight and I'm on my own. Everybody's going out.

2 DECEMBER

Slowly and surely I am being outgunned on Leveson. Even Jenny, or rather especially Jenny, disagrees with me. I cannot understand what Fleet Street is making such a fuss about. We have been exposed, through hacking and blagging, as a bunch of completely scummy bastards and a whole generation of executives turned a blind eye to what was going on. Leveson was the very least that we could have expected and now we are asking everyone to forget about what we were guilty of and carry on regardless.

It is farcical, and Cameron is bowing the knee because he's afraid of the kicking he would get from the hacks. God, it is sickening. Jenny is right, of course, that celebrities like Hugh Grant[377]

---

377 Actor and spokesman for the Hacked Off campaign against press freedom.

are damaging the case for real victims, such as the Dowlers[378] and McCanns.[379] But the press is behaving abominably.

Salmond was right on the *Politics* show to say that we would have to have a separate legal backing if that's the way to go, because of Scots law being different. And Lamont was being plain stupid: she wants legal backing but says Scotland doesn't need a different system. But if England doesn't have a legal underpinning, the only way she's going to get it is by backing the Scottish way of doing it. Mind you, Ruth was probably right to say that Fleet Street, in the shape of Press BoF,[380] won't pay for two Press Councils. And the Scottish papers are completely skint.

3 DECEMBER

Scattering of snow; nothing drastic. Went to see Mither in Dundee. She's in very good nick and in a good mood. I got a bollocking for being overweight and then was force-fed bacon rolls! Took her to her Community Centre Christmas lunch and dance, where we saw all the old dears from her 80th birthday party, seven years ago, all looking exactly the same! No men, they're all deid. Auntie June[381] was there, so it was good to see her, too, although she says Fraser, my cousin, is about to lose his job.

---

378 Family of murdered schoolgirl Milly Dowler, whose phone was hacked.

379 Parents of missing Madeleine McCann who were also phone-hacking victims.

380 Press Standards Board of Finance.

381 June Cochrane, Betty's sister-in-law.

Back in Edinburgh, I columnised on Nicola's 'manifesto'[382] at Strathclyde. Quite interesting, but carefully left-wing, of course, although she's more likely to attract Glasgow Labour voters than is Salmond. And it is interesting how many of the cybernats are now saying they prefer Nicola to Eck. Not many, I admit, but straws in the wind?

4 DECEMBER

Quite a good debate on Leveson and it is clear that Eck is moving towards accepting that he'll have to go for a UK solution, although he does want some sort of fig leaf for Scotland, possibly in the shape of a dual registration scheme. This would mean the papers signing up to a Scottish legal underpinning. But this would be illogical, as we'd have a system where the papers would reject any statutory registration in England but accept it in Scotland. Not a chance.

5 DECEMBER

Told MM that DC Thomson look as if they're weakening on statutory underpinning, as Eck quoted the *Courier* leader last week, backing a separate Scottish system. I said I'd ring them. I eventually got through to Christopher Thomson, who didn't even know what the *Courier* leader had said! And he also said that he had told Eck not to go for a separate Scottish system as he'd be left out on a limb if he did so.

---

382 She outlined her personal vision for independence.

He also told me that the family did not dictate to editors what their line should be. Really? Changed days then. Anyway, he's going to ring Murdoch MacLennan on Thursday morning.

6 DECEMBER

Party leaders appear to think they've talked Eck out of his separate Scottish Press Council thingy. Maybe they have, but in the medium term I'm sure that that's what he wants: after all, he does think that he's going to win the referendum in 2014, doesn't he?

7 DECEMBER

Bugger all happening and then when I got home we got news of how Eck hadn't received those letters of praise over the Megrahi release spontaneously but had actually touted for them.[383] What an absolute creep of the first order. There really are no depths to which that bloke will not stoop. We got it on the front page.

Bad news, however, is that *The Times* has overtaken us after our eighteen months in the lead. Bugger! Simon was a bit worried but Scott,[384] the circulation man, says that we've stopped all marketing and giving away free bottles of water. That, plus *The Times* being cheaper, is working against us. Must try harder.

---

383 Salmond sent a round-robin letter to leading world figures in 2009, begging them to support his early release of the Lockerbie bomber.

384 Scott Lister.

10 DECEMBER

Incredible statement from Barroso, during an interview with the Beeb, that Scotland would definitely have to apply for membership of the EU – AND renegotiate from outside the UK. Fantastic story and naturally we gave it big licks. Poor old Nicola Sturgeon has been landed with cleaning up the mess.

11 DECEMBER

Amazing stuff from Craig Harrow. He wants me to ask Sandy McCall Smith[385] to lob some money into Better Together and to lend his name to the campaign to save the Union. I said how much do you want and he said six figures! I texted back asking if many others had donated that much and he said, 'Yes, several.' But I asked him why Alistair Darling didn't ask Sandy, given that he's a near neighbour. Craig said: 'Alistair doesn't want to ask. He's too embarrassed to do so!' Incredible. But I said I'd do it.

Anyway, I emailed Sandy, asking if he could spare me a few minutes and he emailed right back and then phoned to fix up a meeting.

12 DECEMBER

Had a smashing blether with Sandy at his lovely house in Merchiston. We talked about all manner of things but he politely declined to give any dosh. He said he's got enough pressure just now, without getting any more flak (from the Nats, I took that

---

385 Alexander McCall Smith, bestselling author and Edinburgh resident.

to mean). He's getting a lot for defending the government of Botswana from people like Survival International, who belt them over the plight of the Bushmen.

He says he used to be a Tory, then was a Liberal Democrat for twenty-odd years, but has now left them. 'Leaving the Lib Dems is like trying to leave the Masons; they won't let go and make things very difficult,' he said. He is now a Tory and says they're the best party and protecting his liberties and freedoms. I wonder if he means less tax?

He says he supports the Union but is a pretty ardent devolutionist and denies ever writing that Nat tract forty years ago – even though it's on the Cato Institute website. Very amusing.

He says he might give some money to Better Together but not now. We had a civilised glass of Madeira and a chat about everything, including – and this was nice – about Jose and Harry, especially how the latter was doing at Chets.

On my way out he gave me two signed copies of his latest books AND a lovely bottle of 2000 Medoc. What a nice man.

Back at the bloody Parliament, I wrote a column about the EU and the Nats. AGAIN!

Very nice invite from Archie Stirling to go and stay. Hope we can go.

13 DECEMBER

Europe and the Nats again! Had a brief chat with Nicola before her trial by ordeal.[386] I've never seen her so nervous; she was

---

386 Nicola had to make an emergency statement in Holyrood about EU membership.

almost shaking and she had caked her face in make-up. Perhaps the continued pressure is getting to her. She is a toughie but things are pretty relentless at present, thanks to Eck dumping everything on her.

Bought Simon his Christmas lunch in the White Heather Club and Eck was there as usual, with another load of suits – probably from the wind industry. Lording it over them and they fawning over him, most likely because he's helping them fill their boots with taxpayers' cash. But at least he has a drink with his lunch. Apart from Simon and me, and the FM, nobody in the whole of the restaurant was having wine with their lunch. What a bunch!

Nicola wasn't bad in the chamber but it is clear that their only answer is bravado and bluster and hope that the voters don't notice what a state they're in. And who knows, they may be right.

Jenny is going to Manchester for Harriet tomorrow and is bringing her back on Saturday. Can't wait to see her. Christmas is coming!!!

15 DECEMBER

At last Jenny and Harriet arrive home, having got on the wrong train in Manchester and ending up in Liverpool.

17 DECEMBER

Dinner at Iain and Fiona's[387] rented flat. Typical Edinburgh wel-

---

387 Fiona Martin, wife of Iain.

come: the people renting the flat left them only four knives and forks! You'll have had your cutlery, as well as your tea.

18 DECEMBER

Didn't bother with Salmond's drinks party. Went to the Castle instead for Brig. Mel Jameson's Christmas reception for the Royal Scots Dragoon Guards. Not bad. Nice people.

19 DECEMBER

Tartan Bollocks dinner, which I won.[388] It was a complete stitch-up but a great night and I shall just have to treat it as a big joke.

20 DECEMBER

Last day of Parliament before the Christmas holiday. Thank God. Not feeling great after Bollocks and I wish I didn't have to do STV's stupid programme, especially as it has Lesley Riddoch[389] and Colin Mackay[390] on it. Musn't lose my temper. Keep calm.

Didn't perform very well on STV and Jenny said Riddoch kept making snide remarks. God, what a shitty programme it is. And this is the quality we'll be reduced to if the Nats win. This would be a second-rate country where everything would be third rate.

---

388 AC was awarded the trophy for his story saying there would be no further rebellions within the SNP after the NATO debate. Days later, two of their MSPs resigned.

389 Journalist and Nationalist activist.

390 Radio Clyde political editor.

I've never told them, but it really is a crap programme made by crap people. It was bad enough under Mike Crow, but at least he was good. It is now completely useless.

21 DECEMBER–6 JANUARY

Did three days' work during Christmas week and then took the first week of the New Year off as a holiday.

Had a great, if hectic, time up the Glen for New Year in Graham's[391] cottage. Girls moaned about the décor but it was perfect for a party. Cannot understand why the Mackies keep paying Og-Wed rent for that complete dump of a cottage next door. No water, keeps getting flooded and is really little more than a slum.

And I'm pleased to say that Jamie SD has made a complete mess of Glenuig. I'm glad I went to their New Year party as seeing how much it has lost its character got it out of my system. The people who've got it seem nice enough but I can't see them adding much to the community. And the SDs kept going on about the dinner party they had on Hogmanay. Christ! In fifteen years in the Glen I had a dram there once at New Year. Mustn't keep on about that. I'm boring myself!

Saw Frans and Teresa and everything seems fine with them. Probably best that they didn't let us have their bothy.

It's been wonderful having Harriet back. She's growing up very quickly and is a bit confused about her friendships. She doesn't really appreciate how much she's growing apart from her St G's

---

391 Graham Davie, friend from Angus.

pals. Everyone was very complimentary about her playing.

One of the nicer things is that Josie handles it well. She doesn't seem to mind that her wee sister is the centre of attention. Very mature. She is a beautiful girl, who seems to be very popular. But we cannot compete with all the rich St G parents who give their girls everything they ask for. However, Josie appears to understand this.

2013

7 JANUARY

Terrible day – Harriet had to go back to Manchester. She was quite brave when we said goodbye at the station but we were all very sad.

8 JANUARY

Bloody hell! Back to work in that terrible Parliament. It does bugger all, has an absolute C-list cast of characters – really, really poor-quality people – MSPs, officials, most ministers, most hacks, with few exceptions. Devolution has been a disaster, letting these second-raters believe that they're capable. And I've got years and years of this to go. Retire? What a hope. I've got to deal with this lot forever. Jesus – how will I manage it?

The tragedy is that the only way it could be made to work

would be if Scotland was independent; then the best people would simply have to work there. The English wouldn't stand for any more Jocks at Westminster and anyone who wanted to make a name for themselves in politics would have to be at Holyrood. Devolution buggered everything up. Those blithering idiots who dreamed up that lot of nonsense really have a lot to answer for.

11 JANUARY

Eck has been 'cleared' by a supposedly independent inquiry over his fibs on Europe. And everyone is happy with the result. Complete whitewash, but then that's probably being too kind.

17 JANUARY

Astonishing lunch invitation from Rory Bremner, the impressionist/comedian. He's been missing for some time now, although I think he's got a quiz show, but he's planning to do a show about Scottish politics. Boy, that is going to be difficult. We had a tapas lunch at Iggs with Rory and a team of scriptwriters, who all seemed very jolly, and Patrick Harvie, the leader of the Greens. I'm not sure why he was there, but it appears that he's pals with some of the writers.

Anyway, the whole lunch was taken up with picking our brains – Harvie's and mine – about Scottish politics. The problem Rory is going to have is that there's only one personality: Eck. He didn't appear to 'have' him yet as he didn't 'do' him during lunch, although he kept doing Blair, which is really brilliant. He said that before he'd done Blair for the first time, Blair had joked that he could have a knighthood if he didn't do him, and then after he did do him for the first time he was offered an OBE, which he turned down.

Bremner is a very nice bloke, quite luvvy-ish, but not in a bad way, and struggling very hard to please. Iain M says that his trouble at present is that he can't do Cameron, Clegg, Osborne or Miliband, which does seem to be a bit of a handicap and which also explains why he hasn't been on the box.

18 JANUARY

Jose has finished her exams so we went to the Orchard for supper to celebrate.

19 JANUARY

Thankfully, Jose's hockey was called off because of the quarter-inch of snow. Took Jenny to the station as she's off to see Harriet in Manchester. Wish I was going.

Very cold but no more snow. Rats. Bet there's tons up in Glenuig!

20 JANUARY

Weekend with Jose; it's nice being with her on my own – she actually has a blether with me, which is great fun. She's a very good conversationalist and I even managed to get her to watch *Tunes of Glory*[392] with me. Great Scottish movie.

22 JANUARY

Jenny and I got the train to London, en route for Brussels. Jose has gone to stay with Jackie[393] for a couple of days. We dumped our bags at the Caley and Jenny went off shopping – or at least window shopping – and I wandered over to No. 10 to see Dunlop.

Had a blether with Dunlop, or rather listened to what he was saying. They seem to have cottoned on to my demand that we get more frontline ministers up here. I was especially critical of Hammond and said I couldn't see him going down very well with the hacks and editors; mind you, much of that is due to the fact that most of the Scottish editors don't really know much about politics anyway.

Theresa May[394] is also coming up to warn about the dangers to security following independence – no MI5 or 6 protection. That might be OK although, from what I gather, when she has lunch at the *Telegraph* she says bugger all.

Brilliant dinner with Murdoch and Elsa.[395] We were made very welcome and they made a real fuss of Jenny, which was nice.

---

392 1960 film that pits two Scottish colonels against each other, starring Alec Guinness and John Mills.

393 Jackie Peters, friend.

394 Home Secretary.

395 Elsa McAlonan, journalist and wife of Murdoch MacLennan.

23 JANUARY

Brussels by Eurostar. What a great way to travel. Reasonable hotel in an absolutely freezing city, which looks like a building site. I wouldn't have minded working here, though.

The Burns Supper was OK but some drunken oaf of a Tory MEP kept speaking all the way through my Address.[396] I nearly belted him; it ruined my stuff, although Jenny said the jokes went down well. Never again – there's not enough of them who 'get' Burns. Struan Stevenson[397] is a fantastic bloke; he'd have made a better leader of the Scottish Tories than anyone else they've got. Pity he's packing up next year.

24 JANUARY

Back to Edinburgh, after John McLellan had phoned to say that Ruth was making a major speech, turning everything on its head because focus groups say that the Tories can't go on opposing devolution. Ho, hum.

25 JANUARY

Mundell insists on having a coffee with me, obviously to spin me ahead of Ruth's speech. Had a good natter, where he said I could still have that peerage if I became Tory chairman and then he said I could have that Euro MEP slot, too, that Struan is vacating. He

---

396 AC was giving the Toast to the Immortal Memory of Robert Burns.
397 Conservative MEP; not the one mentioned above.

was laughing but I bet I could get one of them if I set my mind to it and decided to throw my lot in with them. Loads of dosh! And we haven't got any. But I'm afraid I'm just too much of an old hack.

Went to listen to Ruth and was furious. The spin was just so much crap and she didn't take questions so we couldn't find out what the hell her 'changes' meant. I gave it a bit of a panning in my column, so I suppose that's me burned my boats. Oh well.

26 JANUARY

Had a blether with Darling and we're going to try to fix up something for him to meet Gallagher and Murdoch in Edinburgh. The plot thickens!

27 JANUARY

Astonishing balls-up by the Nats: they attacked the Beeb for partisan reporting over what that Irish Europe minister[398] said about their entry to the EU. It was disgusting stuff, slagging off Raymond Buchanan[399] when all he'd done was ask some questions and broadcast the answers. They had a chink of light with Cameron's rubbish about referendums but they've blown it completely now. However, when you leave things to Fiona Hyslop, which is what they've done because she is the so-called 'Europe minister', what can you expect except balls-ups! She's useless.

---

398 Ireland's European minister Lucinda Creighton said that a newly independent Scotland would have to re-apply for EU membership.

399 The BBC Scotland reporter who interviewed Creighton.

Now that I've seen the way the Nats operate and written a column bashing Eck for continually pressurising the hacks and broadcasters, there's no way I'm going to support any kind of legal back-up for a new Press Council. Absolutely no way. I NOW ADMIT I WAS WRONG after Leveson.

28 JANUARY

Wrote a column bashing the coalition over the high-speed rail plans. When is Scotland going to get any benefit? We got nothing from the Chunnel, even though we were supposed to get direct trains and inclusive fares, and I bet it's the same this time. Not good enough, especially when you think of all the money that's being spent. Incredibly, a leading Nat, Kenny Gibson,[400] stopped me in the lobby, said he agreed with me and also said he'd tried to quote me in a question in the chamber. Unfortunately, he wasn't called. Pity!

29 JANUARY

Met the new Chief Constable[401] for an off-the-record chat. Tough as old boots, he is, but really tiny. I've never met a copper as small as he is. Very straight, nothing like my old mate John O'Connor.[402] But I think he'll be okay and he as good as said he's glad he didn't

---

400 SNP MSP for Cunninghame North.

401 Sir Stephen House, the first Chief Constable of the amalgamated Police Scotland, appointed in October 2012.

402 Former commander of the Flying Squad at Scotland Yard.

get the Met, not with all the trouble that they're in thanks to their links with News International. Very traditional; he doesn't want any nonsense about direct entry from the army or anything like street orderlies; just wants coppers – plain ordinary coppers. Worries about the money. Must keep in touch with this guy.

And talking of News International, it looks like poor old Ivens[403] is in the shit for a cartoon about Israel in the *Sunday Times*. He didn't realise it was Holocaust Day. What a fuss. What a row. The Jewish lobby are out to get Rupert Murdoch and Martin is caught in the middle. Poor lad.

Spoke to Graham and Sue[404] later and they both think Ivens is OK. Witherow[405] is backing him, saying he would have passed the cartoon, too. Astonishing!

Tories are in a terrible mess. Simon was the only one who turned up at their wind farm press conferences in Falkirk (Falkirk, for Chrissake) yesterday, and this evening I had a word with Murdo Fraser, who's enjoying the mess. He says that Ruth told the group meeting that, in spite of her speech last Friday and all the hype and spin surrounding it, there was no change in policy.

What the hell's going on then, I asked him. He says that Ruth is under ferocious pressure from London to change tack and that's why Mundell and McLellan are spinning so hard about dramatic change. It sort of fits but we need to check and check and check. Could be a great story.

---

403 Martin Ivens, *Sunday Times* editor.

404 Journalist Graham Paterson and TV executive Sue Robertson, Josephine's godparents.

405 John Witherow, editor of *The Times*.

Finally did my tax return. Skint again.

30 JANUARY

Had a long boozy lunch with Jackson Carlaw. He's pretty loyal all of a sudden and thinks that Ruth is doing OK and that there isn't some great London plot to force her to do things she doesn't want. He also revealed that Ruth's 'wife' has left her – tears all round, I understand.

Hellish toothache which I tried to beat with whisky. Not a chance and woke up in agony when the drink wore off.

31 JANUARY

Ninety minutes at the dentist, infection scraped out and script for antibiotics. Horrible. Went to office briefly and then came home and slept for about eighteen hours!

1 FEBRUARY

Jose said I looked like a chipmunk with face all swollen. Still, it's getting better.

1 FEBRUARY

Sinclair tried to off-load a story onto me about how the Irish government are dumping on their Euro minister for sending a telegram to Nicola supporting Scotland's case for EU entry. But

I decided to pass; this had more to do with Irish politics than anything else. This lady had apparently challenged Enda Kenny, the PM, and that would never do. He tried it on Boothman of the Beeb, too, and he also gave him short shrift.

2 FEBRUARY

Moans from Moley[406] AGAIN about my getting something wrong about his beloved Blair Jenkins. I wish Moley and Jocky[407] would get proper jobs!

Watched Jose playing hockey; she was pretty good and they won. Astonishing! Then United slaughtered Rangers. Fantastic. If only Scotland could beat England. What a hope. Hammered. Still, two out of three ain't bad.

Met Simon Paterson-Brown[408] at the hockey. He's written a new Scottish rugby anthem[409] which just might take off for a Scottish national anthem. Sounds great. If it works he'll make a fortune.

3 FEBRUARY

Mail on Sunday used that Sinclair/Irish story. Not much of a tale. Interesting that Andy Picken[410] is leaving the *MoS* for the

---

406 Ian McKerron, aka the Molecatcher, former journalist, running the publicity for Yes Scotland.

407 Gordon Hay, former journalist, running the publicity for Yes Scotland.

408 St George's parent and eminent surgeon.

409 A reworking of 'Highland Cathedral' to new lyrics.

410 Andrew Picken, political editor of the *Sunday Post*.

Sunday Post. Still, as Simon says, if Williams[411] wanted to keep him, he would have found the money. I'm having lunch in Glasgow with Chris on Tuesday so I can find out there. I'll warn him off Simon, of course.

4 FEBRUARY

Williams lunch cancelled because Chris is retiring and he had a meeting with his financial advisor, who was to tell him how much he's worth. Lucky man. He told Paul Dacre[412] that he planned to retire when he's sixty-five this December and the great ogre merely said: 'I thought I could have got another couple of years out of you.'

Just as well the lunch was off, as the Nats put out this completely fanciful document about life AFTER independence, as if they'd already won the referendum. Complete baloney and it got well hammered by all and sundry, not excluding me.

7 FEBRUARY

Ruth D absolutely useless at FMQs. I should have slaughtered her but I went along with Margo MacDonald, who feels sorry for her, largely because Ruth's partner has left her. It was very bad and she is simply not up to the job. I should write this and can't think why I haven't.

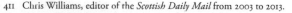

---

411 Chris Williams, editor of the *Scottish Daily Mail* from 2003 to 2013.

412 Editor of the *Daily Mail*.

8 FEBRUARY

Got a very snotty text from John McLellan, telling me that I'd got it wrong about Ruth. What the hell does that bloke do? And is it true that he was in for the *Herald* editor's job? If so, they were wise not to give it to him, but what does it say about how much he likes working for Ruth? Not much.

The knives are out for her and no mistake. Most of the parliamentary party can't stand her; Mundell seems to be ploughing his own furrow and won't give up the chairmanship. Usual shambles.

Another major shambles, this time in Glasgow, and all courtesy of that eejit Ramsay Jones. First of all, it was supposed to be a Chatham House editors-only chat with the Home Secretary. Then the timing was fixed for 2.45 p.m., which everyone knew would end up as 3.30 p.m., and so none of the other editors – save me and the new *Herald* guy[413] – said they'd attend. And so Jones said that reporters could attend in their stead. I blew a fuse with Dunlop but went along anyway.

It was worse than I'd feared. Some of it was on the record and some off but Jones didn't say until the end which was which, leaving us poor hacks scrabbling around to work out what Theresa May had said. If truth be told, she didn't say much, but we managed to drag a line out of her. Or at least me and Alan Crow from the *MoS* did. I filed from his office on some ancient steam-driven laptop left behind by Simon. Interestingly, Eddie Barnes phoned to check a quote. I didn't have it, Crow didn't have it and Jason Allardyce[414]

---

413 Magnus Llewellin, appointed editor at the beginning of February 2013.
414 Scotland editor of the *Sunday Times*.

from the *Sunday Times* didn't have it. But he still went ahead and wrote it! *Scotsman* put it on the front page, too. Extraordinary.

Fiona Cunningham[415] was there, as she's now May's top spad. She used to work at *The Scotsman* but she's done well in politics and she's supposed to be having a fling with the chief of counter-insurgency at the Home Office!

9 FEBRUARY

Went to Murrayfield on my own – very much a last-minute affair – and they won! Incredible.

11 FEBRUARY

Plane to London was ninety minutes late because of one centimetre of snow in London. What a daft way to travel but I had to do it to see Tony G. He was very pleasant and we had a good blether. I told him that Williams had told me that Geordie Greig[416] was now favourite to take over from Dacre at the *Mail*. He said this was all rubbish because Dacre wouldn't retire and pretended that he (Tony) wasn't interested in the job! Oh sure.

However, he does want to come to Scotland to see Eck. I'd better fix that. Had a quick word with MM, who was very pleasant and friendly.

At six I went up to the Caley and had a blether with the great

---

415 Fiona Cunningham, special advisor to Theresa May from 2010 to 2014.

416 Editor of the *Mail on Sunday*.

Hezza, who only lives around the corner. He looked well and said my tree was thriving,[417] but he didn't invite me down to see it, which was a great pity. We live in hope. Jenny would love it. I'm trying to get him up here to make a speech in favour of the Union. He thinks Eck is a very good operator but at least if he comes up they can't do that anti-English stuff; Hezza is Welsh!

12–15 FEBRUARY

Bugger all doing with Parliament in recess. Sent off all my valentines to my daughters and Jenny. Harry liked hers, as did Jenny, but Jose didn't as it was the only one she got. Poor wee thing. And, as usual, Tina said nowt.

Arranged to have dinner à deux with Jenny on Saturday night but had to make it a threesome as Jose hasn't got anything to do and, as Jenny says, she did come on honeymoon with us!

18 FEBRUARY

Jenny went down to get Harriet after her concert in Manchester. Can't wait to see her.

19 FEBRUARY

Curse of Jenny strikes again, as the train that she and Harry got

---

417 AC presented Heseltine, a keen arboriculturalist, with a rowan tree when he visited his home in Oxfordshire around 1990.

was massively delayed by someone committing suicide on the line near Lancaster. They arrived about five hours late and we all went for a Chinese to celebrate. Harry looks great – getting more and more grown-up.

We have to decide what Josie will do for her Highers. She's very good at languages, especially French, Latin, Greek and Chinese. Don't know what will be decided.

22 FEBRUARY

Astonishing announcement by Cardinal O'Brien that he favours priests being allowed to marry – and this from one of the most conservative clergymen around. Amazing. But luckily I heard it on the radio, so we got it in the paper.

23 FEBRUARY

Did loads of gardening – or at least cutting back those bloody bushes. And then went to RSNO Ball. Good craic but too much auction and not enough ball. Don't think I'll go again.

24 FEBRUARY

Scotland beat Ireland. Incredible – they should have been thirty-nil down at half-time. This was Harriet's first game and she clearly thinks that Scotland always win! Great fun.

Fantastic story in *The Observer* that O'Brien has been accused of 'inappropriate behaviour' with not one but four priests. What a story and by Catherine Deveney[418] of all people; never knew she could write news and she probably didn't either.

25 FEBRUARY

Disaster! I have forgotten Fergus's birthday, it was on Saturday. I rushed out and got a present and sent it straight off. Bloody hell, how could I forget that? Felt hellish.

The inevitable happened and the poor old Cardinal resigned/retired/was sacked/whatever by the Pope. And Tom Devine[419] wrote for us, saying that this was the biggest crisis to hit the Catholic Church since the Reformation. Eh? Don't know about that. But then what do I know?

26 FEBRUARY

Got text from Ally saying that the prezzie for Fergus had arrived and that it was a big hit. Phew. Tina has told him to go on an anger management course, so that he could be furious with me. But he's too nice for that.

28 FEBRUARY

Great evening at Campbell Gunn's first retirement 'do'. My wee talk went down quite well and Alex Salmond made a very funny

---

418 Award-winning Scottish feature writer.
419 Professor Sir Tom Devine, Scottish historian.

speech, which he can do about someone he likes and when he's trying not to be catty. Very good occasion but too much wine and not enough food. Felt hellish the next day.

Disaster for Tories at Eastleigh![420] Cameron needs to keep calm.

1 MARCH

Got a 'name' from Tom Cassidy[421] about one of the possible priests in the O'Brien case. He certainly seems a colourful character; it appears that he's fathered at least one, maybe two, bairns. Aus phoned him but he denies everything. Hmmm. Seems he was involved in any number of scrapes, along with two or three other priests, who all got bollocked but not disciplined for various crimes – shagging, boozing and 'crime of all crimes': attending a Proddy church service! What a bunch.

2 MARCH

Harry's going back to Manchester, so we took her to Gusto's in George Street for dinner. Full of stag/hen parties. Christ, what a shower, but management were nice, found us a table.

4 MARCH

Went through to Glasgow for a seminar on whither the press

---

420 By-election following Lib Dem Chris Huhne's resignation, held by the Lib Dems, with UKIP coming second, pushing the Conservatives into third place.

421 Former colleague of AC's on the *Scottish Daily Express*.

– digital or printed. Andrew Neil was chairing but the panel were completely useless. Allan Rennie[422] from the *Record*, however, was much better and more intelligent than I had expected. Philip Schlesinger[423] from Stirling, now translated to a posher post at Glasgow, pretends to be an expert on the press but knows nothing. And there was a new woman from DC Thomson, hired as their digital director. All she knew was jargon. The only half-decent one was the bloke from STV, who at least seemed to know what he was talking about.

We went to dinner with Gerald Warner,[424] who was in a bad mood because he's off the booze for Lent. Christ, what a pair of right-wingers those two are. Neither Neil nor Warner think Cameron has any chance and Warner, especially, hates DC. I reminded them that in the '80s we used to sit around at night betting on there never being another Labour government again. And look what happened. Cameron is the Tories' only option; the rest are headbangers. They cannot be serious about May or Hammond. What jokes.

Wrote a column on yet another education report. Complete waste of time. Consensus rules and decline will continue.

5 MARCH

Total balls-up by Hammond and MoD over bases and troops coming to Scotland; only 600 instead of the 6,000 promised.

---

422 Editor in chief of the *Record* and the *Sunday Mail* from 2011 to 2014.

423 Professor of cultural policy at Glasgow University.

424 Commentator and former policy advisor to Michael Forsyth.

Hammond's spad tried to spin about what a triumph it was ... I think he must admit that he failed to convince me.

6 MARCH

Told Downing Street and Mundell what a load of crap Hammond is, and yet he is talked of as a possible replacement for DC. He is nothing short of a desiccated adding machine. Useless. An accountant. Nuff said.

7 MARCH

Breakfast with Murdoch M, Darling, Harrow and McInnes[425] (for Tories, standing in for poor old McLetchie who is not long for this world, I'm afraid). Brilliant session but still the problem is to get those useless businessmen to both stand up and support the Union and tell the truth about how they are being intimidated and threatened by the Nats. Murdoch offering *Telegraph* facilities but, boy, have I got a lot of work to do!

Brilliant balls-up, this time by Nats, when leaked Swinney document reveals that he thinks their economic policies are all dependent on volatile oil prices. Worst setback for Nats ever and there is a mighty witch-hunt going on at St Andrew's House.

Dunlop texted from Downing Street asking if I'd go down to London to see Hammond. Don't think I should. And then Mundell texted to say that Hammond was coming to Scotland. Left

---

425 Mark McInnes, the Scottish Conservatives' chief executive.

hand doesn't know what right is doing. I told Mundell that it was pointless PH coming to Scotland as it would only give rebirth to the Defence balls-up. He agreed. Texted Dunlop to that effect. No reply. They've obviously had second thoughts. Good, I didn't want to talk to the bugger anyway.

Lunch with Tom Brown (seventy-seven) and Andy Fyall (eighty-two), ex-Expressmen, like me. God, what a life we all had, especially Andy, even though he now has a horrible nervous system ailment which makes him talk and look funny. But by God, they matched me glass for glass. I can't take it any more.

14 MARCH

Did another session with Rory Bremner, who's still trying to have a go at Scottish politics. He talked to me in a funny voice for several minutes and I hadn't a clue who it was. Apparently, or so he told me, it was Alex Salmond; I'd never have guessed. Poor guy. Still, it was good fun.

15 MARCH

Pay day! Thank God. Went through to St Andrews, where I made a speech to a bunch of international lawyers on independence. Pretty boring bunch.

Poor old John (Lord) McCluskey[426] has lost his marbles com-

---

426 His committee to look into regulation of the Scottish press recommended statutory controls underpinned by law.

pletely with his press report. He wants even more shackles than did Leveson. Hopeless; even Eck won't do this lot. One of his problems has been that he doesn't have any proper hacks on his panel. Broon's bairn[427] and that ex-sub from *The Herald*[428] couldn't edit a bus ticket.

Lib Dems in Dundee. Crap conference in a crap conference centre. However, quite a good dinner with them afterwards. Danny Alexander apparently wanted to sit beside me; he's very likeable but, because of purdah, told me bugger all about the Budget. Although he did suggest, although strictly speaking he shouldn't have, that the Office for Budget Responsibility figures on oil and gas revenues would be 'interesting'. Obviously – they'll show that Eck's figures are way over the top. Again.

Changes at the *Telegraph* so took a chance and phoned MM about some cock-and-bull story but did ask him if we were safe on the Scottish edition. He said we'd not to worry.

16 MARCH

Went to Mither's and took her round the usual circuit in the Ferry. Bloody freezing but she coped well and we had a good blether. Bought a very nice plate.

Jenny is in Manchester to see Harriet and I had a bit of ferrying to do with Jose and her pals.

---

427 Ruth Wishart, Scottish journalist and broadcaster.
428 David Sinclair, former president of the National Union of Journalists.

18 MARCH

Cameron has ratted on his 'no deal' over hacks and done a compromise with Clegg and Miliband. Fleet Street in uproar. Load of mince from Fraser Nelson about going to jail. This is the best deal they can get and I think they'll eventually have to accept it. For once in my life I agreed with Polly Toynbee[429] in *The Guardian*!

Had a good lunch with Hugh Munro, the brigadier who's now in charge of the prison inspectorate. Those idiotic civil servants at St Andrew's House have told him he's got to apply for his own job or else he's out. Completely stupid as he's done a great job. Probably too good for those jobsworths in Edinburgh. Unfortunately, Hughie is refusing to make a fuss. Pity.

21 MARCH

Eck has finally announced – to a predictable fanfare – his date for the referendum.[430] Tore it to shreds, of course. One of my better efforts.

Nicola Sturgeon was behaving like an excited wee lassie – all giggly. It doesn't suit her. Alex Neil was insufferable. He really is just a sly old shit, isn't he? I sort of like him, but can you imagine what a leader he'd be? I'm sure he'll stand one day but he'd be hammered.

The one Sturgeon will have to watch is Derek Mackay. The former council leader is very, very good. And he knows it. He's very pally with me.

---

429 Toynbee wrote: 'The press is free, but the balance is tilted a little in favour of the citizen against bare-knuckle thuggery.'

430 18 September 2014.

Lots of moans from all over the place about how low-key Darling is. I know what they mean but if I write that the whole thing will collapse.

22 MARCH

I'm a bit worried about this 30 April dinner.[431] Can't seem to get good guests. And I hope Better Together get their act together!

23 MARCH

Watched Eck on TV. Thought his speech[432] wasn't bad at all, although John Curtice said it wasn't up to much. What does he know? Nicola, however, was very good. Shouldering more and more of the burden. What's going on?

25 MARCH

Tom Strathclyde phoned to tell me he had been 'persuaded' to chair Ruth D's working party on devolution. He's not at all happy at the prospect. Poor bloke – he always gets the sticky end of the lollipop. Then went along to hear Ruth perform her amazing and total U-turn.[433] As well as Tom, she's put Alex Fergusson and Annabel Goldie – both part of the devo-nut

---

431 Fundraiser in London organised by AC and the *Daily Telegraph*.

432 To the SNP spring conference in Inverness.

433 Ruth Davidson had said the Scotland Act was 'a line in the sand' for devolution, but then decided to back further powers for the Scottish Parliament.

faction – on the working party, as well as a couple of academics I've never heard of.

Gave her a bit of a doing on *Newsnicht*, where that little shit Alex Massie[434] patronised me something horrible. I got his number from Iain M and left him a message. He didn't respond. Funny that.

26 MARCH

Labour, and Jackie Baillie in particular, made a complete arse of their attack on the Nats over the bedroom tax.[435] Nicola dealt with it very competently; mind you, it was pretty easy.

28 MARCH

Tom Strathclyde rang again to say that he's not going to make it easy for Ruth to get her way on devolution and more powers for Holyrood. He's been talking to Labour and he's grateful that they're very reluctant to agree a whole slew of new powers. That might get the Tories out of the hole that Ruth is digging for them. I wonder who's behind all of this. Thought it was Dunlop but Tom says no – it's some bloke who's in charge of Tory polling called Andrew Cooper[436] who's persuaded Ruth that more powers is the way to go. Nuts.

---

434 Scottish journalist.

435 Baillie called for legislation to ensure no one was evicted for arrears over the tax.

436 Cameron's director of strategy from 2011 to 2014.

29 MARCH

I'm taking Easter week off. Bashed Tory more powers commission before I finished. Harry's home! And I'm going to see Fergus. Brilliant. Can't wait.

8 APRIL

I was about to write a piece taking pity on the Nats for their continued extremely poor poll showing – *Herald* survey, which is usually over-kind to them, had them down to a bare 30 per cent. Poor darlings. They were saved when the sky fell in with the death of Maggie. Phoned Boothman, who didn't know! It's not often I can put one over on him and I told him I was ready to go on air. BBC John Beattie's[437] programme phoned and I decided to annoy everyone and let rip. Beattie may be 6 ft 19 in., or whatever, and a good no. 8, but he's a very soft broadcaster and knows nothing about politics.

Then that night I did the same on STV's *Scotland Tonight*. They left me standing about in the freezing cold outside their daft, out-of-the-way studio. Maddening.

13–15 APRIL

Mither is working up to a crisis; I can sense it. Something about her weight loss and the fact that they want to take her into Victoria Hospital. Ambulance has been called out again but luckily they

---

437 John Beattie presents the lunchtime news programme on BBC Radio Scotland.

didn't take her to hospital. However, she did go to the Victoria under her own steam but there wasn't a bed for her, so she's a bit confused.

16–17 APRIL

Nothing happening except Maggie's funeral, and on the day itself I did two radio interviews and turned down telly. It was a brilliantly British occasion and who cares if it was triumphal?

18 APRIL

Bloody fools at the hospital; instead of Mither losing six kilos in one month she'd lost only one kilo in six months. Bugger all. And so she was sent home. Billy[438] and Anne[439] are going to see her consultant – first time my siblings have spoken in years, I think.

19 APRIL

Inverness for the Labour conference. Fantastic speech by a fifteen-year-old, bashing Salmond. Great stuff. I was mobbed up by the Labour sisterhood, who all now read my column. Amazing. Miliband speech was very good but I really cannot see him being elected PM.

Still, his linking the divisive nature of both the Tories and the Nats might help with those Labourites, especially in the unions,

---

438 William Cochrane, AC's youngest brother.

439 Anne Cochrane, AC's younger sister.

who don't like being in bed with the Tories. Labour is now to have its own campaign for the Union but I hope it doesn't detract from Better Together. Gordon Banks assured me that it won't ... but I'm not so sure. Seems stupid to me.

Had a long chat with Harriet Harman;[440] very pleasant. I've always liked her from way back in the *Mail on Sunday* days and she is always approachable, no matter what the papers say about the Labour Party. She was drinking Islay malt and says she's off shortly to stay there with Fiona Mactaggart,[441] who owns half of the island.

I'd love to go back to Islay. We had some great holidays there. I'd like to go anywhere, frankly, to get away from this bloody Parliament.

21 APRIL

Have got to get to grips with this speech I'm doing for that defence industries dinner.

22 APRIL

First salvoes in the Treasury assault on the Nats over the pound, but it was pretty crass – threatening to stop Scottish bank notes. I splashed it all the same, as the main edition had some NHS story.

---

440 Former Labour minister, currently shadow Deputy Prime Minister and shadow Culture Minister.

441 Labour MP for Slough.

23 APRIL

More Treasury artillery.

24 APRIL

Osborne and Alexander finally fire the big shots against Eck and his pound plan.[442] Dunlop said that there was quite a bit of unease in Downing Street in advance of their trip to Glasgow, about whether they might be going too far. I told him not to worry and to press on, which is his advice too. Gosh, there are a lot of fearties in Whitehall.

Was taken to lunch by Tory Euro-hopeful Belinda Don and Murdo Fraser, her sponsor. She's OK and that's about it, but given the paucity of the talent, she'll probably get it. Mundell offered me the job but standing for election is a mug's game and, anyway, the money's crap, as is the Tory label. Besides, am I a Tory? Everyone says I am, no matter how often I deny it. Maybe I should stop denying it but I hate to be pigeon-holed.

25 APRIL

St Andrews for that defence contractors' dinner. I thought I had managed a decent array of jokes but my heart sank when, at the pre-dinner drinks, I learned that Jim Leishman[443] had been their speaker last year. He is hilarious and simply reels off a string of

---

442 Osborne said it was unlikely Scotland could keep the pound after independence.

443 Former professional footballer.

fitba jokes. Oh dear. My fears were justified when the company assembled – a pretty dreary lot of engineers determined to get pissed after playing golf – and who knew nothing and cared less about politics.

I'm probably being too hard on them but it was a total disaster, so I went to bed early, got up early, had breakfast and buggered off to the Ferry to see Mither.

26 APRIL

She was in great form. Took her for the messages[444] and went to the Ferry for a wander and a cup of tea. She was in sparkling form.

This must have been the Nats' worst ever week. On top of the pound bashing, we got amazing detail from ICAS[445] about the problems lined up for pensions after independence. I almost feel sorry for them!

Brilliant 'do' at St G's in aid of Jose's Italian trip. We all took food and wine and the Paterson-Brown pop group provided most of the fun, including roping me in to do 'Ruby'.[446] It took Jose by surprise – 'Where did that come from?' she asked afterwards. What a hoot.

---

444 Grocery shopping.

445 Institute of Chartered Accountants of Scotland.

446 The song 'Ruby, Don't Take Your Love to Town', made famous by Kenny Rogers.

29 APRIL

Worrying constantly about this MM dinner. But that lassie Kate[447] at Better Together simply never panics. What a bloody star she is.

30 APRIL

Got train to London for Murdoch dinner. Huge success. Ken Clarke first class if a bit long, and then Darling, Wallace (Jim) and Alexander all did their stuff. The captains of industry thought it was great, but then their ilk always like politicos to sing from the same hymn sheet. Strange people!

1 MAY

Spent too much in the bar at the Caley after the dinner. Still, all in a good cause.

3 MAY

Harry home for the weekend! Hooray.

5 MAY

Sun at last. Spent the day in the garden. Harry going home tomorrow and I've hardly seen her. She's not happy and I'm not happy if she's not.

---

447 Kate Watson, director of operations at Better Together.

6 MAY

Had a nice lunch with Harry, Jose and Jenny before H got ready to go back to Chets. She was braver than me and told me not to worry! What a girl.

9 MAY

Edinburgh dinner with Danny Alexander and the Better Together crowd, along with a few businessmen. Ivor wotsisname[448] from Linn was there, cursing and swearing about Fck. Very colourful but I don't see what that approach will bring. John Boyle,[449] ex Motherwell, was there. Very loud and very Weegie but talked quite a bit of sense.

A couple of useless business types were there as well, including a bloke from PriceWaterhouse. Frightened of their own shadows. Why can't they come out and say that independence is not on? Don't they owe it to their shareholders/customers? I sometimes hope that the Nats win and bugger up all of their businesses. They really are a shower.

11 MAY

Went to Jan Strudwick's[450] memorial service. First-class event. Very moving and very amusing, too. Jan had designed the whole

---

448 Ivor Tiefenbrun, founder and chairman of Linn Products, Glasgow-based hi-fi pioneer.

449 Businessman and former chairman of Motherwell FC.

450 Late wife of General Mark Strudwick.

thing. I wonder if I should do that? Might be tempting fate. Maybe not.

12 MAY

The Great Broon is emerging from his lair tomorrow in a Labour, rival pro-Union event. Can't bring himself to be on the same side as the Tories is the message. That's bollocks, of course; the real reason is that he and Alistair Darling cannot stand each other now – he treated Alistair very badly – and Brown couldn't bear to play second fiddle to Darling.

Labour would rather play silly class-war party games against each other than unite to beat the Nats. Nutters.

13 MAY

Broon delivered his Single Transferable Speech, which is aimed at Labour loyalists, and I suppose that's the sort of stuff they want. Does nothing much for anyone else, I'm afraid.

Nicola tried to trump him with a speech of her own. Predictable stuff.

Can't understand why Broon has to go his own way, but John McLellan at the Tories says that Labour and Better people are at each other's throats, with Sinc badmouthing them and vice versa. Good old Labour; can't resist a fight with each other.

16 MAY

Farage[451] tried to have his presser in the Canons Gait pub,[452] which was where young Roden of the *Mail* advised him to go. Unfortunately for both of them, the Trots got to hear of it and they ambushed the party. Bunch of shits, really, and a lot of them nasty Nat/Trot/racists – telling Farage to go back to England.

17 MAY

Absolutely outrageous interview with poor old Nige by some show-off called David Miller on *GMS*. That programme really is out of control. I hadn't heard it but Simon said Molecatcher had rang him to say that the interview was terribly biased – and this was a pillar of the Yes campaign. So I listened to it on catch-up and it was dreadful – chippy, we Scots are better than the English, how dare that Pom, Farage, come up here; an absolute travesty of supposed neutrality. How the BBC get away with it is beyond me. But Boothman et al. have retreated into the laager and all they do is defend, defend. Still, it gave me a great column and we splashed the story of Farage's row with Eck. The latter was on the news in his creepiest pose – that of the avuncular father of the nation. Christ, no wonder women cannot stand him. Yeeuch.

I had Sinclair and several others agreeing with my column; I don't think that lot at the Beeb are necessarily left-wing or Nat,

---

451 Nigel Farage, leader of UKIP.

452 On Edinburgh's Royal Mile.

they are just crap, downright rubbish broadcasters. Nicola Sturgeon said as much to me one day in the canteen. She can't stand *GMS* either, but like me she's got to listen to it. Except that I'm going to try not to for a wee while and see how I get on. It really is that bad. And that's what Pacific Quay doesn't recognise. There will be trouble.

The SNP have a problem with the Trots, who were the ones who mounted the demo against Farage; they shouldn't have let them on the Yes platform. But they just had to try to prove that they were all one party – just like Better Together. They're failing miserably. Poor old Moley.

19 MAY

Astonishingly, or perhaps not so strange, old Galloway[453] wrote an absolutely brilliant hatchet job on Salmond in the *MoS*. Fantastic. Why? Because the cybernats have been monstering him, too!

20 MAY

I have been traduced by Scotland's stupidest man. Harry Reid[454] had a right go at me in *The Herald*, calling me, throughout, 'the Scottish editor', even though I shared a platform with him a couple of weeks ago. Incredibly, he admitted that that eejit Millar had editorialised during his Farage interviews – so that's all

---

453 George Galloway, Scottish firebrand and Respect Party MP for Bradford West.
454 Former editor of *The Herald*.

right again – but essentially had a go at me for attacking Millar and *GMS*. He may have had a point until he said that *GMS* was better than *Today*! Jesus wept. As I said, easily Scotland's stupidest man. How he ever made it anywhere is beyond me. But then again, he didn't, did he?

23 MAY

Ruth D absolutely useless. Again. And Simon said that Gavin Brown[455] of her front bench was sounding off about how bad she was in the pub last night. I told him to write it, as it came on the day Murdo Fraser had an attack on her in *The Hootsmon*.[456] And as she plumbed new depths at FMQs it all made sense. They have got to get rid of her. But what do I care if they bomb again, as they assuredly shall?

Through to Dundee to RSNO concert in the Caird Hall. The place looked marvellous and huge and the concert was, well, OK but not really to my taste, assuming I've got any. And as I drove, I laid off the sauce. Jim Crumley was there. He's a very good columnist in *The Courier*, mostly about wildlife, but he's a dreadful Nat, too, though a smashing bloke. We worked together eons ago – he was a sub on the old *Evening Tele* and then the *SDE* in Glasgow. He told me that that bloke from *Off the Ball* had a dig at me on Radio Hootsmon about that Farage piece – says I proselytise about *GMS* being all lefties. Not lefties, just useless.

---

455 Conservative MSP for Lothian.

456 Well-known nickname for *The Scotsman*.

24 MAY

Harry home for a whole week! Brill.

25 MAY

Started on that bloody garden rubbish. Far too much for me. Lovely weather.

26 MAY

Start of one week's hols. Had a barbecue, which I said would be too cold for the girls but they persevered – through gritted teeth.

3 JUNE

Back to work today, after smashing week off with Ally, Sue and Fearless up for the latter part of it. Got some gardening done. Not too idle.

And great poll of young people, showing that 80 per cent don't want separation. Poor old Eck. As Freddie Mercury might say: 'Another one bites the dust!'

3 JUNE

Only four weeks to go before we get shot of this bloody parliament.

23 JUNE

Poor old Peter Fraser finally bit the dust. It was very sad but he had the gypsy's warning a few years back and had a triple by-pass. However, he apparently kept on eating and drinking to the extent that towards the end he could hardly walk. Lovely family … poor Fiona.

His youngest daughter, Katie, is involved with Walter Scott investment bank who want me to go to Toronto in November to talk to their clients about the referendum. But I've to do an audition to see if they fancy me! Fingers crossed.

1 JULY

I wrote a piece for today, bashing the idiot Unionists who keep coming up with the stupidest reasons for not backing the Nats. It IS scaremongering and someone should be in charge to put a stop to it. I spoke to Craig Harrow and he said he'd seen the latest stuff they were planning and thought it was crap. It was all about how we'd be charged oodles for using mobile phones in England. Complete rubbish.

And, of course, Rob Shorthouse[457] is in deepest doo-doo for coming up with the ridiculous Project Fear name for the campaign. He really is a stupid boy. I've never rated him and always thought he was massively over-promoted.

---

457 Director of communications for Better Together.

2 JULY

My piece about the Unionists' overkill is taking off. Harrow texted me to compliment me and when I spoke to him he said he had shown the piece to the 'grown-ups', by which I suppose he means Alistair Darling. But I got an angry email from Adam Ingram, whose defence bunch are saying pretty much the same as General Mackay's lot did seven days before! No co-ordination.

Harrow also told me he had referred my piece to the Ginger One, by which he means Danny Alexander, to whom Craig appears to have a direct line. The matter has also been raised by the Cabinet Secretary – the real one, Heywood,[458] not these imposters we have up here – and the word has gone out, apparently, to tone things down.

It appears to have worked because Simon J says that the speeches that Cable and Mundell are due to make in Glasgow have been watered down considerably. Good.

The main problem in all of this is that No. 10 – Dunlop, basically – leaves all the press stuff to that complete and utter idiot, Ramsay Jones. He is too hopeless for words but Dunlop thinks himself far too grand to get his hands dirty. Christ, what a bunch!

Went for my 'audition' with Walter Scott and saw their deputy chairman and their head of client relations or some such. I did my usual song-and-dance act and I think I may have impressed them enough to get some sort of work out of them on a consultancy basis. I hope so; I need the money. We're skint.

---

458 Sir Jeremy Heywood, Cabinet Secretary since 2012.

Very posh offices and when I talked to Robin Peters[459] about them he said that Walter Scott do themselves very well. He says they manage a couple of billion quid for clients, from which they probably cream off a quarter of 1 per cent for themselves, which makes them quite rich. Not bad, if ridiculous. Their clients could probably do just as well by investing their dosh for themselves but they're probably so rich as to be lazy.

Fabulous lunch at the Linklaters', where we celebrated his CBE. Great crowd, including David and Ginny Airlie, both getting older but still in very good nick.

3 JULY

Lunch with Donald Cameron the Younger of Lochiel, who wants to be a Tory MSP. His best bet, he thinks, is to hang on until Jamie McGrigor[460] gives up. Nice bloke, an advocate, and he paid for lunch. Not at all stuffy and he finds all those clan chiefs very amusing, although I bet he takes it very seriously in reality.

He has met David Cameron and told me that when he met the PM, DC said to him: 'Oh, you're one of the posh Camerons!' to which Donald said: 'That's a bit rich coming from an Old Etonian.'

At Prime Minister's Questions, Angus Robertson denounced the stupid attacks on the Nats and quoted me as 'the leading Conservative commentator' for calling them 'tripe'. Kate Devlin[461]

---

459 Friend who knows his way around corporate Edinburgh.
460 Conservative MSP for the Highlands and Islands.
461 *The Herald*'s UK political correspondent.

emailed to tell me I'd got a name check and Simon J has tweeted that it was me they were talking about. And then Bruce A phoned – barely able to speak – to say that he'd been told that I was being talked about at No. 10.

Spent an hour recording a BBC Scotland programme that Richard Holloway is doing about being Scottish and British. I hope I did OK but I fear I got carried away somewhat and I wasn't very nice about the Tories. Holloway is a dreadful old phoney; nice enough but he ain't no intellectual.

4 JULY

History Press, who've been on at me for ages to take part, with George Kerevan,[462] in a book on independence, at last came back with an offer. Iain Martin says it's not great but worth doing. And as I don't have to deliver until Christmas, I shall do it. Murdoch MacL has given me permission.

I have got to start thinking about my Book Festival appearance with Lesley Riddoch. Think I'll do my history as a Nat. But I must also get Better Together to send along some supporters; the Nats will pack the hall, after all. And she's such a bitter cow.

7 JULY

Bad news. Mither's been rushed into hospital again. Anne phoned with the news and, sadly, like her I thought it was the

---

462 Journalist and former SNP Westminster candidate.

old attention-seeking again. However, I now think it's more serious – she is in a lot of pain.

Andy Murray won Wimbledon. What a fantastic day! Incredible. I didn't get bothered by Salmond waving that Saltire behind Cameron's back, although lots of others did. Not Jenny, interestingly enough. Tried to talk to Preston,[463] who's editing the paper in London, out of running a story on it. Failed. Still, I just junked it for the Scottish edition. Power mad, that's me. And I put my own column in instead.

8 JULY

Iain M had me worried when he said I should be bothered about Salmond's behaviour but I do think that the more we attack him, the more support he gets. However, when I go to see Mither in hospital she was furious too and that appears to be one vote he won't be getting. All the staff in the hospital thought the same – all said Eck was a lout.

Mither was in some discomfort but she managed to eat two bowls of thin soup and two jellies. She has tubes in her hand and nose. They're not really sure what's wrong with her.

Murdoch MacL emailed me back, agreeing with me that we shouldn't get too worried about Eck's flag waving. I think Salmond is a fool to himself.

House empty as Harriet has gone to Elie with her pals and Jose is not back from Venice. Very strange.

---

463 Richard Preston.

9 JULY

Woke early because of the heat – in Scotland! There was a text from Campbell Gunn about how he's going to work for Salmond. I sent him one back saying he's a rat joining a sinking ship. Not very nice but he's now the enemy. It's not so long since he was telling me how he thought it was time Eck was replaced by Nicola. I must remind him of that!

What will they get him to do, I wonder? He's not that brilliant. It will be hilarious to see No. 10's reaction. They always thought he was a great guy, even though I told them he was a Nat. Idiots.

13 JULY

Nats are getting themselves in a hopeless tangle – again – over the benefits of North Sea oil and gas revenues, with Eck saying that they'll be worth £300,000 for each of us. Then it turns out that there's another secret Cabinet paper which talks about the 'volatility' of oil. Poor old John Swinney; there is clearly a serious leaker in his department. And why wouldn't there be? After all, they are all members of the British civil service.

2 AUGUST

Back from holidays. Pity. But Salmond is in trouble, or at least should be after barging into an Aberdeen primary school unannounced and uninvited. Needless to say, that idiot Peter Housden[464]

---

464 Head of the civil service in Scotland.

has cleared him of any wrong-doing. Now there's a surprise.

12 AUGUST

Poor old David McLetchie has died after a long and fairly painful illness. He was a smashing bloke and would probably have made a difference if he'd stayed as leader and his chicken-livered colleagues hadn't deserted him over Taxigate.[465]

13–20 AUGUST

Edinburgh Book Festival. Murdoch MacL had asked me to sound them out about us taking it over from *The Guardian*. I'm glad I advised against as they're a hopelessly unreconstructed bunch of nonentities, especially wotsisname the director.[466]

This year the whole thing was dominated by Guardianistas and BBC presenters, which – although I've tried hard to resist the comparison – now amount to just about the same thing.

I wrote a few pieces, as did Jenny, and that blithering idiot of a director told me he'd 'heard' that we had given them a lot of coverage in the *Telegraph*. Heard? Hadn't he read them? Oh no, Frances[467] – his press officer – had told him about it. Christ! Frances is the only decent thing about the whole bloody farce.

---

465 He resigned as Scottish Conservative leader following a row over his taxi bills.

466 Nick Barley, Edinburgh International Book Festival director since 2009.

467 Frances Sutton, press manager of the book festival.

21 AUGUST

Managed to flush out the story about the Yes computer being hacked, thanks to being – or appearing to be – dead straight with them. Of course, the real story was that Yes were paying for nice, favourable pieces to be lobbed as lollipops for hard-up newspapers, like *The Herald*.[468] Jesus, what has this game and this country come to? Moley is furious, of course. But then he always is … about something.

25 AUGUST

Did my 'debate', such as it was, with Lesley Riddoch and some klutz from the Electoral Reform Society who havered away about nothing in particular. La Riddoch was abysmal but the Nat nutters were out in force to heckle me. It was a great shouting match that I quite enjoyed, but the girls were a bit put out by all the insults.

3 SEPTEMBER

Moley and Jocky are furious because of stories that suggest Kevin Pringle is being drafted into the Yes offices in Glasgow to oversee things, which is true but can't be admitted for fear of embarrassing that complete dumpling Blair Jenkins.

---

468 The Yes campaign admitted commissioning and paying for an academic to write an article for *The Herald*. An email relating to the article was hacked.

11 SEPTEMBER

Iain M's book[469] launch at the Travellers Club in London. Great fun. Everybody there, including Bruce, who looked terrible as usual.

22 SEPTEMBER

Fantastic dinner at Gleneagles for editors as there's one year to go before the Ryder Cup. I had a chat – very brief – with Tom Watson[470] (what a gent) and also talked to the boss of Diageo's press team, who, it turns out, used to work for Paddy Ashdown and David Owen.[471] Fantastic reminiscing about the formation of the SDP and the Alliance. I was sitting next to John Boothman, who wandered over to the next table to chat to Moira Salmond, Eck's wife.

I've only ever nodded to her in passing but she said to John: 'Why are you sitting next to that ghastly man from the *Telegraph*?'

I think that's a bit of a badge of honour, which is what Murdoch M said the next morning when I told him. Jenny thinks I should use that name as the title for this diary. Probably a good idea.

25 SEPTEMBER

Got a speeding ticket for doing 90 mph on the way back from Granny's thanks to singing along to 'California Dreamin'' by

---

469 *Making It Happen: Fred Goodwin, RBS and the Men Who Blew Up the British Economy.*

470 America's Ryder Cup captain.

471 Former Labour Foreign Secretary who became one of the Gang of Four who formed the SDP in 1981.

the Mamas and Papas. A hundred quid and three points. Stupid bugger.

29 SEPTEMBER

To Manchester for the Tory conference. But first of all Jenny and I had a night out with Harry. Great stuff.

30 SEPTEMBER

Dinner with David Burnside and his guests. Sat next to the CEO of Arriva, the train company, which is after the ScotRail franchise. I hope they get it as the present lot, First Group, are worse than useless. But he said Arriva would have no chance because Martin Gilbert is chairman of First Group and he is best pals with Wee Eck. Christ, what a country! But, then, is anyone surprised?

1 OCTOBER

Rubbish conference, although Ruth D made quite a good speech. Had a blether with Paxman, who says he's keeping his beard.

5 OCTOBER

Back in Edinburgh ... 64th birthday! God, I do feel old. Still, retirement out of the question. I have mixed feelings about it; sometimes I long to pack it all in, but what would I do? I'd get even fatter, that's for sure.

17 OCTOBER

SNP conference in Perth. As Jenny and the girls are in London, I spent three days there – driving back and forwards every day. Boy, this lot are up for the fight and are an impressive sight when they're all together. They are very much – in class terms – an upper working/lower middle class lot; there are not many toffs and very few horny-handed sons of toil in their midst. But that means that they're very active and very keen to get out there and sell their message. Unlike our lot.

17 OCTOBER

The Nats are being realistic about their chances now and the fact that they're miles behind in the polls; this in spite of those cod-polls that they produced last month (done by Panelbase) which seemed to show that they'd closed the gap. It was all about the way the questions were asked, as even the pollsters – and John Curtice – conceded.

18 OCTOBER

Nicola put on her Scary Sturgeon suit, which was stupid as her warnings about the Brits turning the screw and dismantling the NHS, pensions, and – who knows – killing the first born were totally ridiculous. She can't attack Project Fear as easily now.

Ian Blackford, the former treasurer – and Salmond hater – was there and very friendly and wants me to debate with him. No way, he's too good at numbers and would murder me. He's working his passage back into the SNP's inner councils. He is very able but thankfully Eck doesn't like him at all because he queried Moira's taxi bills way back fifteen years ago! Absolutely true.

19 OCTOBER

Spent a night up the Glen with Frans and Teresa, then went back to Perth to watch Salmond. Quite a good speech – he's not great at them – but he avoided all the hard stuff such as the EU, sterling, NATO and so on, and stuck to lollipops about freebies. But his foot soldiers are an impressive lot. Very committed; very dedicated. And Eck named the day for the White Paper – 26 November – which will be published as a cross between the Declaration of Arbroath and the Magna Carta amid great fanfare, but I doubt if there will be much in it. Thankfully, it's the week after I go to Toronto.

21 OCTOBER

Had a long-ish chat with Darling, who is a bit less than confident. 'I've always thought it would be a close result,' he says. 'Maybe sixty–forty.'

I don't like the sound of that and neither did Murdoch M when I told him. How do we galvanise our bloody support? Or do we just wait and accept that they'll turn out and do the business on referendum day? I'm sure that people would visibly support the cause if BT gave them the opportunity. I'm seeing Shorthouse today. What about some car and window stickers? It's time to go public. I've emailed Harrow – he is usually up for a fight, which for a Lib Dem is refreshing.

22 OCTOBER

Had a chat with Harrow, who's in London to celebrate 'Lord' Purvis of Tweed's[472] ennoblement. As Simon says, 'There's hope for us all if he gets one.' And Harrow says he's having lunch with Michael Moore, no doubt to commiserate with the poor lad over losing his job.[473] What a bloody hypocrite! He's been campaigning and lobbying for Carmichael to get the SoS job for months. I even wrote it once! Politicians – dontcha luv 'em.

He compared Eck's largesse – staying for four nights at Gleneagles – to Carmichael's, who opts for Premier Inns, but it was Nat money that paid for Gleneagles and no doubt they got a deal from Diageo. Must keep an eye on whether Salmond declares it.

Harrow also said there is a demand for Better Together posters and stickers. Must get some.

Shorthouse said everyone at BT is 'shitting themselves' about how successful the SNP conference was, and he said that the Salmond and Sturgeon speeches were seen as especially good, which is right – they were. But he said the numbers were still on the side of the angels, just so long as we keep plugging away and the Nats keep making a balls of the economic arguments.

All a bit unsettling, frankly.

---

472 Jeremy Purvis, former Lib Dem MSP.

473 Alistair Carmichael replaced Michael Moore as Secretary of State for Scotland on 7 October 2013.

23 OCTOBER

Grangemouth blew up and I had to cancel New Club lunch with Harrow. Pity. Phoned John Swinney on the off-chance and – lo and behold – he answered his mobile and chatted away about what a bloody nightmare the management AND the unions are at the plant. He says there's no decision making amongst an 'impenetrable' management and that everything eventually gets referred back to JR – Jim Ratcliffe.[474]

Very little chance of agreement because everyone hates each other. Vile atmosphere. It was good background for my piece and he said it would be difficult for the Nats to find a buyer or to nationalise, which they're not interested in, because Ineos are now going for liquidation. Wrote a piece for op-ed, which they used. I musn't abuse the Swinney link, but must also keep it open.

24 OCTOBER

Incredible. McCluskey[475] of Unite flies up to Grangemouth and caves in on everything – the lot: pensions, wage freeze, everything. Carmichael and Swinney turn up for talks; Cameron and Miliband make supportive noises; everyone is on side. What a turn up. Surely that shit Ratcliffe can't turn down a deal now. But who knows?

Tom P says there's big redundo announcement at *The Scotsman*

---

474 The billionaire chairman of Ineos and owner of Grangemouth, who threatened to close the petrochemical plant after a row with the Unite union.

475 Len McCluskey, Unite general secretary.

next Monday. Ian Stewart[476] has gone away on his mountain bike to 'clear his head', or so they say. Christ, what a poseur. Mark Douglas-Home[477] walked out of *The Herald* when they kept sacking people at his place.

Might try to get Tom back – but he can't be pol. ed. or Scottish corr. Wonder if a) they'd let me hire him and b) he'd come. Can't get an answer from Ellis;[478] he's probably too snowed under and won't appreciate all my emails. Still, it's getting mad, nobody can get any time off. This is my twelfth or thirteenth day in succession at work! I'm too old for this.

25 OCTOBER

Absolutely incredible – the deal is done. Grangemouth stays, the workers keep their jobs, the union is stuffed and everyone is gobsmacked.

27 OCTOBER

Amazing story in the *Sunday Times*: they've got all 1,500 of Stevie Deans's[479] emails – obviously a lollipop from Ineos – that show he spent 25 per cent of his time working to stitch up the Labour candidacy in Falkirk rather than looking after his members at the plant.

---

476 Editor of *The Scotsman* since June 2012.

477 Editor of *The Herald* from 2000 to 2006.

478 Richard Ellis, executive director of Telegraph Media Group.

479 The Unite official at the centre of the Grangemouth dispute.

Incredibly, BBC Scotland make no mention of the story when I go on *Sunday Politics* (with Dennis Canavan[480] and some union bod), presented by Gary Robertson, who tries out some of his O-level Marxist crap about international capitalism. Puerile and just plain wrong. They're not really biased, just rubbish.

Had a bit of a chat with Alistair Carmichael before going on; he says he likes being Secretary of State – he should, as he's been angling for it for long enough – and he also said the management at Ineos were 'f*****g shits' but that the union simply walked into a trap.

28 OCTOBER

Got home to find that I'd been made an assistant editor. Very nice.

5 NOVEMBER

November at last: this year has positively dragged. And we have nothing to do, really, until the Nats publish their bloody White Paper.

The good news is that I'm definitely doing that Walter Scott gig in Toronto.

---

480 Former Labour MP for Falkirk West, Independent MSP from 1999 to 2007, and Yes campaign chairman.

5 NOVEMBER

Did an after-dinner speaking engagement for the Edinburgh/ Moray society – a bunch of well-heeled chaps, mixture of generals and lairds. Very jolly evening and, as usual, not a single Nat; they must be somewhere.

16 NOVEMBER

Jenny's birthday. I've given up trying to buy her anything as she never likes what I buy, so it's best just to give her the money. I did so and guess what? She bought yet another black dress! We went to Café St Honoré, which was very good.

19 NOVEMBER

Went to Toronto with WS. Christ, these money men don't stint themselves. Very comfy business/executive/first-class seats cum beds on the plane and excellent Four Seasons Hotel.

20 NOVEMBER

Brilliant dinner with the WS people. They know absolutely nothing about politics, so I was able to regale them with some of my hoary old anecdotes. They seemed to love it.

Best of all, though, was a fantastic tip-off from Jim Gallagher,[481]

---

481 Academic and former senior civil servant. He joined the Better Together campaign in January 2014 as a policy advisor.

who has a mole in St Andrew's House. The latter says that the White Paper will insist that the Nats will demand sterling union no matter what the English say, and if they win the referendum they will claim they have a mandate to do what they bloody well like! Took a lot of writing and re-writing with Simon but then, wonder of wonders, Swinney stood up our story the very next day. Brilliant work from both sides of the Atlantic … and then some.

21 NOVEMBER

Did my big speech, which seemed to go down quite well. Thank God. Incredible encounter on my way to the event. I met an elderly and very distinguished chap in the lift who said, 'Oh, you are Alan Cochrane, aren't you? My sister sends over *Scottish Field* and I love your articles.' Amazing.

22–23 NOVEMBER

Back to Edinburgh – knackered and fed all the Lessels and Wallaces.[482] Could hardly keep my eyes open.

24 NOVEMBER

Started the White Paper build-up.

---

482 St George's friends.

25 NOVEMBER

Ditto.

26 NOVEMBER

White Paper. Nothing in it – zero, zilch. And no surprises, either. Crap presentation in crap location.

28 NOVEMBER

Eck got slaughtered at FMQs but Nicola apparently murdered Carmichael on STV the night before.

29 NOVEMBER

Total pile of drivel from Fraser Nelson on the great issue. Garbage. He bases it all on Nicola hammering Carmichael and on 'Downing Street' strategists. Total nonsense. He was so confident of his piece that he sent it to Hamish Macdonell to check it out and advise him! Even Hamish said he should tone it down.

Delightful exchange of texts with Fraser, but after a couple of days I decided to call off the war and sent him a Christmas card: I can't keep these feuds going and I know I'm getting far too close to this story; too wrapped up in it. I can't help it but there it is.

CHRISTMAS AND NEW YEAR

Great time was had by all. We had a big crowd on 23 December and had a job getting rid of them all, neighbours mainly, and Jenny's family, who stayed.

Our New Year party on the 2nd was totally different. Brilliant success with (Brian) Steel and Ian[483] and Sarah,[484] plus Alistair Darling, Ming Campbell[485] – who was asked by Sarah what he did for a living, tee hee – and Generals Loudon and Mackay. Great, and Jenny wants to do this every year. Excellent news.

---

483 Ian Hayes, Harriet's godfather.

484 Sarah Hilsley, Ian's girlfriend.

485 Sir Menzies Campbell, former Lib Dem leader.

2014

3 JANUARY

Am on the wagon until ... well, we shall see!

7–17 JANUARY

What a bloody fortnight. We simply cannot keep up this pace, what with both sides of the referendum debate piling on the pressure. It appears that Nicola Sturgeon is making two speeches a day, Alex Salmond is puffing and scheming away, and there are signs that some on the No side are beginning to worry.

But then, all of a sudden, we had another YouGov poll which showed that the Nats are down to 30 per cent. Jesus! They must be worried. However, most of the press decided to focus on the finding that most Scots want more powers for Holyrood. What tripe, especially from the Boy Editor of *The Sun*, who appears to be an out-and-out Nat.

I can't believe that Dinsmore[486] – the London editor, who's a good public schoolboy and Unionist – will allow that to continue. Mind you, that old goat Rupert Murdoch is well into Wee Eck's pocket, so who knows?

15 JANUARY

Iain Martin emailed to say that he had been sitting having a coffee in the Norman Shaw tea room when the Prime Minister came over to him and said, 'I want to reassure you [Iain], and also Cochrane and Fraser Nelson, that I am fully committed to defending the Union.' Incredible, especially as he's lumping me in with Fraser. I texted Dunlop in Downing Street to ask him what that was about but he had no idea.

16 JANUARY

Fell off the wagon at Tom Peterkin's stag lunch. Couldn't do it 'dry'. Felt hellish the next day.

17 JANUARY

Missing three-year-old boy story[487] breaks. Everyone assumes that the estranged father 'done it' but the hacks on the ground

---

486 David Dinsmore.

487 Mikaeel Kular went missing from his Edinburgh home and a day later his body was found. In July, his mother, Rosdeep Adekoya, pleaded guilty to his murder.

reckon it was the mother. Simon still off ill but at least we now have Ben[488] on the staff, who looks to be brilliant; I've already sent him one herogram.

19 JANUARY

Auslan works all weekend, as does Ben, for the *Sunday Telegraph* and then we get this memo from Gallagher moaning about how we didn't do as much as the *Mail* on the mother's dodgy background.

20 JANUARY

Pressure from Tony G and news desk still intense, although the news ed. seems more realistic than his boss. Aus being made to jump through hoops and start background pieces even though we can't use anything until the trial. Mad use of resources.

21 JANUARY

Gallagher sacked! I'm not at all surprised and not much bothered, either. Mind you, he never interfered.

I might well regret his departure, but we'll have to wait and see what the new regime is like.

---

488 Ben Riley-Smith.

23–24 JANUARY

Brilliant bonus from Simon's FOI on Eck's extravagance in America for the Ryder Cup. Lamont led with it, most people had to follow it and then those little shits moved the goalposts by trying to amend the figures involved. Eck is lying and everyone is covering up. We'll get him yet – but probably only if some of those cowardly civil servants shop him. How long can they stay silent as this guy makes an arse of them; he even blamed them for spending all the loot!

I think Labour are right: perhaps Eck spent the missing £3,000 on lavish living and has now paid it back. That's why they've taken so long to reply to the FOI.

25 JANUARY

Have to go through to Glasgow to do a Burns Supper. Wish I hadn't agreed, as Harry's home but goes back tomorrow.

Absolute proof that Nats are all shits – no sense of humour and none of irony, either. I did a jokey speech comparing McGonagall[489] with Burns, in which I said – tongue firmly in cheek – that William's ode to Queen Victoria was greater than Rabbie's 'Scots Wha Hae'. And what happened? Monstering from some old Nat.

And to think I went all the way through to Glasgow for that. What a bunch.

---

489 William Topaz McGonagall (1825–1902), Dundonian widely regarded as the worst poet in the English language.

26 JANUARY

Big poll in the new tabloid *Scotland on Sunday* says Nats have a big jump in support. Worrying, but it's only one poll. However, MM rang when I was making supper, in a very worried frame of mind, and goes on about how useless BT are and how they need a charismatic leader. If I write that, the sky will fall on us. I have got to keep the faith – for now – but it is very difficult.

This is especially so because they are all fighting with each other; Harrow doesn't like Jim Gallagher, and I can understand that; Jim is an arrogant bastard. And he doesn't like Shorthouse, either. And when I set them to arranging MM's dinner in Edinburgh they start squabbling with each other.

27 JANUARY

This trend gets worse when I speak to Billy, my brother, who says he refuses to pick up BT literature when it's dropped off at Lib Dem headquarters. Jesus, what a bloody shower.

28 JANUARY

Wonders will never cease. No sooner has Tony Gallagher buggered off and Deerin flown the coop than I get a piece onto the op-ed pages. Christ, it felt like my birthday. They are apparently all interested in jolly old Jockoland now.

4 FEBRUARY

Went to London on 5.40 a.m. train. No bother getting up and had a nice-ish hot breakfast – well, warm breakfast – read the papers, had a few zeds and got into Kings Cross at 9.40 a.m. Brilliant. Had a very friendly meeting with Chris Evans.[490] He is supposed to be the most hated man in Fleet Street but he's always been very affable towards me. (I'll probably regret writing that.) MM has always said that he was the 'go to' bloke on the paper in London.

Had a meeting with Jason Seiken,[491] the new über-boss, who again was extremely jovial and approachable. He had never heard of the Edinburgh Festival, the Fringe or the Tattoo but was intrigued to hear about Edinburgh in August, when there are upwards of a million in town. He promises to come up and wants me to explore possibilities of sponsoring one of the festivals. Otherwise, it was all about digital gobbledegook of which I understood scarce a word.

5–7 FEBRUARY

Completely knackered, I think by that early start, and things are far too busy.

---

490 Appointed Monday-to-Friday editor of the *Daily Telegraph* in February.
491 Editor in chief at Telegraph Media Group.

10 FEBRUARY

Gave Ben his first bollocking for missing that Oxford Migration survey story.[492] He was extremely chastened but he will survive. I took him to MM's dinner at Centotre which, thankfully, worked out all right, although there was some depressing news about how little money Better Together has got and the fact that the Nats have a £7 million war chest and are about to launch a £2.5 million billboard campaign. This on top of the £800,000 of taxpayers' money they spent on their alleged White Paper, which was, in fact, a manifesto and that arse Peter Housden should have stopped them spending it. But he's terrified of Eck. What a carry-on.

11 FEBRUARY

At last, I have been sent back that book for proofreading. Am taking a couple of days off so had better get started.

12–28 FEBRUARY

Absolutely incredible amount of work – doesn't stop. Every day two or three speeches and we seem to be doing Scottish splashes all the time now.

Bad news is piling up for Eck. Brilliant bit of stuff from Osborne, Balls and Alexander to tell Nats they ain't getting the pound.[493] Had a coffee with Dunlop afterwards and told him

---

492 The survey found that Scottish attitudes to immigration were not much different to the rest of Britain's.

493 The three parties united to crush Salmond's hopes of a currency union.

that there would be a reaction from the huffy Jocks, who would object to posh Englishmen bossing them about.

Needless to say, Eck called it bullying and needless to say, a lot of poor saps at the Beeb and other papers fell for it. But it is all factored into the Grand Plan and everyone expects short-term poll narrowing – which duly happens.

MM worried about the polls but I tried to reassure him, while all the time making Sunday lunch.

The Nats are all over the place on the pound, with Eck and Swinney saying they'll use sterling whatever anyone else says. It's bollocks, of course, and eventually Standard Life drop their expected bombshell by saying that they're clearing off to England with huge parts of their business. There are 5,000 jobs at stake. The Nats bombard the Standard Life offices around the corner from me, and the barber says that one of her customers took 150 complaints by email and phone from people saying they were cancelling their policies. 'I don't give a monkey's about them, we've got four million policy holders,' he told her.

TSB also shifting to London. Poor old Nats.

All this on top of Barroso and that Belgian whatsisname[494] saying that Scotland couldn't waltz into the EU. Rubbish, of course, but it hurts the Nats, so why not.

I was kidding with Alex Neil about the referendum. He says they'll walk it but I can tell he doesn't believe it and I told him to book me early to run his leadership campaign against Eck, as Nicola

---

494 Herman Van Rompuy, president of the European Council, said in December 2013 that any secessionist region would be treated as a new country and would have to submit an application to join.

is also trying to sign me up. Jim Eadie,[495] who's a sensible Nat, concedes they'll lose but insists, 'We are not going to get gubbed now.'

Maybe, maybe.

23 FEBRUARY

Moderated an open primary hustings for the Tories[496] in Kelso. Over three hundred people turned up – two hundred more than normal; normal voters as well as party members. This really is the way to get people to take an active part in politics. Very good stuff from John Lamont,[497] who was the favourite, and a woman[498] who is a former charge nurse or something. Lamont won it very easily and the woman was not best pleased.

The Tories take me for granted a bit. I was rushed down there in a car and then rushed back again. No lunch, not a drink and one measly cup of coffee. Still, they handed in a bottle of malt – which I can add to my large collection. Don't they know I would prefer claret?

25 FEBRUARY

Massive medical. And not good news. I've got to lose two stone, there's a low calcium count in my blood and I'm on the high side

---

495 SNP MSP for Edinburgh Southern.

496 For the Borders seat, currently held by Lib Dem Michael Moore, in the next general election.

497 Conservative MSP for Ettrick, Roxburgh and Berwickshire.

498 Councillor Michelle Ballantyne, Borders Conservative group leader.

towards diabetes. Boring. Must cut back on the booze and start going to the gym again.

3 MARCH

It appears that we are taking a villa in France. No dosh, so it's all going on a credit card. When will that lottery come in?

I'm trying to organise a Better Together dinner for MM, this time in Glasgow.

4 MARCH

Dinner with Jamie McGrigor and some boring Deer man. Jenny came too but I overdid it. Big trouble.

5 MARCH

Went through to Glasgow to see Better. Scruffy little office, manned by kids who didn't seem at all enthused. Looked browbeaten and under the cosh. Very worrying. Shortarse took me for a coffee and I got a great story about Roseanna Cunningham publicising the name and address of a general who supports BT.

6 MARCH

Glasgow dinner not going well at all. The Weegies ain't turning out. It's remarkable, and this was confirmed by both the RSNO and Scottish Ballet, but the idea that they are more generous than the Edinburghers is plain rubbish. Both organisations say that they can raise more money from Edinburgh than they can from Glasgow. And our dinner looks like having a very poor cast list. MM will not be pleased.

7 MARCH

MM says he is going to see Eck on Tuesday, on his own. I'm worried that all Eck will do is complain about us and demand right of reply all the time.

9 MARCH

Did another hustings, this time in Aboyne, where the local laird,[499] who had obviously packed the meeting with his pals, tenants and workers, easily hammered three others, including Big Eck Johnstone,[500] the sitting MSP. It just goes to show that feudalism is alive and well, still, in the Scottish countryside and in the Tory Party!

11 MARCH

MM did indeed see Eck but needless to say Eck wasn't on his own. He had Gunn and Nicolson with him, but there doesn't

---

499 Alexander Burnett, now the 2015 candidate for West Aberdeenshire and Kincardine, currently held by the Lib Dems.

500 Alex Johnstone.

seem to have been any repercussion from their meeting that will affect us. We shall see.

12 MARCH

Looks like we'll get that new office up the lane from the *Scotsman* building. Excellent. And we won't have to cross any roads to get to the pub, or at least the Hemma, which is the best one!

14 MARCH

Went for blood tests, after my medical suggested that there might be too much protein and too little calcium. Must find out what they show.

Then off to the Tory conference at the EICC, where Mundell made sure I met the Prime Minister at a huge crowd scene. Stupid. Embarrassing for both of us.

Met that new Tory chairman a couple of times: Keen.[501] Looks as though he's only in this for a peerage and is extremely chippy towards me, possibly because he's heard that I was once offered the job. That's a laugh: what happened was that Bruce got through to the Downing Street switchboard and demanded to speak to Mundell. Incredibly, they tracked down Mundell and Bruce told him to make me chairman. I remember some vague conversation with Mundell but I've actually been offered just about every kind of job by the Tories.

---

501 Richard Keen, Dean of the Faculty of Advocates, appointed Scottish Conservative Party chairman in November 2013.

The Tories looked almost real in that posh setting and it's very touching that so many people come and say how much they like my column. Maybe I should throw in my lot with them properly; after all, everyone assumes I'm a Tory anyway. *Telegraph* fringe event was a huge success – packed out. But it was a crap debate between Eck Johnstone and Margaret Mitchell.[502]

17 MARCH

Trying to lose weight but I don't think I'm winning. Bloody hard!

21 MARCH

Labour conference in Perth. Good fringe meeting with Ian David-son and Jenny Marra; both very good – Ian the more serious and anti-EU; Jenny stupidly says we should abolish the British Army and have a European version. Bonkers.

Ed Miliband made a perfunctory speech, quite good but not great, to a half-empty hall. If that was Eck for the SNP, it would have been standing room only.

24 MARCH

Polls all over the place. ICM says Nats catching up, TNS says 'no, they're not' and then YouGov says well, yes, they might be. However, the latter is still suggesting that it's sixty–forty against independence.

---

502 Conservative MSP for Coatbridge.

Big 'don't knows' but I think I can guess what's happening. In the '90s, the pollsters discovered a phenomenon, first unearthed with the CSU in Bavaria, where the voters didn't like to admit that they'd be voting for a right-wing party, and thus the survey results were wonky. That's why all the polling organisations got the 1992 general election in the UK so badly wrong – people didn't like to say they were voting Tory, when that's exactly what they were doing.

It became known as the 'Shy Tory' syndrome, although it had another name too, which I can't remember.

I suspect this may be happening in this vote too. People don't want to appear to be anti-Scottish and so may be saying either they're voting Yes or that they don't know – especially the latter. But those don't knows are really won't says and I reckon they'll mostly vote NO in big numbers.

Christ, I hope I'm right!

25 MARCH

Had a great break at the Peat Inn with Jenny. Luxurious and free! *Scottish Field* review piece but had to pay for the wine – spent too much on that, needless to say. It would have cost nearly £500 if we'd been paying. Ridiculous.

28 MARCH

Off to Aberdeen for the Lib Dem conference but astonished to find 'Crisis at Better Together' splash headlines in *Mail*. What's going on? Texted Harrow, Darling and Dunlop. Everyone mystified. Got early train with Ben and Robbie but before I reached Aberdeen saw that my sister Anne was trying to reach me. Eventually got a signal when we got off train and Anne, Billy and Ian[503] told me that Mither had been rushed into Ninewells in the middle of the night with acute pains and very sick.

Luckily, Ian was in Aberdeen and said he'd pick me up after lunch and head for Dundee. Did my fringe meeting, which was well attended, but saw more criticism of Labour from the Lib Dems.

Mum looked terrible – tubes everywhere and an oxygen mask. Stayed at her house in the Ferry and got a bus to Ninewells on Saturday morning.

29 MARCH

Mother much better. Billy took me to Edinburgh but more crap in the *Mail* about Better Together. It appears that Deerin, who is back in Scotland, is now calling the shots there – not Harries, who is a good sub but who knows nothing about politics – and is prattling on about Darling being too negative. Drivel!

Emailed Chris Evans and suggested counter-blast for op-ed.

30 MARCH

Astonishing! Shorthouse tells me that it was Craig Harrow who blabbed to the *Mail*[504] over a boozy lunch and that Phil Ander-

---

503 Ian Cochrane, AC's brother.
504 About in-fighting at Better Together.

ton[505] has been moaning to the *Sunday Times*. Christ, what a shower. Gave the whole thing both barrels and with Phil Johnston[506] doing the page it worked well.

31 MARCH

Ally's birthday but luckily I had sent cards. My op-ed, about Darling being in charge, has gone down well, with the editor of the *FT* saying it was the best analysis he'd seen of Better Together. Everyone dumping on Harrow. What an idiot. Darling happy with the piece too. Incredibly, Harrow texting, saying he wants a blether. Ignore him.

1 APRIL

It gets worse! *FT* run a story saying that the PM has bollocked Darling for calling for a referendum on sterling, which Darling didn't say. Not one bit of the story is true. Kicked up hell with Dunlop, who behaves like a pompous arse, saying the No. 10 press office had been 'less than felicitous' in their answers to *FT*. Christ, what a patrician prat. He says that that idiot Ramsay Jones is ringing round news desks. Jesus, who's going to listen to him? Darling angry but cool; says it's tiresome and talks of 'midterm turbulence'. We're lucky to have him.

Spoke to Chris Evans, who said that he'd had lunch with Cameron and when Evans asked him how he thought the referendum

---

505 Better Together's marketing man.

506 *Daily Telegraph* assistant editor.

campaign was going, he said that a year ago, if he'd been told that he'd be ahead in the polls by the margin he's got now, he would happily have taken it.

Good news: Hezza says he'll do the hacks' lunch in Edinburgh. Excellent.

2 APRIL

My *Yes or No* book is out! Did Border TV with Kerevan and played it for laughs. I had to as I still haven't seen the book!

Harrow very penitent and says he was stitched up by Deerin, whom he didn't know but thought he could trust because he was vouched for by Eddie Barnes of the Tories. Poor bugger Harrow is also going through a domestic crisis and is living in a cottage somewhere.

3 APRIL

Dinner with the Moderator of the General Assembly of the Church of Scotland.[507] Lovely lady but I'm not sure about her successor,[508] who looks a real dry stick and sounds like one, too. Everyone a bit down in the dumps because Margo MacDonald is so ill. She's not expected to last the night.

---

507 Right Reverend Lorna Hood.
508 Right Reverend John Chalmers.

4 APRIL

Sure enough, Margo has died. Did the *Politics Show* for Andrew Neil. Joyce McMillan was my competitor; God, what a smug, boring woman. Not much fun.

5 APRIL

My wee tribute to Margo was much liked by Jim Sillars, her husband, who sent me a very touching email, saying that I was her favourite journalist, even though we seldom agreed about anything.

Did *Good Morning Scotland* with Brian Taylor about Margo. Happy/sad occasion with lots of anecdotes about the lady.

8 APRIL

Missed dentist's appointment! Idiot. Dropped in for lunch at the New Club. Good grub, boring members – except for Angus Grossart, who came and sat at the Members' Table. I like Angus. He is completely his own man, with a finger in most pies, but he does a lot of good for Scotland. He is almost certainly a Nat but, as he says himself, he is all for and only for the Grossart Party.

10 APRIL

Plugged the book mercilessly on *Newsnicht*. Good fun.

11 APRIL

SNP conference in Aberdeen. Have at last got copies of the book. Not sure if I like it all that much. But, interestingly, before she goes off to Lyon, Josephine asks to read it and says that she likes it, even if she points out that my bit is tiny compared to George's and often starts with the first person singular. Oops!

Very good, left-wing speech from Nicola. She is a class act and she knows it. Dreadful conference centre but some of the Nats turned up at the book event that George had arranged and they behaved very well – and bought lots of books. I had met Ian Rankin the day before in George Street and he told me to have a fast car sitting outside the centre with the engine running so that I could make a speedy getaway. No need in the end.

12 APRIL

Very ordinary speech by Salmond, in which he announced that he was promoting Shona Robison and Angela Constance to his Cabinet. On merit, he says. Balls! It's because the polls show that women still don't like him. Horrible pre-speech preview of a show that some Nat actors are doing at the Fringe this year, called *Pure Dead Brilliant*.[509] Racist tripe but the delegates screamed for more. What a bloody shower!

Got a lift home with Sev. Great to escape. There were lots of Nats in Aberdeen but not quite as many, nor as loud, as I'd feared.

---

509 *The Pure, The Dead and The Brilliant*, a pro-independence play by Alan Bissett.

13 APRIL

Jenny and Harry in Twickers, Jose in Lyon, so I'm on my own at home but luckily got dinner with the Inwoods. Roast lamb – smashing.

14 APRIL

Slob of a day, doing the garden, after again plugging the book mercilessly on *Good Morning Scotland*. Good laugh and everyone was pleased with it.

15 APRIL

Incredible day. That complete idiot Philip Hammond gave an interview to *The Herald* in which he said that everything was negotiable after independence, which means – as the Nats seized on – that sterling and Trident could be on the table. Stupid, stupid man.

Texted Dunlop to ask what the hell was going on and he said he was angry about Hammond doing the interview – especially with *The Herald* – and that he didn't know it was happening. This is mind-boggling, as that useless bugger Ramsay Jones sat in on it and he is supposed to work for Dunlop. And yet Dunlop doesn't know about it. Kate Devlin confirmed Jones's presence but swore me to secrecy.

Had a chat with Shorthouse and was determined to hammer Downing Street for being so bloody useless. A piece by Brogan didn't help. In it he said that Cameron should set up a personal headquarters in Glasgow from whence to fight the campaign. Christ, it would be burned down overnight.

Then Darling rang and asked me not to publish my bashing of Downing Street as it would simply add fuel to the flames, already raging because, in part, of Brogan's piece. He said Brogan's commentary was like a 'stream of consciousness' and that his idea of a Glasgow HQ for Cameron would lead to daily riots in the street. How did Brogan make it so far?

I had already thought about not filing it and told Darling that.

However, after I picked up Jenny and Harry I started to have second thoughts and sent Darling my piece. He rang back and again asked me not to publish but, instead, to send it to Dunlop. I said I would and sent it to Mundell, too. Jenny said I should do what Darling asks. He's in charge after all. It's not really good journalism but what the hell does journalism matter? This is much more important.

Darling manages to have a laugh and says if the Tories behave like this during next year's election, Labour will walk it. I think he's right and I also think he may well fancy his chances a bit more of a new career with Labour.

Darling is just the best man to have in a crisis – very cool. Brilliant in the face of all those London idiots looking at Scotland from 400 miles away through the wrong end of a telescope.

Chris Evans's secretary emailed to arrange that summit about referendum coverage for next Wednesday. It can't come soon enough. I sounded off a bit to Phil Johnston, who is an excellent scout and understands the situation. Hopefully, he will go to the meeting on Wednesday. I need an ally.

16 APRIL

Mundell phoned to say that he'd got my piece and assured me that there will be changes, although he refused to tell me what they were. Still, that sounds promising and it seems my diatribe may well have done some good.

19 APRIL

Paul Sinclair's wedding to Clare, a Glasgow lawyer he knew when they were both at Glasgow University. Very 'Labour family' affair, what with the Darlings, the Lamonts, the Smith-Robertsons (Jane Smith[510] and Malcolm Robertson) all there. Lovely ceremony in the university chapel and then a cracking dinner after lashings of Monopole champagne in the sunny quadrangle. Nice table with Murray Foote and wife of the *Record*, Andy Nicol and Annie, Magnus Gardham and Julie, his wife.

Towards the end of the evening, Alistair came over to show me a text he'd had from Helen Liddell,[511] the former Secretary of State for Scotland, saying that civil servants were being ordered to resign from the CBI[512] because it was now backing Better Together. Then Malcolm Robertson said George Foulkes was saying the same thing on Twitter.

Absolutely outrageous! Prompted much joking about

---

510 Middle daughter of former Labour leader John Smith.

511 Baroness Liddell, former Scottish Labour MP and British High Commissioner to Australia from 2005 to 2009.

512 The Confederation of British Industry registered with the Electoral Commission as a supporter of Better Together, allowing it to spend up to £150,000 campaigning.

Kristallnacht (mostly from me) and Gestapo tactics. Tried to wind Labour up about it but Johann Lamont predicted that the civil service unions were too cowardly to do much. Sadly, she was proved right.

Had a nice night in the Hilton; I think it's my favourite hotel. I much prefer places like that to those twee wee hotels like the Peat Inn, which I've got to review for the *Field*.

20 APRIL

Drove home and tried to do a story about the CBI boycott. Very difficult: no one knows anything, apparently, although Fiona Wilson[513] said that 'everyone is too scared to talk'. Hellish situation and it's all being done by that 'nice' John Swinney. His behaviour is a real eye-opener. Apparently, or so the rumour goes, he had a furious row with Sir Peter Housden over his edict that civil servants should boycott the CBI, before Housden eventually backed down. Still, if true, at least old Pete is at last showing some fight.

21 APRIL

More tripe, this time in the *Mail*, about 'top Tories' bashing Darling. Christ, they're useless and I'm surprised Darling doesn't quit – then we'd really be in trouble. Cameron and Osborne have got to get a grip of their party. I hope to hell the Tories lose the next

---

513 Head of news for the Scottish government.

election; that would serve them right for bashing Darling at every turn. They are a useless lot, they really are!

Had a chat with Ben Wallace about the situation. He's quite good on it but wants to undermine his old enemy Mundell all the time, which detracts from what he says. Still, he agrees, as does everyone, that the No. 10 team is completely useless.

Aberdeen, Glasgow and Edinburgh universities have now pulled out of the CBI – what a shower of cowards. Still, with that 'nice' John Swinney putting the arm on them, what can they do? I must keep using that description of JS; it might annoy him. We shall see.

I expect more trouble on the CBI front but the Great Broon speaks tomorrow on pensions. That's much more important, always assuming that people believe his apparently secret figures. Hope they're right.

23 APRIL

London for a meeting on the referendum. Quite good – everybody listened to me but I suspect they understood about half of what I was saying. The English just don't get it. However, Evans is on my side; I think.

Story doing the rounds about how Cameron asked to meet the new editor of the *Telegraph* and three people turned up: Evans, Seiken and Kate Day, the woman who's in charge of the online stuff. Evans told me that there was a funny moment when one of the three – he didn't say which – asked the PM how he thought the referendum campaign was going and he said: 'What does Cochers think?' Amazing. He's apparently quite relaxed and, like me, reckons it will be all right if everyone keeps calm – especially the bloody Tories in London.

25 APRIL

Margo's memorial service. Fantastic occasion and sat in the old Press Box at the Assembly Hall.[514] Wasn't going to write anything but just had to, which delayed our departure for Oxford.

Dreadful journey; I hate driving in England, it's got too many people! Took about seven and a half hours but what a house and what a life Dame Elish Angiolini has. She is now principal of St Hugh's College, Oxford, and that's what we should all aspire to be. Lovely house and grounds and Dom, her husband, made us very welcome.

On the drive down, Ben RS phoned to say that the idiots at the CBI had admitted that they'd made a mistake and that the decision to register with the No lot had been taken by some junior clerk and they were now withdrawing. They will never EVER be taken seriously in Scotland again.

26 APRIL

Smashing day walking around Oxford with Dom and Harry, while Jose and Jenny went to the open day. Jose is hooked and is going to have a try for Oxford. Fantastic.

---

514 The site of the Scottish Parliament from devolution in 1999 until completion of the new building at Holyrood in 2004.

Wonderful meal cooked by Dom – he even makes his own ravioli. What a lovely man. What a marvellous cook. He told us a horrible story about Helena Kennedy[515] trying to stop Elish going for the St Hugh's post because, as she said, 'What will Dom do?' Patronising old cow – confirms everything I'd ever thought about that woman. It was all to do with her wanting Charlie Falconer[516] to get the job. There's socialist solidarity for you.

27 APRIL

Drove Harry to Manchester. She's had a great holiday and it's great to have her home but she does love Chets.

28 APRIL

Parliament back and normal service resumes. God, what a bore.

Salmond in terrible trouble for saying he liked Putin. Excellent news!

1 MAY

May Day and it's freezing! Salmond got the hiding of his life over the Putin business from all three opposition leaders. I've never seen the Nats look so subdued, especially Nicola. Her face was

---

515 Baroness Kennedy, human rights champion and principal of Mansfield College, Oxford.
516 Lord Falconer, Labour peer.

like thunder throughout his pathetic attempt to justify his stupidity. And all he had to do was apologise. Fat chance.

Went to a nice party for the Continis'[517] 10th anniversary, where Andrew Wilson agreed that Salmond 'got a doing'. And he's one of the inner circle.

2 MAY

Spoke to Ian Blackford, who thinks Salmond is in serious trouble, especially as the situation in Ukraine is getting worse. But then he and Salmond have always been at daggers drawn, ever since he was SNP treasurer and he queried Alex's and, worse, Moira's taxi expenses.

Great poll for Channel 4 which puts the good guys sixteen points ahead. The polls have been making an arse of this – they are ignoring the spiral of silence, all those people who don't want to be thought of as anti-Scottish by saying No.

3 MAY

Stupid *Week in Westminster* from Jackie Ashley,[518] who had a go at the No campaign. I emailed her to tell her the facts and to point out that she'd missed the Channel 4 poll. Still, the two pollsters on her programme said No would win. And, interestingly, there was agreement about the spiral of silence – the fact that people

---

517 Restaurateurs Victor and Carina.

518 *Guardian* columnist.

are saying they'll vote Yes or Don't Know because they don't want to sound anti-Scottish.

Jackie is a nice lady and a very good columnist; she emailed me back to say her programme had been recorded before the C4 poll came out. And she agrees that there is something to this 'spiral' thingy.

5 MAY

Amazing email from some young lad who says he works for Gordon Brown, who, apparently, has read the *Yes or No* book, likes it and wants to have a meeting. Of course I say I will, but then I wake up in the middle of the night thinking that maybe this is a hoax!

6 MAY

I phoned Sinclair, who says he's never heard of this Brown emissary but that he will check him out. However, he says Brown did mention me a couple of weeks ago and claimed that I hated him. How come, asked Sinc? It's all due, apparently, to a column Jenny wrote for *The Courier* lambasting Broon for taking so long to get into the Better Together fight. Funny old world.

7 MAY

Wrote a column repeating my view about the spiral of silence – the fact that people are saying they'll vote Yes because they don't want to sound anti-Scottish. And I backed it up with that stuff from the bosses of ICM and Ipsos Mori supporting it. Hope I'm right.

Sinclair says that the Brown email was kosher. I wonder what happens now. Strange man, Broon.

8 MAY

Helluva lot of work on that Radio 4 stuff on Willies[519] – more than I thought I'd have to do and still no contract. Still, I don't want to fall out with the BBC, especially the Radio 4 lot. I love hearing the sound of my own voice. And so do they, apparently.

Dreadful book event at Waterstones. George K and I had to take our own wine to supplement the miserable amount supplied by the History Press. They had insisted that David Torrance[520] and Dr Peter Lynch from Stirling (and Dundee) should be there too, to have some kind of debate. George havered on too long and the other two added bugger all to proceedings. Jenny and Catherine Burns[521] thought the whole thing was crap, but Jose seemed to like it; she's getting really interested now.

Several people buggered off without buying. What a complete waste of time and money.

---

519 People who work in London but live in Edinburgh.

520 Author and commentator.

521 Better Together volunteer.

9 MAY

Great day 'up country'. Went to Alyth to have a look at their referendum roadshow. First-class event and really good that the local newspaper (*The Courier*) is engaging with the public; come to think of it, it's patronising to say it's local newspaper stuff. We should all be doing it – instead of this digital crap. Got a column out of it. This is what I like doing, rather than all this editor rubbish in Edinburgh. Must get out more.

On my way back from Alyth I looked into John Swinney's house to mooch a cup of tea. He wasn't in but phoned later. Still like John and really like Elizabeth, but Mr Swinney's tone was different, as well it might be. Wonder how he'll take defeat? Wonder how I will? He will probably cope better than me and will probably retire on his money to look after Elizabeth. I hope we can stay pals with them both.

11 MAY

Went up to Aberdeen to do a Turcan Connell presentation to some of their clients. They are a very influential but also very below-the-radar sort of firm who have oodles of rich clients, and Douglas Connell, the founding partner, is very careful not to declare for one side or the other of the referendum argument. Mind you, he makes no secret of the fact that he's as black-hearted a Unionist as they come when in private. Very nice but also extremely shrewd man.

I wish I could charge for these things but it's all about Saving the Union. The dinner was attended by a host of understated, but I suspect quite well-heeled, executives from the oil industry; just the sort of people Salmond says are on his side. On the evidence of last night, none of them are! They are all hard-headed blokes who want to remain British and don't believe a word of Eck's claims on the pound.

Quite a good dinner in a nice hotel – at least they're putting me up – and they had Alex Bell along to give the opposite side of the story to mine. He's the former aide to Salmond who quit last July after falling out, spectacularly I hear, with Nat One over the direction of the White Paper. Apparently, Bell thought it should have been much more radical but Alex has chickened out.

However, he delivered a real surprise, at least as far as most of the guests and me were concerned, by declaring that there was no way that the Nats would win. Very strange – and it suggests that the split with Salmond was even more profound than we imagined. Chatham House rules so I couldn't write about it.

13 MAY

Absolutely stupid story in the *Mail* saying that Darling is being sidelined by, of all people, wee Douglas.[522] Hilarious, if it wasn't so damaging. Alistair was furious when I phoned him at 7.30 a.m. I've never heard him swear so much. Completely and utterly stupid – how could anyone believe that wee Dougie could replace anyone? Is there nobody in charge at the *Mail*?

Did a ring-round and the verdict from all – Harrow, Shorthouse,

522 Douglas Alexander.

Mundell – was that it was Dougie himself, and his pals, who had put the story round. What an idiot.

Managed to write an op-ed.

Got another email from the Great Broon's laddie and I'm meeting Broon at the Sheraton. What's this all about? He must want something.

Needless to say I told Darling what Bell had said and, wisely, he commented: 'Chatham House rules are dangerous. The word always gets out.'

14 MAY

Astonishing meeting with Gordon Brown. He was sitting alone, except for his two protection officers, in that vast Sheraton lounge. They moved to the next table when I turned up, leaving Gordon to talk to me alone. He's actually read my bit of the book and cross-questioned me carefully about my background, slagged off poor old Kerevan for being a Trot – 'He was IMG, you know' – and interrogated me about my family – especially the girls. Interestingly, he said he'd been offered a place at Oxford but chose to go to Edinburgh. 'I wish now that I had gone. I think I missed something by not going.' He said that he had lost out as a result; I said he hadn't done badly – Prime Minister and all.

His main theme was essentially that the Better Together team, and especially the Tories, were pitching the campaign as Scotland versus Britain, which he, rightly, says is wrong. It should be that Scotland will be better if it remains within the UK. Osborne, Cameron etc. were wrong – totally wrong – in their approach.

Basically, he thinks everyone is wrong except him. I don't think the campaign is wrong but I can see what he means.

Strange man but quite friendly, and by choosing me I think that suggests he's pretty friendless. Two protection officers were still sitting nearby. What a thankless task.

He was furious and bitter about what he says were lies from Tony Gallagher and Rupert Murdoch over promises he says they made before the 2010 election not to monster him. He cannot believe, surely, that the *Telegraph* would back anyone other than the Tories, can he? Very odd.

However, after pondering all of this for a bit, I think this meeting was all about a piece Jenny wrote for *The Courier*, in which she bashed him for undermining Darling. He was pretty angry about that and kept referring to 'your friend'. 'Your friend said this, your friend said that.' I wondered what he was on about but then I finally twigged that he was talking about Jenny and I said, 'Oh, you mean my wife?'

To which he replied, 'Oh, you married her, did you?' Incredible. He also said he'd read my piece in that day's *Telegraph* where I'd told everyone to calm down and that the good guys were winning. It was an attempt to kill that nonsense story in the *Mail* about Douglas Alexander taking over from Darling.

Gordon said I had got it wrong and that it wasn't Douglas or No. 10 who had planted the story. 'I know what's going on,' he said. But when I asked him to tell me, he repeatedly said that he wouldn't.

Hilarious exchange!

I left, having promised to send a memo to Chris Evans.

Walking back to the office, I then took a frantic call from Michael Forsyth, saying that all his old constituents in Stirling were fed up with a lack of action, they say, from Better Together. I lost my rag with him and told him that I was fed up with such moaning and that if they wanted something done they should bloody well go out and stick some leaflets through letterboxes, like Josephine is doing.

15 MAY

Nice lunch with the new Irish consul, Pat Bourne. Excellent bloke and I introduced him to Angus Grossart and John Swinney in the Parliament restaurant.

Through to Glasgow for drinks with David Cameron. He was in sparkling form, although he looked a bit knackered. He came into the room and immediately took off his tie. He looked slim and fit and held court with the Scottish editors brilliantly. Lots of jokes about the Cup Final, which somebody had told him was between Dundee United and St Johnstone; he said he knew that Brian Taylor was a United fan, to which I told him that there were three or four others in the room, me included.

He thinks that the referendum campaign is going OK and says they had to make the currency announcement early to give it time to seep into the public consciousness. He was surprised to learn that that's what the *Record* leader had said, too, and said he would cut it out and take it back to George Osborne. Thinks Eck is more interested in process than in debating the issues and said he only wanted the debate because it would be against an

English Tory; I said he could forget about the Tory bit as it was only the English bit that Alex wanted to highlight.

He was very preoccupied with giving Holyrood more powers. I said that he was pre-empting Tom Strathclyde's commission, which, needless to say, he denied, and then he went on to, incredibly to my mind, say that there were was nothing wrong with different tax rates in the different parts of the UK.

Eh? Did I hear right?

He says that he's got to stop the Tories being seen as the anti-devolutionists but it seems that he wants them to be the most ardent (and bugger the consequences?).

He made a very good joke about Salmond and Farage. Someone asked him who he disliked most, Salmond or Farage. And he got on to thinking about both of them standing on the cliff edge at Beachy Head. Who would he push off first? 'Oh, Salmond,' he said with a grin. 'Business before pleasure.' Gales of laughter.

This was all supposed to be Chatham House and nobody is supposed to write anything but I bet that joke will get out. And then some po-faced hack – most probably from the *Sunday Herald* – will denounce Cameron. Jesus, what a bloody country.

16 MAY

I texted Tom Strathclyde to warn him that the PM was stitching him up and pre-judging his commission, and he replied that he knew what was going on. Poor old Tom, he'll have to come up with a sell-out on more powers even though he hates the idea.

I then phoned Sinclair to get more gen on that phone call he'd had from Broon about my meeting. He told me yesterday that GB had said I was completely under the sway of Jim Murphy and when I rang Sinclair today he repeated all of that.

According to the Brown analysis, Murphy has now ingratiated himself with Better Together to the extent that he is taking it over, and that it was Murphy and Frank Roy[523] who were now running BT in Murphy's interest so that Murphy could look good with all that Tory money backing him, whereas the United with Labour effort[524] would look puny by comparison. And by saying that it was good for BT that Murphy, Roy and, oh yes, Reid, were all now in the fold, I was effectively saying that they had recruited all of GB's enemies.

Sinclair seemed to go along with this and said it was clear to him and GB that it was Murphy and Roy who had stitched up Alexander over the *Mail* story. Sinky said that Douglas knew what Murphy was up to in advance but had done nothing about it because he never likes to get involved with that sort of stuff.

I thought all of this was absolutely incredible. Here we were fighting to save the Union and those stupid Labour bastards, including the former PM, are more interested in fighting each other. Sinky said he agreed, adding: 'That's why I want to get out of the Labour Party.'

What a mess. If any of this gets out, the BT campaign will be sunk. We are having dinner with the Darlings on Wednesday. I shall tell him everything then, if not before.

---

523 Scottish Labour MP for Motherwell and Wishaw and Better Together's grassroots co-ordinator.

524 Brown's initiative.

Went to dinner with the Linklaters and told Magnus and Jim Naughtie some of the above but NOT the Murphy stuff. That would prove very damaging to the BT campaign if it ever got out. They were both aghast and said I should write it for my memoirs; little do they know! Jim, especially, was very troubled about Broon and said he'd hardly spoken to him since he did that smashing book about Brown and Blair.[525] Mind you, it's no wonder.

18–20 MAY

Took Granny to Sheffield to see brilliant new grandson – Eddie Cochrane. Smashing time had by all, even if the drive was pretty bloody.

21 MAY

Dinner with the Darlings, and what a feast. Maggie is a great cook – fish lasagne preceded by the kind of duck/pancake dish that you normally only get in Chinese restaurants.

Great craic, too. I told Alistair all about the Brown encounter and the Sinclair read-out. His most prominent reaction was to shake his head in bemusement and wonder at the rubbish Brown talked. He was also very funny about his conversations with Gordon.

Broon would castigate him about something that had been said in his book, to which Alistair would say: 'But Gordon, you always say you haven't read my book!'

---

525 *The Rivals: The Intimate Story of a Political Marriage*, published in 2001.

And Gordon always says he never reads the newspapers and yet he can quote whole pages back to you.

Both were very sad about Gordon – incredulous about his reaction to Jenny's piece in *The Courier* but also genuinely concerned about him. Not just the Darlings, but many of Brown's friends, and former friends, are worried about him, stuck in that house in North Queensferry all week with the boys, while his wife is in London.

On the Alexander/Murphy stuff, Alistair was very disparaging about both of them, believing that neither was up to much, but doubted whether the latter was using Better Together to mount a challenge to Miliband, as Gordon seemed to be suggesting. However, he did think that Douglas was the author or at least the mainspring for that rubbish *Mail* story last week which proposed that he should take over from Darling as boss of BT. Laughable that Douglas could run anything.

Darling also doubted if either of them was much use to BT and instead said that he intended to put a great deal of faith into young female MSPs such as Jenny Marra and Kezia Dugdale,[526] who were sharper and much more likely to attract new voters.

And he was hugely enthusiastic about Frank Roy. 'He gets things done and rings up every afternoon to find out what's going on, what needs doing and who's doing what. He has transformed the office.'

Oh yes and Maggie – Darling always calls her Margaret – says she is collating all the cybernat stuff but I don't think she'll have much chance in identifying the culprits, although Alistair is very

---

526 Labour MSP for the Lothian region.

frustrated that somebody – he means newspapers like the *Telegraph* – cannot devote more resources to cracking this. He's probably right but I've no idea how to go about it.

They are very funny together – him always talking about how bad a time he had at Loretto and her teasing him about it and telling him to shut up. She can't wait until the referendum campaign is over and Jenny is right that she'd kill him if he tried to be a major figure in British politics again. It's obvious that Miliband is useless but I don't think Balls or anyone else has anything to worry about from Darling. Especially as Labour won't win.

Thank God Darling is in charge here.

22 MAY

Out of interest I had a look at some of the cybernat reaction to Jenny's *Telegraph* blog and was amazed to find that one of them – Guga – had stated that he knew where we both lived. Why would he need to know that? He also denounced me as a fascist – Quisling – and pointed out that Jenny was South African and presumably also a neo-Nazi (even though her father fought apartheid and had to flee the country) and therefore not entitled to have a view on independence.

They really are a creepy lot.

Incredible story whereby the professors of all of Scotland's top medical schools have written an open letter saying that independence would be terrible for research funding, and saying that because they had been browbeaten into silence it did not mean that they were supporters of separation.

As usual, not a bloody word on the BBC news, even though I rang Boothman and Mullin.[527] All they had were endless tales about the Celtic manager resigning. When they eventually did it the following morning, they played it all down and took the Nat line. No wonder Mullin is fed up with BBC Scotland; they are really, really useless. Crap from top to bottom. They wouldn't know a story if it hit them between the bloody eyes. Their best political reporter, Glen Campbell, had a silly wee story about the CBI, whereas their 'referendum reporter', somebody called Laura Bicker, completely missed the professors' story. Jesus.

Voted early in the Euro elections for that Lib Dem shit George Lyon.[528] I only did it to try to stop that even bigger shit Tasmina whatshername[529] getting the third Euro-seat for the Nats. I should have voted for UKIP but couldn't bring myself to, but Salmond et al. are very worried that they'll win that seat, which would disprove once and for all the nonsense that Scots are massively in love with the EU. The fact that he keeps telling people not to vote UKIP means that he's worried that they'll win a seat. Fingers crossed.

25 MAY

Trouble looms for the Treasury over too many briefings on their set-up figures. Both the *Sunday Herald* and the *Sunday Times* have splashed with attacks by Eck on their figures. No surprise about

---

527 John Mullin, referendum editor at BBC Scotland.

528 Lib Dem MEP and former MSP for Argyll and Bute.

529 Tasmina Ahmed-Sheikh, a former Conservative candidate for the Scottish Parliament and Labour Party member before joining the SNP in 2000.

either – the latter is just as bad as the former when it comes to supporting the Nats.

26 MAY

UKIP win that third seat! Wonderful scenes – Nats furious, as are Labour, but David Martin, the veteran Labour MEP, says the UKIP bloke should write a thank-you letter to Eck for talking up their chances. The UKIP MEP says he will. He looks and sounds like a complete idiot. The first thing he said to Bernard Ponsonby of STV was: 'Oh good, you'll know where all the gay bars in Brussels are!'

Salmond has completely lost it, blaming the BBC for UKIP's success, whereas Nicola was sensible about EU powers, saying that she'd stick up for Scotland.

27 MAY

Stupid, totally stupid *Record* and *Sun* – seriously stupid leaders. They just don't get it rc: immigrants, wittering on about how they oppose UKIP's policy on immigration and blethering about how Scotland rejects all that stuff. Don't they realise that it's their readers who're voting for UKIP and who hate immigrants?

28 MAY

Huge Treasury balls-up materialises after all. *FT* attacks them on the front page for misquoting that LSE professor over start-up costs.[530] The *FT* was right to blast them but, not for the first time, the *FT* is totally wrong to say that Dunleavy's words formed the basis of the Treasury start-up costs document. Unfortunately, the idiots in the Treasury press office have been briefing about that bloody document since last Friday and the Nats have got hold of Dunleavy, who's having a fit about being misquoted, and have monstered the Treasury thanks to their tame hacks – starting with the *Sunday Herald* and *Sunday Times*. Stupid, really stupid. Needless to say, Downing Street deny all knowledge. Danny Alexander tried to rescue the issue by repeating again and again that the Dunleavy assessment was NOT the total basis for their paper. But nobody is listening. Why can't London get anything right?

Luckily, Swinney saved the day by refusing to say, umpteen times, what the SNP estimate of start-up costs was. Astonishing difference between Scottish and London papers in reporting what happened. The London lot are still havering on about the balls-up, whereas the Scottish ones have moved on. *FT* leader seriously and incredibly wrong but everyone genuflects to the *FT*. It's pretty crap, really. Just as well none of the punters read it.

Went through to Glasgow for lunch with Tom Strathclyde. The noble lord gave me the full SP on his commission report, which, as I suspected, is a total cave-in to the Nats. Tom has simply followed orders and come up with what Cameron wants. Amazingly stupid.

---

530 Professor Patrick Dunleavy said an independent Scotland would have to spend £150–£200 million on new administrative structures to replace existing UK bodies. The Treasury quoted a figure of £2.7 billion.

29 MAY

Lunch with Eddie Barnes, who, surprisingly, didn't want to tell me about the Strathclyde Commission; he wants, quite rightly, to do it as a one-hit wonder. I didn't tell him that I knew all about it.

30 MAY

Brilliant. Eck in real trouble over his made-up figures over the cost of independence, but again the London columnists – Simon Jenkins in *The Guardian* – get it wrong, although they have a great story about how, surprise, surprise, Scotland isn't the richest country in the world. Jenkins doesn't seem to know what devo max really is; mind you, nor do most punters.

Got Simon to write up the Strathclyde stuff and then, much later, I texted Eddie Barnes, as well as Ben Thomson,[531] to tell them we were doing it. Courtesy, really. Also spoke to Forsyth, who's been squared and isn't going to bash the plans, at least not until after the referendum. He said that the *Sunday Times* had been on to him about the story. He didn't tell them anything.

1 JUNE

Shouldn't have bothered telling Barnes; he's playing a double game – he didn't tell me that Ruth D had written a piece for the *SoS*. No more deals with him!

---

531 The chairman of the Reform think tank is an advocate of devo plus and so had an interest in the Strathclyde Commission.

1 JUNE

It had to happen but now the journalists at BBC Scotland are threatening to go on strike over the sacking, or rather the termination of contract, of Gary Robertson. The NUJ claim that the Beeb say they can't afford Robertson any more because they have hired loads of expensive hacks from London – specifically Jim Naughtie, Sarah Smith[532] and John Mullin. It's not really Robertson's plight that they're moaning about, it's more that they object to émigré Jocks being brought back in time for the referendum. The reality is that the BBC had to as there's just not enough depth of talent in Scotland to handle such a big story.

Jim is really brilliant. Everyone takes the piss – quite rightly – when he does his flowery 'word pictures' about all sorts of squitter. But he really is a class act and the fact that he has bought a house in Edinburgh now means he can spend half a week presenting *Good Morning Scotland* and the other half doing *Today*.

He is far from complimentary about what he found when he arrived at Pacific Quay but he is diplomatic enough to keep schtum about it. He is a huge and very welcome addition to the Scottish journalistic community – a genuine lad o'pairts.

I do like Sarah and think she was a very good Washington correspondent for Channel 4, but she lost her way with them when she came back and didn't get the presenter's job. It's been absolutely outrageous the way she's been monstered by the cybernats about her Labour credentials. And I've never watched her *Scotland 2014* programme.

---

532 Television journalist and eldest daughter of John Smith, former Labour leader.

John Mullin, who was deputy editor of *The Scotsman* and recently editor of the *Independent on Sunday*, has been brought up by Boothman to run BBC Scotland's referendum unit. Mind you, nobody seems to know what he does and neither, if truth be told, does he. I've had a couple of beers with John, who's an old pal, and he says that all he seems to do is go to meetings, and sometimes it's meetings about more meetings.

He's hopeful that things will get better as we head for the big day ... but I wouldn't bet on it.

Overall, BBC Scotland does need a major kick up the arse but I can't see why they picked on Gary Robertson – he's one of their very best.

2 JUNE

To Glasgow for the Great Strathclyde sell-out. That's being a bit harsh, I know, and poor old Tom was just following orders, but it really is a load of total mince. And I said as much on TV.

But then I walked to the Better Together offices and the transformation was startling. Lots of activity – people running around, getting things done. Frank Roy masterminding everything from the top table with Mark McInnes, who's the director general or something of the Scottish Tories, sitting next to him and saying that he's the most left-wing of them all.

I was persuaded by all those eager young people that what the Tories were doing was 'for the greater good'. Hmmm, we'll see.

4 JUNE

First things first: I would have much preferred it if Alistair Darling hadn't likened Alex Salmond to that odious North Korean dictator or used those 'blood and soil' comparisons.[533] Such language always cheapens political debate. But in saying that, I'm bound to add that it could only have been a matter of time before the former Chancellor responded in kind to the type of abuse he's had to suffer since agreeing to front the Better Together campaign.

And if the referendum debate is now plumbing new depths, Salmond need look no further than his own mirror for the principal culprit. He has stood by for years while his followers have traduced and grossly insulted all and everyone who opposed them. All he had to do to stop it was say the word, call off his dogs, and those appalling nutters – there's no better word for them – would have been silenced.

All we got instead were weasel words which purported to suggest that both sides of the referendum debate were as guilty as each other. That was a damn lie and Alex Salmond knew it to be so.

The first time I was called Quisling, I laughed it off, as I probably did quite a few of the later times, too. But Vidkun Quisling was a fascist traitor to Norway, his homeland, and that's what they still call me. Why should anyone have to put up with that kind of insult?

Why does Salmond allow his cybernats to roam at will over the internet, spreading their poison wherever they choose to land?

---

533 The *New Statesman* said Darling, in an interview with the magazine, compared Salmond to Kim Jong-il.

Why, for instance, do they take perverse delight in telling their opponents that they know their addresses, if it's not to issue a veiled threat?

As ye sow, so shall ye reap.

Labour presser in Edinburgh at which the Great Broon outlines his, frankly remarkable, speaking tour: thirteen venues from Inverness to the Borders. Brilliant, and he was in great form, too, cracking jokes, smiling – truly amazing – but he still looks, well, not all there. Gave it an over-the-top write-up. Hope I'm right.

5 JUNE

I'm always asking this bloody question but it keeps cropping up: is anyone with even half a brain in charge of the London end of presentation for the anti-separatist campaign?

The latest from the maniacs in the Treasury is a bunch of unbelievably crass, stupid and patronising decisions to use Lego figures and a load of tripe about how many fish suppers and portions of mushy peas could be bought with the £1,400 per head that the Treasury says we'll all get if we vote No in the referendum.

The Whitehall geniuses who dreamed up this rubbish refused to listen when Better Together headquarters in Glasgow told them that they shouldn't proceed with their loony tunes idea. The upshot has been a deserved kicking from every corner of the media, most notably from my colleague Fraser Nelson in the *Telegraph* yesterday.

And, as usual, both sides of the coalition are blaming each other. Mundell said it was all signed off by Danny Alexander. Oh no, it wasn't, say the Lib Dems. Oh yes, it was, say the Tories. And so it goes on.

Anyway, let's say it again: everything, but everything, connected with the No campaign must be approved by the Better Together team in Glasgow. No exceptions whatsoever – and with a bit of luck that might mean no more Lego men or squitter about fish suppers.

Fantastic news. Obama has pitched in against the Nats and grabbed all the headlines. Brilliant. Eck caught completely off guard. Wonderful.

6 JUNE

Lunch with John Reid in Glasgow. He insisted on curry at the Koh-i-Noor. Delicious, but I can't eat curry at this time of day. Great craic, much of it slagging off Broon, who, John reckons, is certifiable and he's probably right. He told me that he once pushed Brown up against the wall in the Members' Lobby, when they were both in the Cabinet, and threatened to punch him unless he stopped seeing conspiracies everywhere. Wish I'd been there to see it, but there is nothing strange in any of this as everyone knows they hate each other.

What I didn't know is that, according to John, Brown begged him to stay in his Cabinet when he took over from Blair. No way, said Reid.

But he does admit that Brown can be a brilliantly successful player in this campaign.

JR is in great form and about to enter the campaign proper

himself, thank goodness, insisting quite properly that voting No does not make you any less of a Scot. He's doing it in Stirling, where he studied, taught and got his doctorate in some Marxist nonsense or other.

He is fully engaged with BT and really does believe in the all-party nature of the thing. I think some of those Labour guys deserve recognition for doing what they're doing in this all-party format. They're getting a terrible kicking from the Nats for being in bed with the Tories. Mind you, they hate the Nats and they know that if Scotland leaves the UK, Labour is sunk.

7 JUNE

Jose off to London. House empty. Jenny bereft.

8 JUNE

ONLY 100 days to go. Christ! I can't imagine anything will change. Everyone is behind their entrenched positions and defending them to the death. Will I survive? Will anyone?

9 JUNE

Glasgow again! This time for a Better Together event in Maryhill which was 'pure dead brilliant'. Really good, with lots of ordinary people. Unfortunately, word keeps seeping through that Brown is causing trouble – slagging off Cameron for making it a Scotland versus England contest, which is what he said to me. Idiot. And then to make it worse he said, in London at the Press Gallery lunch, that Cameron should debate with Salmond. That did it. I got back to Edinburgh and monstered him, good and proper. But then I phoned Reid and persuaded him that lots of Labour people, such as him, attacking Brown would do more harm than good and he agreed, although he said if he was cornered by TV he might say something. Brown must have known that the agreed BT position is that if Salmond wants a debate, he can have one with Darling, but that would never do.

Had a long chat with Tom Brown[534] while writing my Broon diatribe and even Tom says he's finished with Gordon. He says his whole behaviour is about looking good and saving the Union single-handedly. And of course he wants Alistair to get none of the credit – absolutely none.

Brown thinks that the whole of BT is an anti-Gordon conspiracy and Jim Murphy is the ringleader. Said Jim to me at the BT thing in Glasgow: 'We are bending over backwards to help that guy and this is what we get.'

Got a midnight 'well done' from John Reid, who'd read my piece online. Very funny. Says I won't get invited back for coffee in North Queensferry.

10 JUNE

Helluva story. Simon J told me that he had had an email from Campbell Gunn which, although it pretended to be 'clarifying'

---

534 Scottish political journalist, now retired.

the fact that that Lally[535] woman who'd featured in yesterday's Better Together re-launch wasn't all she appeared, was actually a very clumsy attempt at blackening her character. And worse, the stupid bugger wrote it down in black and white. Although Gunn is a mate, or rather, until he went over to the dark side was a mate, I had no second thoughts.

Once these hacks decide to work for a political party – any political party – they're the enemy as far as I'm concerned.

I have attacked all of them at one time or another since the start of the Scottish Parliament – David Whitton,[536] who worked on *The Courier* with me and played in the same football team in Dundee, and who was Dewar's spad; Peter MacMahon,[537] who worked for Henry, and who dreamed up the phrase when poor old H had to resign, saying it was 'a muddle not a fiddle' and who was horrified when I told him he was now the 'enemy' when he got the job. And Ramsay Jones has been lambasted all of the time for what I've always thought was his uselessness for the Tories.

Gunn should be sacked for attempting to denigrate Lally, saying she wasn't just an ordinary mum but actually a Labour activist and, worse, in Gunn's eyes, a relative of Pat Lally, the former Labour Lord Provost of Glasgow. In fact, she wasn't anything of the sort – a huge mistake.

We went to town on it – splashing it and calling for his head. I got a bit of flak; after all, Gunn was a popular bloke when he

---

535 Clare Lally, former Mum of the Year and Carers' Champion.
536 Former Labour MSP for Strathkelvin and Bearsden.
537 Former press spokesman for Henry McLeish.

was on the press corridor, and I expected to get a battering. I said again on TV that he was a pal but that he still had to be sacked or resign.

12 JUNE

Huge follow-ups everywhere – with most people calling for his head on the grounds that what he'd done was a clear breach of the code that is supposed to govern the work of special advisors. Eck was at his most unctuous but he was also pretty good in defending his man, aided and abetted by the fact that Johann Lamont tried to fit Gunn up with all sorts of other offences committed by the cybernats.

Gunn survived that day and as a result he'll probably stay in post. It's ridiculous but not entirely unexpected. Nobody will believe me when I say it's not personal but they should believe me when I say this is a serious business. I'm determined not to let the Nats away with anything in this campaign. It's much too important.

I'm not surprised I'm not very popular. Campbell is extremely well liked by both hacks and politicians and, of course, that's why he got the job. It was an entirely cynical move by Salmond to make him a spad, and furthermore to make him the 'go-to' spad for the hacks. The latter, went the thinking, would always believe what Campbell said. No longer, I hope.

14 JUNE

Jose had a great time in London – working at Westminster. She did half a week with Margaret Curran and the other half with David Mundell. In both cases she effectively worked with their researchers/secretaries but both Margaret and David put in a fair bit of time with her, which was very good of them.

I knew that Mundell and Andrew Dunlop had a huge surprise prepared but I didn't tip her off. After giving her a tour of No. 10, she was ushered into the presence of the Prime Minister. She saw him in the Cabinet Room and was so surprised that she says she couldn't think of anything to say to him. He was, needless to say, charm personified. Great.

16 JUNE

Wee Eck's arrogance knows no bounds. 'I'll still be in charge in two years' time,' he says in a *Daily Record* interview.

Now, if he wins the referendum, I've no doubt at all that he would still be top dog. But if he loses? I suppose it does depend on the margin but I'd be very surprised indeed if there wasn't a glint in the eyes of several leading Nats in such circumstances.

Principal amongst them would be Alex Neil – definitely – Derek Mackay – maybe – and Nicola Sturgeon – without a shadow of a scintilla of a doubt.

She's a very ambitious lady is Nicola. As always: cherchez la femme!

18 JUNE

I don't know why I bother sometimes. I did a favour for Brigadier Mel Jameson, the regimental colonel of the Royal Scots Dragoon Guards, Scotland's only armoured regiment. I publicised their commemoration of the fact that there's a year to go before they celebrate the 200th anniversary of Waterloo, where the Scots Greys launched their famous charge. That's right, a year to go!

I was a bit miffed to be asked, as the brigadier who's now in charge of the Tattoo – as Mel used to be – didn't invite me to last year's event. Oh, what the hell, I like Mel and enjoy doing army things and maybe I'll get invited this year.[538]

19 JUNE

Astonishing scenes at FMQs when we were attacked, or at least mentioned in disparaging terms, ten times by Eck over Simon J's great story about how his civil servants had been tasked to produce a rushed report on the start-up costs for an independent Scotland.

He really does look like he's losing it and from the look on the faces of Nicola Sturgeon and John Swinney – who both seemed to be studying their shoes – they thought so too.

Still, I can't complain about this sort of publicity: it proves what Salmond said to me ages ago: 'The *Telegraph* IS the opposition.' Quite right, too.

It also allowed me to write a fairly pompous column, about how we will never be silenced. Pure hokum, of course.

---

538 He wasn't.

25 JUNE

The Nats have signalled the end of council house sales. A sad day, made worse by some of the rubbish talked by the Nats and Labour. The Housing Minister Margaret Burgess,[539] who can read a brief written for her but that's about all, said that council house sales had 'no place in the Scotland we want to build'.

Jesus, what kind of Scotland would that be? Her views were echoed with knobs on by Labour's Mary Fee,[540] who wanted the ban accelerated to one year instead of two. It's pure class war. These people don't understand, or actually hate, the freedom council house sales gave to people like my parents and thousands of others like them.

And Ms Fee would certainly not have known that the policy was almost in the Labour manifesto in the '70s. According to the fascinating memoirs of Bernard Donoughue,[541] Callaghan's[542] policy advisor, it was only Douglas Jay[543] who blocked Labour bringing in the policy that Thatcher later championed, enabling her to win over Essex Man and the C2s.

Douglas Jay, for God's sake! And I confirmed the fact of his father's opposition with Peter Jay,[544] his son, when I met him up in the Glen a couple of years ago.

---

539 SNP MSP for Cunninghame South.

540 Labour MSP for West Scotland.

541 Head of the No. 10 Policy Unit from 1974 to 1979, first under Harold Wilson, then under Callaghan. He became a life peer in 1985.

542 Labour Prime Minister from 1976 to 1979.

543 Labour MP for Battersea North from 1946 to 1983. He became a life peer in 1987.

544 Broadcaster and diplomat who was married to James Callaghan's daughter Margaret (now Baroness) Jay.

27 JUNE

It really does piss me off, the amount of moaning and groaning that those opposed to independence do. Why isn't there more passion, why can't we get more No posters, why are Yes always on the telly. Jesus – what a shower.

When Jose went to a canvassing meeting the other night at Better Together with a lot of middle-aged, middle-class wifies, she discovered that none of them – not one – had ever knocked on a door or handed out a leaflet. It's all been a bit beneath them. Still, I suppose that now that they're turning up at the Better Together offices means something; they are at last prepared to stir themselves.

30 JUNE

Definite signs of the beginning of the Nat campaign to keep BBC Scotland under their thumb when around 350 nutters staged a demo outside Pacific Quay in Glasgow, bearing banners complaining about the 'one-sided conveyor belt of scare stories' being run by the Beeb. I wonder who thought up that wee phrase for them. Needless to say, the Nats claim it's nowt to do with them. Oh sure.

Jim Murphy is quite right – it is bullying, pure and simple.

2 JULY

Op-ed for main edition about the Queen's role in Scotland – mostly colour but did suggest (gently, cos I'm a coward) that she needn't be so bloody neutral about the whole independence thing.

23 JULY

Back from holidays to discover – surprise, surprise – that Eck's vow not to allow politics intrude into the Commonwealth Games didn't last very long. Singing Glasgow's praises on the eve of the opening ceremony, he calls it 'Freedom City' because he reckons it's going to vote Yes in the referendum. Freedom from what, pray? And anyway, Labour say they haven't given up on holding the Dear Green Place.

24 JULY

Cabinet reshuffle. Great relief that Hammond is out of the MoD – he must be the worst Defence Secretary we've ever had since poor old Fred Mulley,[545] perhaps, who fell asleep watching a fly-past. Hammond caused any amount of damage in Scotland and I can't believe he's been promoted, even if, as Foreign Secretary, he can't do too much damage.

Games opening ceremony. Jenny and the girls thought it was dreadful. I agreed that the start was awful, truly awful, but the rest made up for it.

25 JULY

Mother of poor little Mikaeel Kular jailed for killing him. Dreadful circumstances again – yet another child battered to death by the very person who is supposed to love and cherish him.

---

545 Labour Secretary of State for Defence from 1976 to 1979.

Hellish. Wrote one of those 'something must be done' type columns. Dreadful story.

30 JULY

Panic! Went to the Orchard for a quiet drink with Jenny. Andy S[546] was there and we were having a blether when I got an emergency text from George Kerevan, saying that he was in Blackwell's book shop doing a stint about our book. 'Where the hell are you?' he asked. Shit, I'd forgotten all about it. This was around 6.45 p.m., the event started at 6.30 p.m. and Blackwell's is at the other end of town. Jenny said I had to go anyway so I rushed out of the pub, wearing a scabby old short-sleeved T-shirt and some gnarled flip-flops, and eventually got a taxi up to the book shop opposite the university.

There was the usual mixed bag of Nats, oddballs, people with nothing better to do – maybe thirty in all. George had done his bit and so I was on straight away to talk to the assembled throng. Did quite well, even if I say so myself, completely off the cuff, and then we took questions, which were, frankly, a complete waste of time.

We sold the grand total of four books; George signed three and I signed one. What a farce. I spent about twenty quid on taxis and for what? Really useless, that so-called marketing department for the History Press.

---

546 Andy Speight, neighbour.

6 AUGUST

Who would really have thought it? Darling smashed Eck in the first debate last night. Everyone on the Nat side of the argument, including that eejit Blair Jenkins, supposed boss of the Yes campaign, has been crowing about how much of a hammering Darling was going to get. I wasn't especially worried as these debates never add much to the sum of human knowledge or affect the result much. But, still, I texted a 'break a leg' message to Alistair all the same – more in hope than expectation, I'm bound to say.

However, it wasn't needed. Not at all. Salmond was hopeless. It looked like he hadn't done any preparation at all and got absolutely skewered on the pound, which Darling returned to again and again.

Darling's best moment, and the one that had the over-confident Salmond stuck for an answer, came when he asked his opponent to 'contemplate for one moment that you might be wrong'. Of course, Alex Salmond never believes he's wrong – so he was stumped.

But the strangest Eck moment came when he used his bit of the exchanges to witter on about some claims from the No side that we'd have to drive on the other side of the road after independence. And even more bizarre was when he asked Darling if Better Together believed that an independent Scotland would be 'more susceptible to attack by aliens'. Eh?

The Nats are shell-shocked this morning. Their hero has been hammered. Is this their worst moment? I bloody well hope so – BT have got to get cracking now and keep up the pressure.

10 AUGUST

Absolutely hilarious article in the Nat-supporting *Sunday Herald*. Some weeks ago, Gina next door said that they'd rented their house out to some actors. I wasn't really listening to her until she said the name of the principal lodger: David Hayman. My God, I thought, he is a real Nat, wears his nationalism on his sleeve, and the play he's in is a real Nat-fest.

Jenny wrote a blog for the *Telegraph* a few weeks ago, with tongue firmly in cheek, about what it would be like to have the 'enemy' living next door. She never mentioned who it was and refused to say when people began asking.

Now that stupid prat, Hayman, has 'outed' himself in a state of high dudgeon and complained about Jenny's 'worrying attack', expressing his bewilderment at the venom directed against him. He is clearly typical of most Nats in completely lacking a sense of humour and has made himself look an even bigger fool by talking to the po-faced *Sunday Herald*.

The article is all the more daft, given that Jose has been baby-sitting for some of the people in Hayman's party, I have been moving their rubbish bags to the street bins and Jenny even offered to let them have showers in our house when they discovered that their boiler had broken down. Why would we have done any of those things if we had really believed that Hayman was an 'enemy'? I actually think he's a smashing actor but on this showing he's not much of a human being.

And, sad to say, I never got round to seeing his play.

14 AUGUST

I am completely fed up with the Book Festival: it's little more than a *Guardian* love-in. OK, they sponsor the bloody thing, but under the present direction it's like *The Guardian* writ large, a whole host of right-on chairpersons introducing a similar bunch of authors. That's a bit of an exaggeration, I admit, but not too much of one.

The upshot is that I don't plan to attend much or give it much space this year.

The exception is Roy Hattersley[547] but, infuriatingly, his is the one lecture that, because of too much referendum stuff going on, I couldn't attend.

However, Mark and Colette Douglas-Home[548] rescued everything by having us to dinner with the Hatts, as well as Ming and Elspeth Campbell.[549]

Great night – fabulous cooking by Colette – and lots of anti Nat plotting and insulting. A great deal of time was also taken up by me singing the praises of Stevie May, whom Roy's beloved Sheffield Wednesday has just signed from St Johnstone. I told him what a great player he is – and how he ruined my hopes of Dundee United winning the Scottish Cup this year by scoring the Saints' second goal. Swine!

There's no point in trying to out-anecdote Roy; he's done everything, been everywhere and knows everyone. But he is great company and I like him a lot. He is still staunch Labour and he

---

547 Former Labour MP for Sheffield and former deputy party leader.

548 Columnist for *The Herald*.

549 Former Lib Dem leader and his wife.

had a bet on next year's election. I said the Tories would be the biggest party. He said Labour. Stake? Dinner at Rules in Maiden Lane!

16 AUGUST

Bad news for No – Prof. Tom Devine has announced that he is to vote Yes. It's not all that surprising, given that Tom has immersed himself in Scottish culture and Scottish history, but his reasons for doing so, outlined in an interview with *The Observer*, include a great deal of havers about how he thinks that Scotland now embodies all the virtues of fairness and the like that used to be associated with Britishness. Tripe. But, still, I've always admired Devine and fear people will listen to him. I hope not.

17 AUGUST

Fantastic story from a financial services 'Deep Throat', who must remain nameless. He gave me chapter and verse of a letter being sent out by Speirs and Jeffrey, a 100-year-old Glasgow stockbrokers, warning that they'd set up new companies and bank accounts in England so that all their customers' assets could be transferred at a moment's notice if there's a Yes vote. I gave it big licks on the front page.

In radio interviews Eck says he has a Plan B, after all, on the currency but he won't say what it is. Jesus, what a klutz. He also still insists that the Treasury is bluffing. In his dreams.

18 AUGUST

Salmond has set up a new nutty Nat outfit called N-56 – something to do with Scotland's latitude or longitude – and which is run by a bloke[550] who used to work for Eck. It says that there's oodles of oil left in the North Sea, enough to last forever apparently. Good old Prof. Jim Gallagher was on *Today* programme and called it 'the economics of the tooth fairy'. Brilliant.

20 AUGUST

It had to happen. Alex Neil has taken the Nats' NHS campaign to the ultimate, claiming that a No vote will lead to the health service being ABOLISHED. Christ, what a bunch.

I did another of these interminable debates with George Kerevan on our wee book, only this time in the Scottish Parliament with Tricia Marwick, the Presiding Officer, in the chair. Not much of a debate and we sold about ten books. Afterwards I was assailed by a very posh lady who moaned at me for equating the Yes campaign with Alex Salmond. She said there was more to them than him. 'Well, tell him that, then,' I advised her. What a joke – Eck is their campaign. If they don't like that they should get rid of him.

---

550 Dan Macdonald was on the advisory board of Yes Scotland when he launched N-56.

21 AUGUST

London are really getting interested in this story – which will be a pity, I fear. Ben Clissitt,[551] wants a full memo on who's doing what in the referendum campaign. I tell him … but I bet I never hear another word about it. Typical waste of bloody time.

22 AUGUST

Was told by some Labour eejit that former Labour First Minister Henry McLeish was going to vote Yes, so I wrote it.[552]

25 AUGUST

Disaster! Darling hammered.[553] The whole thing was terrible. It was pretty clear that the Better Together side were playing for a draw and, as Alex Ferguson[554] would have told them, if you play for a draw you get a hiding. I texted Darling beforehand to wish him all the best but my 'break a leg' message didn't seem to encourage him. The BBC buggered up the thing in spades.

They were so determined to make it bigger and better and different from the poor old STV one a few weeks earlier that they made a complete and utter gutter of the whole bloody thing.

---

551 Then the *Telegraph*'s director of visual journalism.

552 He didn't come out for Yes.

553 In the second televised debate between Darling and Salmond.

554 Former manager of Manchester United.

For starters, the venue[555] was much too grand and instead of having Glenn Campbell – the moderator – between the two contestants, they made him stand to one side. Stupid. Both Sinclair and Kevin Pringle had said that he should stand between the two contestants, but the Beeb decided to be different and made him stand to one side. The upshot was that he couldn't hear – or at least didn't seem to be able to hear – what Salmond and Darling were shouting at each other. The whole thing was chaotic, but much worse than anything the two principals were saying were the questions from the audience.

Unlike Ponsonby in the first debate, Campbell didn't seem to know where the Nats, anti-Nats and don't knows were sitting. The upshot was that out of thirteen questions, ten were from Nats attacking Darling – including one calling him a hypocrite – and only three from the No side.

But that aside, Alistair wasn't good ... in fact, he was less than that. It was very bad. And worst of all, it will put new heart in the Nats.

Afterwards, I tried to gee him up, but Alistair simply replied to my text with the understatement 'audience two-thirds Nat'.

26 AUGUST

All the papers, including me, give the verdict to Salmond; there's not much point in pissing about. Jose says that her pal, whose sister works at the BT headquarters in Glasgow, says that the

---

555   Kelvingrove Art Gallery and Museum in Glasgow.

atmosphere there is very subdued today. Is this the worst moment in the campaign? Or is there more to come? Christ, I hope not.

27 AUGUST

I wrote a column accusing the Nats of being desperate but the truth is that it's me who's desperate for some good news. Jesus, we are in a bad place at present; I wonder if the Nats know how buggered we are.

The only good news is that Charlie Kennedy did a TV debate with John Swinney and slaughtered him on the currency, telling him 'you're stuffed' if the Nats don't come up with a better economic policy.

Why can't we have Charlie down here in the Central Belt where he's needed? He'd go down a treat. And we have pubs here, too, Charlie! Sorry, that's a cheap trick.

27 AUGUST

John Swinney has long ago cast off his 'Honest John' mantle and I don't get much out of him now. The days when he used to phone me for advice, when he was party leader, are gone. There was one strange day – it must have been more than ten years ago because I remember we were still living in Great King Street – when John Swinney and Jack McConnell, who was then Labour leader and First Minister, both phoned me for advice within ten or twenty minutes of each other.

And, of course, both were at one of the girls' christenings.

Bridget McConnell[556] accused me of 'trophy collecting' after I'd fallen out with Jack.

Anyway, John is as brazen as Eck now about the currency issue, repeating in a TV debate (with Charlie Kennedy) Salmond's daft claim that Darling admitted that 'of course' Scotland could use sterling. What Darling had actually said, in the BBC debate, was that Scotland could go down the sterlingisation[557] route but that that was not much of a solution.

28 AUGUST

Had lunch with Mundell in the new Mussel and Steak Bar to thank him and his son for looking after Jose when she was working as an intern at the Commons. Very good session, during which he repeated the story that Alistair Carmichael is to be replaced by Jo Swinson[558] as Scottish Secretary.

Jesus – Big Al has been pretty crap as SoS, nothing like as good as Michael Moore, but Jo Swinson! Gimme a break. Not more than three people in Scotland know who the hell she is, and they're all probably related to her. For Chrissake, when she was first an elected MP the late and great John Farquhar Munro[559] thought she was the new Lib Dem group typist! Very sexist, I know, but then John wasn't very PC. There's still hope for Alistair – he needs some better advice – but not her. Please.

---

556   Wife of Jack and chief executive of Culture and Sport for Glasgow City Council.

557   Using sterling without the approval of the rest of the UK.

558   Lib Dem MP for East Dunbartonshire and Minister for Employment Relations.

559   Lib Dem MSP (d. January 2014).

It's pretty clear that the Nats and their goons are targeting Jim Murphy on his round-Scotland tour. He's getting more and more nutters at his meetings and things are increasingly ugly. But when I speak to Jim he's perfectly happy. The truth is that, perhaps, he is a lightning conductor and is content to attract the bad guys. Why not – they make Yes look very bad!

29 AUGUST

Big, big day. We had a major story reporting that as well as the 100-plus businessmen[560] who are backing No, there are at least as many who're saying that they couldn't back the No cause because they'd been leant on and were frightened of dire repercussions if they'd signed the letter.

Fantastic stuff.

Then we got two videos of Jim Murphy. The first was of his treatment in Dundee the day before, when the mob turned out to monster him. Very ugly, but actually made out to be even uglier by the fact that the reporters from *The Courier* in Dundee had never seen such a political confrontation in their lives. Still, good stuff.

But then, and too late for my edition, we had the egg-throwing incident against Jim in Kirkcaldy and then, brilliantly dramatic, Jim called off – on police advice, he says – the rest of his tour until he got assurances there'd be no more attacks. Puts Eck on the spot a bit and he looks like a prat for attacking

---

560 More than 120 business leaders signed a letter on 20 August backing the Union.

Murphy but actually Jim is playing up to it. All in a good cause, of course.

All through these hectic days I keep getting emails from Archie Stirling – mostly very funny but also serious – about how he's worried about the result, about how he thinks BT are 'crap', about how the Nats are tearing down his No posters from his fields, and about how I've – ME – got to do something. Neither he nor I have any idea what I'm supposed to be doing!

Still, he is a great bloke, very committed, and says that Eck is dividing this country in a terrible way – with massive repercussions. I don't quote him in my column, instead call him a 'Stirling farmer'. That's a bit rich; it's not many farmers who give their name to the whole county. But as Archie says: 'We've been here for 800 years but if that bastard wins, I'm off.' And as for there being a 'mature debate' on the issue, he says that's absolute nonsense. He's right on that.

The *Scotsman* newspaper gets stranger and stranger. They were given that letter signed by Scots businessmen backing No as an exclusive but, incredibly, they buried it on an inside page. Absolutely bonkers. But more than that, it's a dereliction of duty. However, today they put the opposite side of the story – that is, those businessmen who support Yes – on their front page, in spite of the fact that it was given to their arch-rivals on *The Herald*! What the bloody hell is happening at that paper?

29 AUGUST

Thank God for the *Today* programme. It had a mad Business for Scotland spokesman[561] on talking about how much support there was for the Nats in their ranks and claiming that British embassies abroad were in the habit of charging Scottish companies for using their premises when English companies got it gratis. He was repeatedly challenged on this by Justin Wotsisname[562] and kept repeating it. Eventually, the Foreign Office minister in charge of such things[563] phoned in to rubbish the entire claim. But not before that idiot Angus Brendan McNeil MP said that voting No would see Scotland kicked out of international football. No evidence, of course. Another case of 'post-ceilidh foolishness', no doubt.

30 AUGUST

Phone call from Bill Jamieson,[564] who congratulates me on monstering *The Scotsman* about their ludicrous failure to do their own story big but instead give top billing to a stupid story in *The Herald* about a bunch of businessmen who're tiny by comparison, apart from a few exceptions. What the hell's going on in that paper? But, then, who cares?

---

561 Sandy Adam, a property developer.

562 *Today* presenter Justin Webb.

563 Lord Livingston of Parkhead.

564 *Scotsman* journalist.

31 AUGUST

Anonymous information from a health service worker in Glasgow, whose whole department is about to be privatised – sold off to Weight Watchers. Great story[565] – but will anyone listen? Bunch of lying Nats.

1 SEPTEMBER

It's a bit of a bloody nuisance having to do all this digital nonsense as well as reporting the campaign properly; the trouble with instant digital is that it is just churning out what the broadcasters call 'actualite', with no political insight or judgement applied; complete rubbish. However, Ben is a star and can cope with all of it, as can Simon, and Aus isn't bad, either. It's just me!

Speaking of Ben, he is getting a lot of hassle from Eck. Basically, what he's doing is continually putting Eck on the spot and asking hard questions and, as he often does, Salmond is trying to patronise him and asked him today, 'What kind of sweeties are your favourites, son?' Now this may sound like innocent fun but it is actually disgusting bullying, and in other circumstances if an old man like Salmond was to ask a young bloke like Ben what were his favourite sweets, people might think that he fancied him!

---

565 The *Daily Telegraph* accused Salmond of hypocrisy for warning about the privatisation of the NHS when his own government was selling parts of Glasgow NHS to a private company.

3 SEPTEMBER

Ben was due to have a set-to with Salmond in Ayr on one of his stop-overs. And, as usual, Eck would have what they call a 'huddle' with the writing hacks – no TV cameras or radio mikes present. We reckoned that this would be the time that he produced the bag of sweets and we tried to work out how Ben should respond.

There is no doubt that Ben is embarrassed by the whole thing and hates being treated this way; he is a very serious young reporter, better than most of those around him in Scotland, including many who are much older. Being offered sweets is just a way of putting him down. But what to do?

Simon suggested that if and when Eck offered the sweets, Ben should hand him a copy of the book *Economics for Dummies*. We all had a laugh at this but after a think we decided that it would make the whole thing a joke, which it clearly isn't.

And so off Ben went, knowing that he was going to be humiliated, but determined to tough it out and give Salmond as good as he got.

So it turned out. Yet again and after a tough question-and-answer session, Salmond produced a bag of liquorice allsorts for Ben, at which he bridled and said he didn't think it was a joke to be patronised like this by the First Minister of Scotland. Salmond backed down for a bit but when the questions got tasty again, he handed Ben the sweets – stating quite clearly that he enjoyed patronising Ben.

That did it! I got Ben to file every cough and fart of the exchanges and while Simon tweeted about this outrageous treatment, I wrote up a thunderous attack on this total shit of a man.

Then we put it all online and BANG, the whole issue exploded right in Salmond's face. It was brilliant. Salmond looked like the arrogant bully he is.

Fantastic reaction within minutes of the thing going digital (which is, I suppose, something in its favour) and in no time the whole world, or so it seemed, knew about his appalling behaviour.

Even if we'd planned the whole thing – which we didn't really – it couldn't have gone better for us or worse for Salmond. A good day's work.

3 SEPTEMBER

Amazing blether with (Sir) Charlie Maclean, son of Fitzroy and general good egg. His daughter is in Jose's year at St George's and he's invited us in the past to have a holiday with him on that Croatian island that old Tito[566] gave his father for services rendered during the war. One day we should go. Contrary to what I'd always believed, Tito didn't give him the whole island – just a very nice house on it.

Anyway, Charlie is, like many people, very exercised about the referendum result and is getting increasingly angry about the intimidation by the Nats. He says that most No posters that he's seen have been defaced and/or destroyed.

When he wanted to put some up, he went along to his local builders in Argyll, where they were being made, and asked the

---

566 Josip Broz Tito, Yugoslav resistance leader in World War II and President of Yugoslavia from 1953 to 1980.

girl at reception: 'Could I have those No posters that I ordered, please?' A sudden hush fell over proceedings and one of the firm's directors came out of his adjoining office, looked around a couple of times, and whispered to Charlie, 'Keep your voice down and come with me.'

He told Charlie that the firm's 200 or so employees were mostly No voters but that they were keeping schtum in case of trouble from the Nats. He ushered Charlie into the front seat of a big four-wheel drive van of some description and set off through a couple of fields and up to a large barn with a heavily padlocked door. Then, looking around him all the time to make sure nobody was watching, he brought out several big No posters, which Charlie plans to put in a few fields but which had been made in conditions of totally secrecy. Jesus – even the Manhattan Project[567] wasn't as clandestine as this.

4 SEPTEMBER

Massive Nat rally in Glasgow, which looked good on telly but then BBC Scotland always fall for the stunts – such as Nats being bussed in from all over to make it look bigger than it was. And Salmond was on his best behaviour. I sent Ben to tackle him again and there was no nonsense this time; there were no sweeties.

---

567 The research project that produced the first atomic bombs in World War II.

4 SEPTEMBER

Helluva row thanks to what looked like a mistake by Ruth Davidson, saying that she thought it was 'not likely' that the Tories would win the general election next year. In fact, she said this in answer to a hostile question about why a Yes vote would keep the Tories out of an independent Scotland. What she meant to do was help Labour by saying that, according to the opinion polls at that time, there was a big chance that Labour would win next May.

But that stupid bugger Miliband decided to play the party card and he started quoting Ruth, saying, 'Even the leader of the Scottish Tories doesn't think David Cameron will win next year.' This caused understandable outrage from the erstwhile Better Together allies. Alistair Darling told me he had spoken to Miliband and asked him, in effect, to lay off and said that he'd told the Labour leader that Ruth 'was taking one for the team' in saying what she did.

Those were the words that both Harrow and Shortarse used too.

But Miliband pays absolutely no attention to Darling's appeal to lay off Ruth and repeats what he thinks is his best line, and snide stuff about Ruth, several more times during the day, in spite of being told twice by Darling to desist. What a useless bugger.

This is the thing that continually infuriates me, this partisan bickering between the supposed allies. They're all at it to a greater or lesser extent and English Labour can't help bashing the Tories in the same way as English Tories are always moaning and groaning about Labour in Scotland, especially Darling. The main thing, of course, is that the Tories are shit-scared that Alistair will return to the shadow Cabinet and take Ed Balls's job as shadow Chancellor.

The Lib Dems are not averse to a bit of stirring it, either, with Harrow always moaning about Labour's helpers – he calls Douglas Alexander 'Rain Man' because nobody knows what he's talking about.

However, everyone thinks that, in general, the so-called top table at Better Together's new HQ in Sauchiehall Street – donated by John Boyle, ex-Motherwell FC boss – works well, with, variously, Jim Murphy, Douglas Alexander, Jackie Baillie and Mark McInnes, the Tories' campaigns director in Scotland (by the way, he says he's the most left-wing of that lot and he's not wrong) all beavering away. However, they are all under the direction of Frank Roy, the hard-nosed Motherwell MP. He runs everything. Brilliant bloke – hard as nails.

5 SEPTEMBER

Really went for it, with an emotional 'special' – telling the faithful to get out there, stop whinging and bloody well campaign. There is still too much moaning about lack of tough leadership from BT, lack of posters, lack of handbills, too much Salmond on the TV etc. etc. It really does get you down after a while. So I called for an end to the moaning and said if their posters were torn down to put up new ones, and if they didn't have enough posters to make them! All they needed, I said, was a sheet of A4 paper and a felt-tip pen (apparently, I should have said a 'marker pen') and the ability to write the word No on it.

Astonishingly, people took me at my word and one of my neighbours made a home-knitted poster as I'd directed. But it looked so bad that her kids tore it down and they eventually put up proper ones, complete with Saltire and Union Jack flags flapping at the upstairs windows. Brilliant.

7 SEPTEMBER

The inevitable, but still horrid, happened, with a YouGov poll in the *Sunday Times* showing that the Nats had taken a two-point lead. Panic stations all round. But not me. Nobody believes me but I just don't think that poll is right and I still can't see where the Nats will get the numbers they need to win. Oh sure, they'll probably win Glasgow and maybe Dundee, too, but they've got to win them by absolutely massive numbers to sway the result.

Osborne was in the brown stuff for saying on Marr that more powers were on the way, when all that he meant or should have said was that there would soon be a timetable for the transfer of powers that all the parties had already announced.

Still, it seemed like everyone was queuing up for the window ledges. This looks bad.

6–7 SEPTEMBER

Alarm bells ringing in royal and Tory circles surrounding Cameron's visit to the Queen at Balmoral, which has coincided with that bloody poll in the *Sunday Times*.

Massive stories (rumours?) about how the Queen gave Cameron a bit of a bollocking for appearing to be the man in charge when her kingdom gets disunited!

But on Saturday (6 September), and so as not to appear to be backing a No vote, the Queen didn't take her Prime Minister to the Braemar Gathering, where he would have been seated right alongside her. A bit pathetic, especially as there surely can be little doubt that she doesn't want 'her' kingdom broken up, no matter how much she's supposed to get on with Eck. And I'm not all that sure – from what we used to hear from one close to her – that she likes him all that much anyway.

But there was the potential for a huge embarrassment, with Aberdeen Asset Management pitching their marquee right next to the Royal Pavilion at the Games. And as Martin Gilbert, that company's boss, seems to worship the ground on which Eck walks, would the Nat leader turn up at the Games when the PM couldn't? It didn't happen in the end, much to everyone's relief – not least, I'm sure, the Queen's.

8 SEPTEMBER

I got a call from Bruce Waddell, former editor of the *Daily Record* and *Scottish Sun*, who now appears to be Broon's apostle on earth – who's paying him, I wonder? He says that the great man wants to talk to me and that I could expect a phone call within ten minutes.

Sure enough, almost on the dot of ten minutes later Gordon comes on the line, in fairly friendly tones, to give me a précis of the speech he's due to make. However, that's not before he gives me a bit of a bollocking: 'The last time we talked (that was presumably that strange meeting in the Sheraton) you didn't seem to accept what I said. I hope you will this time because your views carry a lot of weight with the other political journalists in Scotland.'

Gosh, why is Gordon being so nice? He proceeded to tell me – or rather repeat – his view that Cameron and Osborne had been presenting the campaign as something akin to Scotland versus Britain, instead of the two visions of Scotland. The first is the SNP version, the second is Labour's or (although he didn't say it) the Gordon Brown version.

He told me:

> It has been absolutely central to what's been going on here that we [Labour] have got to have a vision of Scotland's future. Although the campaign on the pound has worked over the summer, we don't want to always be relying on the negative.
>
> We have to make our country feel proud.

He then told me about the blueprint he was to announce later – a firm timetable for the new powers for Holyrood, with work beginning immediately after the vote, on 19 September, then preliminary agreement by St Andrew's Day on 30 November and draft legislation ready by 25 January – these dates will piss off Eck mightily but are a great gimmick by GB; only he could have thought of them. But more importantly, only he could have delivered this promise and got people to believe that something was in the offing.

In truth, however, this is merely warmed-over broth – brilliantly served up, sure, but there's nothing new in the details.

And, of course, the parties are miles apart. I said to Gordon: 'But, look, Labour want only 75 per cent of income tax raised by Holyrood, whereas the Tories want 100 per cent.' To which he replied: '100 per cent versus 75 per cent – there's surely room for compromise there.'

The speech was a brilliant coup and could have been delivered by no one other than Gordon. It will make a difference because, apart from any other consideration, the Nats are scared of the Great Broon and the effect he has on the populace, many of whom still like him and believe he got a raw deal in 2010.

There is no doubt that Gordon is a superstar here, but he is an extremely difficult bugger to work with, according to the Labour and Better Together people. One of his minders, who I'd better not name, told me the following stories:

Gordon had been due to make a speech in his native Fife but told everyone that as Nicola Sturgeon had had a crowd of 400 the day before at the same location, he couldn't possibly do his effort unless Labour could guarantee the same number at his speech. It was pointed out to him that the Nats had bussed in the audience for the Sturgeon speech from all over Central Scotland and there was just no time for Labour to do the same. Outcome? No speech!

On another occasion, Gordon was due to make a speech somewhere in Central Scotland when it was discovered at the last minute that David Cameron was due in Scotland at the same time, also to make a speech, so could Gordon postpone his?

He grumpily agreed but then, surprise, surprise, he issued the text of what he would have said to the press anyway.

9 SEPTEMBER

Everyone is watching and waiting to see which way the *Scottish Sun* will jump, given Eck's friendship and admiration for old Rupert. I've now heard the same story from two different sources, although to be fair, given the sources, it's probably a case of one of them telling the other and swearing him to secrecy. But then he told me, someone who can't keep secrets!

It went like this: Rupert summoned David Dinsmore, the London editor in chief, as well as Gordon Smart, the Scottish editor, as well as – bizarrely – Kelvin MacKenzie,[568] to New York and asked the three of them what the Scottish edition should do on Referendum Day?

Dinsmore was very firm that the paper shouldn't back the Nats, whereas the new kid on the block was equally determined that the Scottish edition should say 'Vote Yes' loud and clear. I wasn't told how Kelvin voted but given his antipathy for all things Scottish – in spite of his name – he'd probably have backed the Scottish editor. (I think that Kelvin and Craig, both public school boys and both of whom I've worked with, must have had a horrible Scottish nanny to give them this hatred for the Jocks; still, we'll manage without them.)

Anyway, the meeting passed off without a firm decision being taken. Still, I was determined to write something and phoned Sinclair and Shortarse to see if Labour and/or BT were prepared to kick up hell about the way the *Scottish Sun* was cheerleading for the Nats. No way, they both said. '*The Sun* hasn't actually

---

568 Editor of *The Sun* from 1981 to 1994.

come out totally against us, so we don't want to antagonise it; not yet at any rate.'

Bloody cowards. So I wrote the piece, denouncing Rupert anyway. It died a very swift death. Ho, hum.

(I subsequently found out what happened later. Although massively pro-Salmond, Rupert was appalled to discover what kind of people the SNP leader was keeping company with. During a trip to Scotland the week before the vote he found out that the Nats' bedfellows were none other than the Scottish Greens, who so hate the idea of economic growth that I've dubbed them the Iron Age Appreciation Society, and an assorted bunch of Trots and Marxists in the Scottish Socialist Party. Rupe tweeted his disgust at this bunch and so ended any chance of the *Scottish Sun* backing Yes.)

It was all put down to a stunning triumph for Dinsmore over the young upstart Gordon Smart. I've no idea if that's true but I'm happy for David to take the credit. A brilliant victory, whose ever it was.

9 SEPTEMBER

Wild rumours that Prime Minister's Question Time is to be cancelled and everybody is heading for Scotland. This, like most political rumours, turns out to be true. Astonishing.

10 SEPTEMBER

Cameron in Edinburgh, Miliband in Glasgow, Clegg in the Borders. What a carry-on. I was told there wasn't enough room for me or Simon at the Cameron event. I told Downing Street and the Scotland Office to get stuffed and also what a good story it would be if the *Telegraph*'s Scottish editor couldn't attend a PM presser on Scotland.

I went anyway and waltzed into the Scottish Widows HQ, where Cameron gave a brilliant speech, which sounded like he meant it – which he did. The bad lads like me and a few others in the front rows agreed that we could see a tear in his eye and so that's what appeared in the papers next day! Disgraceful behaviour.

11 SEPTEMBER

Salmond declares war on the BBC. Amazing – he lost it completely at a presser supposedly for the foreign press corps that he normally loves to lord it over. I watched it on the box from the office and it was obvious he was in a ratty mood anyway – it's always easy to tell with Eck. Wodehouse's old remark about a ray of sunshine[569] could have been written for him.

But this was serious. He dismissed Nick Robinson's[570] persistent questioning of him over the RBS decision to move its headquarters to London and said that, essentially, it didn't matter a damn because all it involved was the shifting of a brass plate – there was no intention to move or lose jobs in Scotland.

And he accused Robinson of not only heckling him – which the BBC pol. ed. was perfectly entitled to do thanks to the fact

---

569 P. G. Wodehouse said, 'It has never been hard to tell the difference between a Scotsman with a grievance and a ray of sunshine.'

570 The BBC's political editor.

that he wasn't getting a proper answer – but also of being, some-how, in cahoots with some dirty Treasury tricks over the RBS announcement.

But what happened then was very interesting. The whole of the Nat media machine began to move against Robinson. All the cybernat websites – collective and individual – started monstering the BBC man, accusing him of selective editing and of biased reporting. Spontaneous? I don't believe that for a moment.

As for Robinson, I do think he makes a meal of things from time to time but he is a smashing political editor, easily the best in the broadcasting world, and thank God we've had him up here to give Eck a run for his money.

13 SEPTEMBER

Feelings of relief shattered by a 9.30 a.m. phone call from Mur-doch MacLennan. Having weathered the storm caused by that YouGov/*Sunday Times* poll of last week, it was hellish to be told by MM that a *Sunday Telegraph*/ICM poll showed an eight-point lead for the Nats. Jesus Christ – I was in a terrible state and furi-ous that someone had commissioned a poll after we'd got things back to equilibrium. I had visions of 'It was the *Telegraph* wot lost it!' headlines if the referendum went the wrong way.

Jenny and Josephine told me not to be so pathetic but I really did have the jitters. Anyway, I went up town with Jenny to dish out No leaflets at St Mary's Cathedral and everyone took one except Steve Cardownie,[571] a local Nat councillor, who was raging about the Orange walk along Princes Street that day. 'You've got the Orangemen and George Galloway on your side,' Steve shouted. 'And you've got Tommy Sheridan,' I replied. But Salmond can't attack the Orange Unionists because he needs their vote desperately in Glasgow.

I plucked up courage to tell Darling about our stupid poll and I was amazed at how calm he was. Incredible. I asked him if Better Together had any canvass returns or anything to counter our poll, but he didn't reply.

Then about half an hour later, Darling called me back. In view of our poll, he had decided to publish one of their own – by Survation – which showed an 8 per cent No lead, but which they had been saving for later in the week. Phew!

That trumped our poll brilliantly, even if it did spoil BT's plans for a big hit in the final countdown to the referendum. What a relief. Easily my very worst day in the whole campaign.

But also, from Darling's cool reaction, the day I knew we'd win for certain!

Watched Last Night of the Proms with the London hacks, who've decamped to Edinburgh for the campaign finale. A very *Telegraph* – and British – occasion. Great fun. Everyone a bit pissed, but it had an end-of-Empire feel about it. Chris Hope[572] led the singing of 'Land of Hope and Glory' lustily, as if it really was the Last Night for us. Poor Chris was heading to the TUC conference

---

571 Deputy leader of Edinburgh Council.

572 The *Daily Telegraph*'s senior political correspondent.

in Liverpool last week, with just an overnight bag, when he was told to get off his train at Coventry and divert to Edinburgh instead. He's been here ever since and needs to change his clothes.

14 SEPTEMBER

Brilliant, brilliant story. The Queen, after the weekly service at Crathie Kirk, walked over to some well-wishers and told them that she hoped everyone 'would think very carefully about the referendum'. But that was only half the story. This was a completely deliberate and put-up job by the Palace.

My old pal Jim Lawson was the only reporter outside Crathie Kirk when the royal party came out and as usual he and the photographers were corralled some way away from Her Majesty and the usual crowd of royalists who gather there every Sunday. But on this occasion, the police were told that the press – Jim and the snappers – could get over to where they could hear what was going on and that's how the story about the Queen's remarks got out.

I was a wee bit concerned that Jim was the only reporter there – after all, he's been in a few scrapes over the years – but it was a great success for him to get that story. But it was also a bit of a coup for the Palace and the Queen herself. There is absolutely no doubt that she did it deliberately; and knew exactly what the effect would be – it was the splash everywhere. Fantastic.

I wouldn't be at all surprised if she was provoked into it by Salmond saying last week, when there was a bit of a stushie about whether she should speak her mind on the issue or not, that he thought she would be 'proud to be Queen of Scots'. That implied some sort of support for independence.

A very bad move by Our Great Leader and one that must have convinced Her Majesty to speak out. It was also a bit of a triumph for Chris Evans, who began a 'Queen should speak' campaign a couple of weeks ago. I bet he didn't think it would work.

14 SEPTEMBER

Everyone is always looking for a 'Sheffield' moment from Eck – similar to Kinnock's major balls-up in the 1992 election – and he came close to it today on *Andy Marr*, announcing his so-called Team Scotland, in other words all those from all sorts of parties that he'd invite to help him take Scotland onwards and upwards. Amazing confidence, or is it just the normal braggadocio we've come to expect from him? Darling, who was also on *Marr*, just sat there and smiled.

15 SEPTEMBER

Who says all those Nat rallies are spontaneous? Over 1,000 turn up at Pacific Quay in Glasgow to protest about the BBC's 'bias' and especially that of Nick Robinson. This is vicious stuff and I don't believe that it's not organised by the Nat hierarchy. Oh sure, they can point to the fact that it's all done by the Radical Independence[573] lot but the impetus comes from the Nats, of

---

573 A political campaign promoting independence, which describes itself as a collective of Scottish Greens, Scottish Socialists, the more militant trade unionists, nuclear disarmament campaigners and anti-monarchist republicans.

that I'm sure. I'm sure also that Nick Robinson will cope with it but I'm much less sure about BBC Scotland. They've been dancing to the Nats' tune for years now, to the extent that they are terrified of offending them.

16 SEPTEMBER

The day of the Vow. Amazing front-page declaration in the *Record* from all three party leaders, signing up to deliver a solemn promise that they would grant Scotland massive extra powers AND keep the Barnett formula. Gordon Brown is getting all the credit for making sure that this was done, but I hear that the man responsible was Murray Foote, the *Record*'s editor.[574] He is a brilliant tabloid operator and has made the *Record* one of the most intelligent red tops around – taking it back to the way it was thirty years ago, before it was ruined by a bunch of nonentities who made it a joke.

It was Murray who invented the concept of the Vow and put all their signatures on what looked like vellum on a 'poster' front page.

It was pure journalistic hokum. Still, it has become a sort of second Magna Carta. It would be hilarious if it wasn't being taken so seriously.

Great stroke and put it one ahead of *The Sun*, which, since it's no longer backing the Nats, looks absolutely crap.

---

574 Appointed *Daily Record* editor in February 2014.

17 SEPTEMBER

Wrote heartfelt appeal – and no matter what the cynics will say, I meant it! Appealing to the Brits to get out and vote. Bit sugary, I suppose, but these pieces go down very well. There are lots of desperate, absolutely terrified Brits out there, wetting themselves that the Nats will win.

Very surprising call from Donald Findlay QC. 'Look, Cochrane, are we going to win this fucking referendum?' Tough-as-boots old Findlay, Scotland's premier criminal advocate (barrister), is panicking about the prospect of defeat tomorrow. I reassured him as best I could, but I'm not sure he was all that convinced. But I really don't think we'll lose. I just can't see where the Nats will get the numbers they need.

I was walking home with Peter D,[575] the London political editor, and Chris Hope, when a bloody car roared up the Royal Mile, mounted the pavement and came to a halt a few yards in front of us.

It was an old banger driven by Jim Murphy, who was on his way to speak at a public meeting but just stopped for a chat when he saw me. He was in great form – completely fired up for the fray and having relished all that shit he's taken from the Nats.

And he told us that he'd just been stopped in the street by one angry Nat who said: 'I'm going to fucking kill you, you bastard, when this is over.' That's what he's been putting up with. Amazing.

---

575 Peter Dominiczak.

18 SEPTEMBER

Fantastic day. Very, very proud as I walked to the polling station at 7.30 a.m. with Jose, where she voted for the first time. I doubt if she'll ever vote on a more important issue for the rest of her life. I certainly hope not. She was very pleased with herself as there were quite a lot of neighbours there, too.

Had a few pints in the Café Royal, where I met, amongst others, John Ivison,[576] ex-*Scotsman* now a big cheese in Canadian journalism. He gave me a great line re: Carney,[577] who said he told Salmond before his first visit early this year: 'I'm only here for one day, Alex, but don't fuck with me or I'll be up here a lot more often.' It worked because Salmond kept praising Carney for holding a middle line.

However, the truth is that the Governor was actually sticking it to the Nats about their loony currency plan but they insisted for their own reasons that Carney was sitting on the fence. Like hell he was.

I wrote a column saying that he had, at the end of the campaign, begun to follow orders from the Treasury, otherwise they had threatened to stick him on an Air Eskimo, no-frills flight back to Winnipeg.

Pretty relaxed mood in the Café Royal; it seemed to be full of No voters, including one very loud Lib Dem who shouted at the top of his voice that he wanted Salmond to not only lose the referendum but also the Ryder Cup, just to wipe the smug

---

576 Political columnist for the *National Post* in Ottawa.

577 Canadian Mark Carney, Governor of the Bank of England since 2013.

grin off his face. I could see what he meant but that was taking things a bit too far.

18–19 SEPTEMBER

Used our house as media centre for the great overnight stint. Peter D and Simon J in the house, along with Iain M, Aus with Eck in Aberdeenshire, and Ben at the count centre.

Sinclair phoned around 11.30 p.m. to say that the council estates weren't turning out in large enough numbers in Glasgow to help the Nats to a big victory, whereas the middle-class areas in the Glasgow suburbs were pouring out – in some cases up to 90 per cent. But that tends to be in what's now East Dunbartonshire – Milngavie and Bearsden. Still, it all sounds good. And if the Nats don't have enough troops to get those traditional non-voters in the council schemes out to the polling stations, then they're sunk.

It was obvious from the first results that No had won, and as all the results began to pour in – Clackmannan first[578] – it was a shoo-in for the forces of truth and justice. I thought it would be a much better lead but then Glasgow ruined it, even though by not a big enough margin, pegging it back to 55 per cent. And Dundee came through for the Nats, too, but the turn-out in both cities was way down on other areas – 75 per cent in Glasgow and 79 per cent in Dundee, much less than everywhere else.

And the best news of the night was seeing Eck slinking away

---

578 Clackmannanshire declared around 1.30 a.m.; 54 per cent voted No, 46 per cent Yes.

and failing to go to the Aberdeenshire count, which showed a huge majority for No. Brilliant.

We opened champagne after putting a 5 a.m. edition together but then Jenny had to drive Simon to a Salmond press conference at 6 a.m ... no taxis at that hour ... at Dynamic Earth.

One and a half hours' sleep then off to work – first to LBC, where I saw David Mellor[579] for the first time in maybe twenty years. Smashing phone calls from Nick Soames and Alistair Carmichael, saying thanks for help in the campaign, although the latter wants help on more powers stuff. That can wait a while, I reckon.

Offered Ian McGregor[580] 2,000 words on the road to victory and he bought it. Great.

Ploughed through it all day as all sorts of nonsense kept emanating from Nat Control about how Westminster was already ratting on its promise of more powers.

The problem was that Cameron, clearly flushed with the success of the referendum, announced that he wanted to not only give Scotland that extra devolution but also to sort out the English votes for English legislation stuff. I didn't think he linked it directly to Scottish powers but everyone else did so maybe I missed something. Anyway, everyone started howling. There's bound to be trouble from Labour. But they'll just have to swallow it.

A truly hectic day, with the office packed and everyone pounding away – just like newspaper offices should be. I got a phone call from some wine merchants saying they had a case of champagne

---

579 Cabinet minister in John Major's government; Conservative MP for Putney from 1979 to 1997.

580 Weekend editor of the *Telegraph*.

for us and would we like it delivered and when. Very nice, too, a dozen bottles of fizz arrived about 5 p.m. in the *Telegraph* office from MM – so we drank a toast to 'absent friends', once Eck announced he was resigning.

But he did a truly incredible and spiteful thing – him and his civil service lackeys. They banned the *Telegraph*, the *Mail* and the *Express* from his final presser, along with Severin Carrell of *The Guardian*. They said there wasn't enough room in Bute House for everyone, so they had to restrict some of the writing hacks. It was pure co-incidence, presumably, that Eck decided on the *Telegraph*, *Mail* and *Express* as being the ones to ban. And he tried to tell *The Guardian* that they couldn't send Sev but had to choose some other reporter, who presumably Eck likes a bit better – and Sev does actually loathe Eck. Brilliant that *The Guardian* said 'we'll decide who does our reporting, not you' and sent no one.

I wish the Scottish hacks behaved as honourably. What a bunch. Chris Hope and Ben went along and videoed those shits – that's the civil servants – not letting in the *Telegraph*, and also the bigger shits of all, our colleagues walking past the officials as they barred our entry. Appalling behaviour by a bunch of pygmies. What a shower!

Still, the bugger said he was resigning so it wasn't all bad, even If we did get the usual drivel – something about the dream living on. Gibberish.

Brilliant, fantastic day – which Eck's banning us did nothing to spoil. A great victory for US.

Celebratory drinks at the Burns's house – Catherine and Richard. People like them, ordinary mortals but avid Unionists, are the real heroes.

And I'm sure that the majority could have been higher if BT had saved their weekend poll until closer to the voting day – bloody *Sunday Telegraph* poll mucked that up.

21 SEPTEMBER

Met a buoyant Sarah Boyack,[581] a Holyrood Labour shadow Cabinet member, in the street. She was very pleased with the result but is worried about the extra powers stuff – because she fears that Scottish Labour MPs in the Commons will wreck things. But she was extra conciliatory. 'We shall just have to help them to understand that they must make concessions so that more devolution helps us see off the SNP.' Hmmm – more hope than expectation there.

Later: admission to the inner sanctum of the Labour 'family'. Extraordinary. Invited to a discreet party, beginning at the Darlings' house and then moving across to Professor Alice Brown's[582] house round the corner. Smashing evening and smashing people – the Darlings, of course, and Maggie makes us so welcome. Kezia Dugdale, whom AD says is a star in the making – and I agree – pumped me all night about what I thought about things, much of which appeared in her *Record* column a couple of days later.

Oh yes, and J. K. Rowling was there too with her husband, a quiet, extremely clever doctor.[583] She was easily the nicest multi-

---

581 Labour MSP for Edinburgh Central since 1999.

582 Chair of the Scottish Funding Council, former Public Services Ombudsman.

583 Dr Neil Murray.

millionaire I've ever met. Had plenty of opinions but is in no way a show-off and, amazingly for a Labour supporter, she likes the *Telegraph* and reads my column!

The girls will be dead jealous.

Got grilled by Catherine MacLeod[584] – AD's former aide – 'Why are you a Tory?' Not quite a St Peter moment but I said I always voted against the Nats in Edinburgh North, which seemed to satisfy AD, if nobody else. Darling in great form, although I've never heard him use the 'F' word as often! Still, who can blame him?

22 SEPTEMBER

Early train to Manchester, ostensibly for the Labour conference but actually to see Harriet. Got a great reception everywhere from Labourites – Margaret Curran, George Foulkes – for my part in the campaign. Dreadful Ed Balls speech; this lot are going nowhere. Andrew Neil told me it was Crosby[585] who got Cameron to bugger up Labour over English votes.

24 SEPTEMBER

Got back to Edinburgh double quick. Labour looked hopeless.

Eddie Barnes (Tory spinner) says he has a story for us but it turns out to be a load of crap about some renegades trying to form

---

584 Special advisor to Darling when he was Chancellor and former political editor of *The Herald*.

585 Lynton Crosby, the Australian who is Cameron's election director.

a breakaway. He wants us to flush them out. He can get stuffed.

Sinclair was surprised that I'm not going to the Tory conference: 'You'll be a hero there,' he said. I told him that I hadn't heard a word from the Tories (actually, Forsyth did ring to thank me for my efforts), although both Libs and Labour had been generous in their praise. And, sure enough, a couple of hours later Ruth D rang me to express surprise and to say she wanted to buy me a drink.

25 SEPTEMBER

Told Murdoch I wasn't going to the Tory conference and he said he'd even cover for me.

AFTERWORD

B Y ANY STANDARDS it was a pretty conclusive result. The exhausting and, at times, bitterly fought campaign over whether Scotland should remain part of the United Kingdom of Great Britain and Northern Ireland produced an astonishingly high turn-out of over 84 per cent and a comfortable majority for those who said 'No' to the question on the ballot paper: 'Should Scotland be an independent country?'

Twenty-eight of Scotland's thirty-two local authority areas produced No votes, against only four voting Yes. A total of 2,001,926 voters rejected independence compared to only 1,617,989 in favour – 55.3 per cent against 44.7 per cent, a majority of 10.6 per cent; all in all a satisfying, if not overwhelming, victory.

Astonishingly, however, the days and weeks following the 18 September referendum have been dominated not so much by a 'we wuz robbed' feeling amongst Nationalists – that was always

likely – but by a sense almost of guilt amongst the Unionist community that they'd won.

At the root of this strange phenomenon was the Vow. A piece
of brilliant tabloid journalism by the editor of the *Daily Record*
newspaper – whereby he got the leaders of the Conservative,
Labour and Liberal Democrat parties to promise 'extensive' extra
powers for the Holyrood Parliament – has been transformed in
the public mind into something resembling the Magna Carta in
importance. It is talked of in hushed tones, and is normally now
referred to as 'the solemn Vow' which must be honoured and
which Nationalists insist pledges so much devolution as to make
it indistinguishable from 'pure' independence.

The truth, however, is somewhat different. The three party
leaders – egged on and choreographed by Gordon Brown, who
emerged in this campaign renewed and lusty from the hiberna-
tion brought on by his 2010 election defeat – did not say in their
Vow exactly what new powers they were prepared to deliver.

But the Nationalists insisted that it was this eleventh-hour
promise – and only this eleventh-hour promise – that convinced
Scots to reject separation and make do with the extra powers coming the way of the Holyrood Parliament. The only poll conducted
on this issue – by Lord Ashcroft, on referendum day itself – tells
a different story. This showed that the vast majority of No voters had made up their minds how they'd vote over a year before
the referendum and 57 per cent put economic concerns – especially over what currency an independent Scotland would use – at
the top of their list of priorities. These figures support anecdotal
evidence from canvas returns from both sides, which suggested

that the issue of extra powers for the Holyrood Parliament rarely cropped up on doorsteps.

And yet, post-referendum Scotland appears to have gone mad for more powers. A crass statement by David Cameron in the first flush of success after the result was known, in which he appeared to link more devolution for Scotland with what's known as 'English votes for English laws', has taken a great deal of unravelling. But although the wilder fringes of nationalism will forever believe they're to be short changed, it is to be hoped that a commission to rule on these new powers, headed by the sober-sided Lord Smith of Kelvin, will be capable of soothing all but the most savage breasts.

Looking back at the campaign from this vantage point and from this biased viewpoint, it was perhaps remarkable for the fact that at no stage did the Nationalists ever look like winning. Except once: on the Saturday before the vote I most certainly did panic when told the news that an opinion poll to be published in the *Sunday Telegraph* showed a substantial lead for No. However, as I relate elsewhere, it turned out to be a short-term scare, with my hero of the hour, and of the entire campaign – Alistair Darling – shrugging it off and never, ever wavering, or at least not that I could see, in his belief in victory.

The principal players in the campaign were, of course, Darling and Alex Salmond, both men scoring one head-to-head debate victory each. But although he was frequently criticised for his low-key approach, the former Chancellor stuck manfully to what he saw as his main task – holding Salmond's feet to the flames over the SNP leader's, in the end, stupid insistence that he could continue to use sterling in an independent Scotland, no matter what

England, Wales and Northern Ireland said about the matter. The economic unease this policy generated proved ultimately fatal to the Nationalists' chances.

But if Darling was the overall star of the marathon campaign, the man who won most of the plaudits for the sprint in the final weeks was undoubtedly Gordon Brown. No team player he, the Great Clunking Fist showed, with remarkable displays of passion and emotion, that he can remain a tremendously influential figure on the British political scene. And although at all times difficult to work with – especially given his distaste for sharing platforms with Tories – Gordon Brown produced a magnificent effort to help traditional Labour voters stick with their party's opposition to separation.

The No campaign was also brilliantly, and in the highest-profile way, served by Jim Murphy's incredible 100 venues in 100 days barnstormer, which saw him egged on – literally – by angry Nats. But beneath the radar, most of those involved with Better Together would pay enormous tribute to Labour's Frank Roy and the Tories' Mark McInnes, who manned the bridge and kept their heads when all about were losing theirs.

In my, admittedly, jaundiced opinion, the biggest weakness in the Yes campaign was allowing itself to be totally dominated by Alex Salmond. He makes and made as many enemies as friends, but that's not my problem.

I'm delighted that separation was comprehensively defeated and that my family and I are to be allowed to remain British. That, for me, was what this battle has been all about. It wasn't about politics, it wasn't about journalism. It was about who I am.

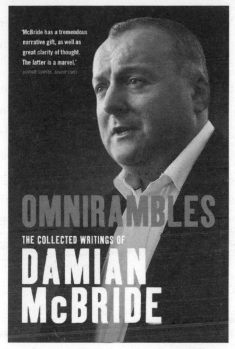

384PP PAPERBACK, £14.99

A 300-year-old union. A comprehensive debate.
A historic decision.

On 18 September 2014, Scots will decide their future: should the country quit the United Kingdom and take control of its own destiny, or should it remain part of what advocates call the most successful political and economic union of modern times?

Everyone in the country has a stake in this decision. Now, in this fascinating and insightful new book, David Torrance charts the countdown to the big day, weaving his way through a minefield of claim and counterclaim, and knocking down fictions and fallacies from both Nationalists and Unionists. He plunges into the key questions that have shaped an often-fraught argument, from the future of the pound to the shape of an independent Scottish army.

With access to the strategists and opinion-makers on both sides of the political divide, this book goes straight to the heart of the great debate, providing an incisive, authoritative, occasionally trenchant guide to the most dramatic constitutional question of our times – the battle for Britain.